ARCHITECTURE FOR PSYCHIATRIC ENVIRONMENTS AND THERAPEUTIC SPACES

Architecture for Psychiatric Environments and Therapeutic Spaces

Evangelia Chrysikou

Architect Medical Planner

Press

Amsterdam • Berlin • Tokyo • Washington, DC

ISBN 978-1-61499-459-6 (print)
ISBN 978-1-61499-460-2 (online)
Library of Congress Control Number: 2014956424
doi:10.3233/978-1-61499-460-2-i

Publisher
IOS Press BV
Nieuwe Hemweg 6B
1013 BG Amsterdam
Netherlands
fax: +31 20 687 0019
e-mail: order@iospress.nl

Distributor in the USA and Canada
IOS Press, Inc.
4502 Rachael Manor Drive
Fairfax, VA 22032
USA
fax: +1 703 323 3668
e-mail: iosbooks@iospress.com

LEGAL NOTICE

The publisher is not responsible for the use which might be made of the following information.

PRINTED IN THE NETHERLANDS

Acknowledgements

First, I would like to thank the people living in the mental health facilities that I visited who allowed me to intrude in their private space. Even more I would like to thank the staff and the service users who trusted me to conduct the interviews, even though there was always the risk of touching sensitive issues and causing disruption in the life of the wards, and having the focus and the patience to answer my questions. I would also like to thank the health authorities in several parts of Europe, and mostly in France and the UK that enabled me to access their facilities and provided me the information that I needed.

There are no words to express my gratitude to Professor Julienne Hanson and I would also like to thank the people that encouraged me in my first steps of working on mental health Professor Kyriaki Tsoukala, Professor Fani Vavyli, Professor Dimitris Kandylis, Professor Nick Bouras, Susan Francis and Professor Alan Penn, as well as those who encouraged me closer to the end, Professor Theodoros Konstandinides, Professor Lionis and Professor Gabbirel Ivbijaro. Special thanks to Dr Marios Hatzopoulos for his invaluable advice regarding this book. My special thanks to Professor Helias Mossialos and John Wells Thorp. I would like to express my gratitude to Alexander S Onassis Public benefit foundation for the active support.

Furthermore, I would like to express my thanks to my family, especially to my father, whose love and belief in me proved endless. Finally, I have to express my gratitude to Dimitris for the fact that he is always there with his warmth and love.

Finally, many thanks to Public Benefit Foundation Alexander S. Onassis for its contribution through granted scholarship for the conduction of this research, as well as for the publication of this book.

Short CV: Dr EVANGELIA CHRYSIKOU

Dr Evangelia Chrysikou is a registered architect, researcher and academic. She is the owner of SynThesis Architects, an awarded architectural practice specialising in healthcare facilities. She is one of the very few architects around the world holding a PhD in healthcare facilities and especially in facilities for the therapeutic qualities of psychiatric space. Her architecture and her extensive research on the environment and health, has received **several awards** including the Highly Commended award at the category: International Research Project in International Academy for Design and Health Awards in Kuala Lumpur in 2012. Parallel activities to architecture include teaching at medical and architectural schools in Athens and London, research, and advisory for professional bodies and the Greek Ministry of Health. Dr. Chrysikou is a published author, editor and reviewer. She is also a Trustee, Member of the Board and Director of Research and Education at DIMHN (UK).

She graduated from AUTH, acquired an MA in Health Care Buildings Planning Management and Design from LSBU and her PhD from the Bartlett School of Graduate Studies UCL. For her PhD she received a scholarship from Alexander S. Onassis Public Benefit Foundation.

Table of Contents

Chapter 1

Introduction

Therapeutic architecture could be described as the people-centered, evidence-based discipline of the Built Environment that aims to identify and support ways of incorporating into design those spatial elements that interact with people's physiology and psychology. It is a significant field of architecture that relates to the lives of the people when they are in wellbeing, yet it becomes even more important when people experience ill health, as it is in this state that they present the least abilities to cope.

From this perspective, this book explores the design of specialised residential architecture for people with mental health problems. It sets out to show how building design can support medical and health-related procedures and practices, leading to a better therapeutic outcome and a higher quality of life for residents and their carers. It is a scholar work and comprises the outcome of almost two decades of visiting and researching environments for the mentally ill people in several European countries. The main aim of this work has been **to understand how the therapeutic milieu, the care programmes and the actual life in those spaces interacted with the architectural design, which provided an envelope for those activities**. This required an integrated approach, viewing the architecture of those facilities from the perspective of the people who spent a considerable amount of time in them.

As mental health has been associated with stigma even from ancient times, it was important **to locate the meaning and expression of stigma and prejudice in mental health facilities**. In that respect, it was essential to establish the meaning of 'institution' as a factor that might still exist in therapeutic practice and which could in effect hinder therapeutic results. The next step **was to recognize the unevenness of the foundations of mental health care systems, and to try to explore and understand their concepts in order to locate the role of buildings designed to facilitate the delivery of care therein**. Once the broader systems for the delivery of care became clearer, it was essential to see how the buildings corresponded to each particular system. To fully understand this, one had to locate the therapeutic aim of those places and identify how the aim was facilitated by the buildings hosting the therapy. This required an understanding of the parts that constituted the therapeutic procedure, together with its goals and stages. Finally, it was essential to focus on the service users' experience of those premises, and **understand their needs in respect of mental health care, psychosocial rehabilitation and wellbeing during their stay**. This required a critical examination of the idea of domesticity as opposed to institutionalization, and through an independent, scientific approach to explore its redefinition or even its adequacy for the design of environments for the mentally ill in the community.

For that reason, and in view of the multi-disciplinary, user-centred, integrated and experimental nature of this work, a case study approach will be our main evidence path to construct the argument. The empirical research that formed the spine of this narrative,

took place in two neighbouring countries, the UK and France. This has not been acciden-
tal. These two countries formed strong cultural affiliations lasting over many centuries
and yet at the same time held diametrically opposed theories and practices in respect of
cultural norms and values, science and philosophy. Mental health facilities in both contexts were examined in architectural and policy terms, and in terms of the users' experiences, to enable a distinction to be made between local variations and global trends.

1.1. Care in the Community

Throughout history, changes to institutions that dealt with mental illness were able to
transform society's attitude to the illness and subsequently to affect its buildings and
treatment regimes. Each new concept would question and subsequently substitute the
previous one with a fresh approach. In the nineteen fifties, the discovery of anti-psychotic
drugs orientated mental health care towards the hospital setting and set the medical model
as the predominant model of care. As drugs were expected to provide permanent solutions, the main building type for the delivery of care became the psychiatric department
of the general hospital.

Yet, as the limitations of drug treatments soon became apparent, together with the
need for long term care policies that would deal with chronic cases or relapse episodes,
new questions were raised about institutionalization within the hospital environment, and
even in regard to aspects of the medical model, shifting their validity from that of an
undeniably efficacious regime to one that did not comply with de-institutionalisation approaches, that succeeded the medical model from the nineteen sixties onwards, depending on the country. This new approach became known as 'care in the community'. Under that prism, the positive contribution of the paramedical disciplines began to be rec-
ognized and functions previously attributed to the hospitals were gradually replaced by
experimental residential facilities located in the community.

Another trend that was closely connected to shifting care towards the community
was that of 'normalization theory', which was imported into mental health from the
neighbouring field of learning difficulties during the nineteen sixties. Under this concept,
mentally ill people should be accepted with regard to their illness. They should have the
same rights as able members of the community and be enabled to participate, as far as
possible, in the ordinary life of the community rather than living the life that the hospital
rules imposed.

Architecturally, environments bearing the least possible resemblance to hospital settings, being as close to the generic equivalent function as possible and located in the
community, were considered the optimum setting for the care of the mentally ill and
their social reintegration. Normalisation theory implied that environments that hosted accommodation for those with mental health problems should bear as many references as
possible to an ordinary family home.

In the UK, care in the community ushered in a paradigm shift in mental health provision, which altogether changed social attitudes to both patient services and the types of
buildings that were deemed necessary to support the provision of mental health care of
all kinds. It led to a greatly reduced demand for the types of hospital architecture associated with in-patient care and a corresponding increase in demand for people with mental
health problems to be enabled to live in an ordinary house within a local neighbourhood

setting. Therefore, normalisation theory became one of the main architectural results of de-institutionalisation as it related to care within the community. The expression of these goals for mental health facilities was to be achieved through buildings which appeared domestic in character, as opposed to institutional.

Care in the community was an international movement, and some influential approaches were pioneered in the USA. The US National Institute for Mental Health, among the essential components of community care, included factors relating to target group identification and outreach, assistance with benefits, crisis intervention preferably in the community, psychosocial rehabilitation, comprehensive support network, medical and mental care, community involvement, service user advocacy and case management [178]. This definition of care was obviously more integrated than the medication-led model. Moreover, it recognised the unpredictability of mental illness, expanding services to involve all stages of service users' competence, even via outreach teams. Service models opened up to include the 'able' parts of the community, from volunteers to family and friends, assisting those who might experience burden and distress [178]. In the light of all the above components of community care, psychosocial rehabilitation was more relevant to the study of mental illness.

Wherever these new community-based practices were introduced, they were clearly opposed to institutional frameworks. However, as practice might not always align with current thinking, institutional practices intruded into the care in the community reality, pending their gradual replacement. The persistence of old values and practices was perhaps most apparent in the building stock, as buildings tend to adapt slower to change [48]. Additionally, designers' limited knowledge on user experience resulted in buildings based on assumptions [184].

The experimentation, the lack of sound scientific knowledge and the lack of a clear direction was reflected in the complexity of the terminology regarding de-institutionalisation and community care. Indicatively, Ekdawi and Conning [85] summarised the three different uses of de-institutionalisation:

- the fact of institutions' closure;
- the process enabling the movement of people from hospital to the community; and
- the philosophy behind that movement

Similarly, NAHA [180] gave two interpretations of 'community care'. One referred to the move of patients from hospital to the community and the second assumed that people stayed in their homes and received care by community services. Ekdawi and Conning [85] also put together three uses of the term:

- non-hospital care;
- care by the community, as in the foster family model, where families offered shelter to mentally ill people; and
- care delivered in communities such as hostels, group homes etc.

This unclarity of contexts created a plethora of approaches and policies. Even the role of the hospital varied, from central in the system to being altogether replaced by community- based services, sometimes even inside the same country. [180] stated that the confusion about the term 'community care' negatively affected the planning and implementation of community projects. As this is a scholar work that aimed to identify a suitable physical milieu for the delivery of a modern care regime that would break this line of assumptions, prejudices and confusions, it concentrated on the first (non-hospital) use of the term 'community care'. As a result it has explored a range of facilities that replaced functions once provided in hospitals, such as acute care or the care closest to the acute stage that is not provided in a hospital setting, whilst acknowledging that some instances of the term could include the other two.

At the point when the first part of this research began in the mid-1990s, the very presence of such a large number of varying approaches provided a web of non-thoroughly researched options for the design of environmental settings, so that the progression from experimentation to an evolved model of care was being hindered. The wide variety of options that replaced hospitals, such as CMHCs (community mental health centres), day hospitals, night hospitals, crisis centres, rehabilitation hostels, supported housing of full or partial supervision, half way homes and clubhouses, to name but a few, combined with inadequate funding regarding the architectural research of those settings, generated a hiatus in scientific knowledge regarding the design of care environments.

In other words, when asked to design for mental health the architects, until very recently, could not refer to evidence-based guidelines on which to base their solutions. Anecdotal evidence and 'personal' references were the available 'tools' for design professionals. This dearth of evidence-based knowledge was often complicated by inadequate briefing on the part of the health and care providers. This was due to the lack of understanding about how to translate the concept of community care into a fully-functioning building.

1.2. Design for Domesticity

At the onset of this work in the mid-1990s till very recently, care in the community and normalisation theory have been the major theoretical concepts in current use for the planning and design of mental health facilities and they have not yet been seriously questioned. Under that prism, the hospital has been accused of cultivating institutional behaviours and preventing the reintegration of the mentally ill back into the society, especially of those who remained there more than the minimum amount of time required by an acute episode.

On the contrary, the optimum milieux for care has been assumed to be those that bore immediate references to the equivalent structures of a normal life in the community. The optimum solution for service user accommodation has been the one closer to that of the home. The main architectural responses to the concept were therefore to shift the location of the residential facility towards the local community, to reduce the overall scale and massing of the building, and to design facades that included references to the local residential environment in order to arrive at a new form for in-patient settings. The metaphor of an environment with domestic references for facilities that provided accommodation was a fundamental part of the paradigm shift.

When residential architecture was considered in the context of in-patient care, it was assumed that it should have a domestic character, as the examples show in figures 1 and 2, yet further, more precise definition was still missing. The lack of pre-existing research on the architecture of the facilities for the mentally ill in the community, the lack of clarity regarding community care and the variety of options for facilities that

Figure 1. London Clubhouse common room

Figure 2. Courtyard of a hostel for homeless mentally ill people, South London

replaced the hospital wards, as well as the lack of definition of the meaning of 'domestic' in a psychiatric context, all demanded that the research conducted should be exploratory in its nature. However, as mental illness compromises seriously several aspects of the life of the individual, domestic environments have been questioned for the adequacy for the treatment and the care of mentally ill people [66]. In short, the aim of this project was to address service users' needs, explore how these needs were expressed in existing facilities and eventually to identify the limits that should be set to domesticity in order not to compromise the therapeutic outcome in the name of a so called return to a 'home' that could be in fact a substitution of one institutional form (hospital) by another (the so-called home).

Discussing spatial qualities of inpatient psychiatric facilities, the term that is most often used is therefore that of 'domesticity', which also expresses the shift towards community-based options. However, domesticity needs critical examination for its possible re-definition to include environments that deal with cases of increasing severity. In other words, what does 'domestic' mean in psychiatric environments that provide accommodation? What, if any, should be the limits to domesticity so that oversimplification does not compromise the therapeutic role of the environment? Or, can a case be made that domesticity could be overrated and some other expression would be more appropriate?

The use of the word 'domesticity' in psychiatric care differs from its meaning when applied to ordinary family housing. One of the key questions was to identify and pinpoint the meaning of the term 'domestic' in the context of architecture for people with mental health problems. Even if facilities display a clinical environment with 'touches of normality' such as a picture on the wall, domestic has been the adjective predominantly used by both architects and professionals in the description of psychiatric environments that offered alternatives to institutional references. General health-care architecture, on the contrary, would usually name other accommodation forms such as student hostels or hotels as positive building stereotypes. It was essential, therefore, to revisit the concept of domesticity as it has been interpreted within psychiatric environments for the acute mentally ill, as opposed to designs that have an institutional origin, in a critical and independent fashion, through evidence based, empirical research.

During the first decade of the new millennium, though, as the normalisation theory model was increasingly tested in practice by everyday experience, its inadequacies started to appear wherever it was implemented. That was more apparent in the UK, where the hospital model had been replaced by acute mental health facilities in the community and where its limitations, especially with respect to safety, reached the media headlines. This concerned unfortunate incidents in which forensic service users slipped through gaps in the care system back to the community, where they committed violent criminal offences against innocent victims. In France, on the other hand, where hospitals had been retained as the provider of acute care, the move towards more community-based structures had only just begun as a result of the partial closure of the psychiatric hospitals. Deinstitutionalisation was therefore at a different stage in the process of implementation, which allowed for a fruitful comparison of the different solutions adopted by the two countries.

Those limitations on safety identified in the case of the UK, as well as other limitations in the therapeutic role of the existing facilities, had already been pinpointed by the web of the main fieldwork presented in this book and especially during the service user and staff interviews, between 2002 and 2003. Yet, because mental illness was not regarded as life threatening in the same way as coronary heart disease or cancer, the Great Recession of that decade and the shortage of government funding took its toll on the efforts to establish new standards in mental health care and in implementing the new frameworks in both countries, so although there were changes in mental health care during this decade, they have not been as dramatic as they would otherwise have been or taken the directions they would have done if there was less shortage of funds. In that respect, many of the issues explored by the thesis are still of substantial relevance, not only for countries like Greece or Eastern European countries, that lagged behind in its psychiatric revolution, but also to the UK and France.

1.3. Mental health service users and their needs

Buildings for people with mental health problems have to respond to the needs of a wide variety of service users with very different symptoms. Under these circumstances, what was meant by a 'normal' environment took on an added significance, as normal accommodation in mental health had different connotations from the environment found in a typical family home as expressed by the local cultures. Moreover, as far as the design implications were concerned, service users could be divided into two groups: one group would comprise the agitated and aggressive whilst the second would include the depressed who are quiet and withdrawn [73]. The stage of the illness and the exact pathology, i.e., the two broad classification criteria, influenced behaviour and needs.

Historically there had been attempts to segregate service users according to pathology, but psychiatric wards tend to cater for a variety of diagnoses. In consequence of that the two groups coexist spatially and the environment then has to cater for contradictory situations. Dependency levels might also vary from low to high. Up to now, the terminology has been unclear and there have been misunderstandings and misinterpretations of all those terms. Moreover, once the de-institutionalisation movement gained weight, changes in treatment and care affected population characteristics. With the shift of vast numbers of people from hospitals to the community and the help of drugs, the average length of stay in hospital decreased, contrary to the needs of the acutely ill and the severity of some cases [214], [249].

In the UK, attempting to define the needs of the acute mentally ill, the Sainsbury Centre (now Centre for Mental Health), a research and development centre on the quality of life of people with mental health problems which played an important role in the development and implementation of the National Service Framework around the opening of the twenty first century, stated the following aims for care provision: high- quality treatments, information, support, good food and leisure. The same organisation underlined the requirement to address other functional needs that could even trigger an admission, such as 'benefits, employment and housing'. In greater detail, they presented the following matrix of needs, using the Camberwell Assessment of needs. At first glance, the environment is directly related to basic needs. However, this is not so straightforward as the arrangement, the design and the amenities included in a facility can interact with more aspects of the needs of the individual than finding shelter. For example, danger is related to spatial aspects, as are social relations. With regard to the latter, the organisation or location of a facility could enable service users to perform tasks or provide local integration opportunities. This realisation has justified the integrated and service user-centred approach adopted by the author.

At the same time, within the wider health care systems, an integrated framework for looking at service users' interface with the psychiatric system resulted in many old facilities becoming unsuitable environments for the new, more inclusive, concept of needs. When defining suitable environments for healthcare architecture, Scher [216] placed the concepts of curing, healing and caring in association with the environment. The emphasis for curing was placed on the best medical provision in the best environment that promoted concentration for the staff, and corresponded to the medical model. Healing, on the other hand, was related to the ability of the body to repair itself, as in the examples of closing wounds or growing bones. Cleanliness, nourishment and rest were essential for that process and the quality of the environment could affect the result. Finally, caring incorporated physical and mental help, comfort and reassurance, to which the environment was a major contributor.

Figure 3. Psychiatric hospital in Belgium

Figure 4. Haringey Mental Health Unit, UK

When assessed in the light of Scher's model, some psychiatric hospitals (figure 3) and some in-patient psychiatric wards in general hospitals (for example Haringey Mental Health Unit, shown in figure 4) might be regarded as having a clinical environment, even though psychiatric hospital buildings lack the sophisticated electronic systems and complicated engineering of operating theatres, pathology wards or diagnostic imaging centres. Yet, despite the fact that "cure" sounds very optimistic for mental health, it also needs to be acknowledged that the progress of the illness is not linear and relapse episodes may reoccur. By contrast with the settings illustrated above, environments for

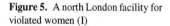

Figure 5. A north London facility for   **Figure 6.** A north London facility for   **Figure 7.** Symbolic use of
violated women (I)   violated women (II)   art in a unit for mothers

abused mothers and children extant in the broader scope of mental health provision, may take healing into consideration (figures 5-7). However, in regard to mental health, "caring" tends to be the dominant word as more recent concepts in health care design, such as salutogenics focus on psycho-social issues like service users' rights to privacy and dignity, and should emphasise health to increase the service users' sense of coherence [163], [80].

1.4. Towards a Model for Rehabilitation

The psychosocial reintegration of the mentally ill could be viewed as a process, instead of being purely restricted to discharge policies and re-settlement. Service users, staff and the community could be in partnership for its effective implementation to boost service users' skills, where these have been impaired by the illness and the hospital stay. The physical settings of rehabilitation might even be the hospital and in that sense acute settings and facilities for service users that are more stable could be included, even if they were not to be called 'rehabilitation units'. This agrees with Butcher's [53] inclusion of all service users as potential receivers of the benefits of rehabilitation in a procedure to enhance their social and mental capabilities. Even at its most rudimentary level it could include any efforts made to modify the psychiatric disability of the service user [85]. Thus, rehabilitation could benefit even the most disabled service users or only those that have just relapsed, contrary to the preceding medical treatment model which focused on symptoms reduction, set a limited time span and ignored residual disability and social handicap [177].

Rehabilitation approaches assumed that service users could gradually and with carefully structured help increase their skills, following a procedure that required patience from staff and confidence that it was possible to achieve greater independence than their current state [176]. The staff was considered to be a key element in the process. Shephed [218] supported the view that rehabilitation was more about the reassuring and supportive attitude of staff and the creation of connections with ordinary life to prevent isolation, than the provision of facilities.

As the past has shown, it takes more than a house in the community for service users to re-integrate and there can be loneliness in the community too. Nevertheless, this book suggests that carefully designed and sensitive residential architecture for people with mental health problems does have an important contribution to make in the overall process of rehabilitation, and poor and unsupportive environments may obstruct this process or prevent it from taking place at all.

1.5. Structure of the Book and Presentation of Ideas

The book consists of two main parts, the theoretical and the research one.
Part 1 comprises of three main chapters.

- Chapter 2 is a brief introduction to old practices, from the onset of mental illness, to establish the awareness of the stigma associated with the illness and its exposure in today's reality.
- Chapter 3 targets the current medical, psychosocial and architectural thinking, bringing them together to identify current influences and views on the planning of mental health facilities.
- Chapter 4 presents the alternative to the current thinking for the planning and the design on mental health, in the form of a theoretical model put together for that very purpose.

Part 2: Comprises the research and conclusion as they derived from fieldwork.

- Chapter 5 presents the methodology and the main findings from physical milieu of the research.
- Chapter 6 concentrates on the architectural checklist tool and its related findings.
- Chapter 7 readdresses policy in respect of spatial organization and design decisions and key findings stemming from users' opinions.
- Chapter 8 provides a short discussion of the implications form the findings and how these can be generalised as lessons for everyone concerned with the design and management of facilities for people with mental health problems.

Chapter 2

History of mental health and its expression in architecture

2.1. The onset of psychiatry: from God-given medicine to the deep roots of Western psychiatry and "back" to the Great Confinement

Initially, psychiatric issues were dealt with by drawing upon pagan and mystic concepts targeting Evil, even in cases where the mental patient was treated as a sacred person [87], [106]. In Ancient Greece, in Asclepeia, priests "prescribed" treatments that involved physical exercise or baths and employed God Asclepius's healing snakes that crawled on the floor of the patients' dormitories. Later, the pre-Socratic philosophers rejected divine intervention as a cause of mental illness, which was the birth of rational medicine and set the roots for Hippocrates's somatic interpretations [106]. Plato emphasised personal responsibility, giving rise to the duality of character (between morality and medicine) of psychiatry, a term that developed further in the 19th century and expressed this very duality. Aristotle introduced a more systematic approach to psychology and the Epicurean and Stoic ideas on the importance of experience and human relationships created the grounds for the English empirical school [65]. The Romans categorised medical cases and syndromes and Galen considered the brain as the centre of mental functions and spoke of psychosomatic illnesses [65], [106]. So far, one can see the absence of the stigma that still 'haunts' mental health institutions.

Between AD 354 and 430, St Augustine initiated the theological discussion on demons relating to mental illness and in about the 6th to7th century, the Church concluded that psychiatric illnesses were the Devil's work. However, the influence of Greek antiquity retained a respect for the medical theory until the 11th century, when the taxonomy of demons by Psellos ushered in the era of Demonology for the Christian countries [65], [92], [106].

In the early 14th century, the Edwardian "Statute de Prearogativa Regis" distinguished between the person of "unsound mind", the "lunatic", and the "idiot" or "natural fool", a distinction that remained until the Mental Health Act of 1959 [84]. The Bethlehem Hospital in London, accepted mentally ill patients from 1377. During the 15th century the Spanish built the first institutions in Europe to accommodate only the mentally ill [65], [141], [197]. Those were on a large scale, imposing and compact and were characterised by the strong symmetry of cruciform buildings. Spatially they were ornamentally and structurally heavy, denoting authority rather than care.

Towards the end of the 15th century, "Malleus Maleficarum" (The Witches' Hammer) related psychiatric disorders with witchcraft and heresy [65]. Mental illness was classified as a sin. Foucault [101] described the attitude of the late Middle Ages towards mental health as a procedure of salvation through segregation and social exclusion. The structures that had existed earlier for leprosy prevailed to ensure the mental restoration of the rest [101].

In the Renaissance, doctors promoted a clinical approach to psychiatric pathology [65], [11]. Gradually, cases of humanitarian psychotherapy implementations appeared, including staff hosting mentally ill people in their homes. In that transitional period, Christianity showed a new face [106]. In the Belgian town of Gheel, mentally ill people were placed in foster families to take care of their elder parents [97], [137], [206]. Gheel was the "inspiration" for the current "foster family model". Under that scheme, some service users with a past history of institutionalisation that do not have a level of independence to support themselves are placed near normative families to keep an eye on them.

The 16th century saw the first systematic efforts to design buildings for the mentally ill. Restrictive and controlling practices prevailed. The Hospital General in Paris, known as the Hotel Dieu, opened in 1586. It was something between a prison and an isolation site gathering under one administration all the previous institutions for paupers, the handicapped, the old and the sick, under rather poor conditions [197], [81], [65], [11]. This enormous hospital comprised four wards only, ignoring the number of inmates and their "diagnosis". Its L-shaped arrangement by the river did not allow space for a courtyard, emphasising the "out of sight out of mind" purpose of the institution. Yet, its lack of order was not a characteristic of its time.

Hotel Dieu-like arrangements are expressions of the 'asylum', where people are treated as clutter: hidden from society and at the minimum financial cost, despite its central location next to Notre Dame by the Seine. What today would be considered an ideal location for community architecture, due to its integration and the views it offered, was in those days an exile within the city walls due to its compact claustrophobic architecture.

Between 1650 and the 19th century, it was all over Europe a time of confinement and incarceration for all those who deviated from the social norms [32]. Bicetre and Salpetriere, in Paris accepted the mentally ill among a greater diversity of those confined. In 1676, in the rebuilt Bethlehem Hospital, special cells for lunatics were positioned on both sides of each corridor, leaving the narrow middle (gallery) for controlled interaction [161]. Later on, they separated the groups confined in different buildings. The exception was still the Hotel Dieu, where there was considerable overcrowding (some mentioned 8 patients per bed), at least until 1790 [197]. In Britain, the Vagrancy Act of 1714 enabled the incarceration of thousands of people in mad-houses, associating lunacy with criminal behaviour [32]. Restraint was a means of cure. Asylums were perceived as meeting the needs of both inmates and society, and the middle class influence on the issue gave a social dimension to the illness: the mentally ill became the pauper lunatics [81].

Social, medical and historical events gave a new outlook on the illness. The first legislation on English madhouses appeared in 1774, and related to their inspection and licensing [84]. A little earlier, in 1766, at the Bethlehem Hospital the "exhibition" of the "mad" for fun was stopped and gender segregation was enforced to protect the female service users [236], [84].

By the end of the 18th century, the historical event of the "madness" of King George III (1738- 1820) stressed the fact that the illness could affect anyone. Nevertheless, while Arnold in 1809 condemned the use of chains, he made an exception for paupers who remained treated with the same old purgatorial practices [81]. A bigger debate was on its way, when the "scourge of gaol", was associated with poor hygiene and ventilation as well as overcrowding [161]. Therefore, the doctor was called to protect the rest from the disaster that was going to spread from these places [101]. This brought environmental changes, such as fresher, mechanically ventilated air, sanitary facilities and laundries in sanitary blocks, fresh running water, as well as choice of airy locations with clear benefits for the inmates, even if for public protection motives [161].

In 1776 a committee responsible for the improvement of the French Hospitals, re-built some parts of the Salpetriere classifying and segregating the inmates [161]. Francois Viel in 1786, tried to improve ventilation by a double row of small (2.3m x 1.86m) rooms corresponding with open-air corridors. Arranging the pavilions around courtyards and providing areas with trees for walks, created a sense of freedom and comfort combined with concern for safety and security [236], [161].

The new asylum building was in accordance with the new ideas. The pavilions pro-vided an airy, better ventilated atmosphere and enabled the separation of the inmates that were not perceived as 'clutter' any more. Moreover, the idea of the pavilion redefined the open spaces of the asylums as a campus ground, with distinct-typologies and stand-alone volumes, arranged on north-south and east-west orientation around a central point. There was large economy of the ground, in terms of passages-streets left for ventilation and communication rather than open grounds that would provide views. The pavilion-type psychiatric campus is an arrangement that is still present, as a means to break the volumes and create village-like psychiatric settings.

2.2. From the ideals of the French Revolution to the asylums

The French Revolution in 1789 brought changes regarding the premises for the mentally ill. After the Declaration of the Rights of Man and the Citizens' Bill of Rights (1789), the mentally ill had to be treated in purpose-built premises by wardens who were interrogated by the judges. Doctors visited the patients and were responsible for their treatment and discharge [56]. The municipality was responsible after their discharge to observe relapse episodes, according to a 1790 law, and a year later the family was responsible for their safe keeping. Family could also place a mentally ill relative in a hospice or a maison de la sante at their own expense. For the poor, there was nothing but disorganised hospices [56].

In Central Europe, prisons and buildings for psychiatric patients were located out of towns for civilian protection. In Germany particularly, they were built out of the towns so that they did not pose any threat to the local inhabitants. At the early German prison of Celle (1710) prisoners were separated from the mentally ill, whose windows faced into the courtyard to promote security [236]. This difference of orientation compared to prisoners' cells that were facing outwards, could be interpreted as a difference in the concept for their reform [161]. This seems to be a first attempt to use the design of the building as a therapeutic means. However, there could be another possible explanation for the arrangements of the windows: the different status between a psychiatric and a criminal inmate. Perhaps the stigma of the mentally ill was stronger and they had to be well hidden from the public eye, while prisoners had to face the condemnation of the disapproving public gaze.

Later the Narentrum was built in 1783, in Vienna. It was a five-storey round building with 28 cells per floor around a central courtyard, with inadequate supervision and ventilation [197], [236]. Supervision was solved with Jeremy Bentham's Panopticon in 1791, a six-floor cylinder with cells along the periphery and a tower at the core enabling supervision from a central, raised point, invisible to the prisoners and the supervision of wardens by the director [236].

Pevsner [197] mentions that "the Panopticon was rarely and fragmentally imitated" and Markus recognises that a very limited number of buildings reached the same "asymmetry of power (as) inmates could see and hear each other, or they could see their keepers, or there were periods when they escaped surveillance" [161]. Yet, the double function of the asylum as a place of confinement and "therapy" was reflected in its architecture, which was an amalgam of prison and hospital: the cells were isolated while the ward-like gallery allowed some pseudo-freedom and social interaction, within an already isolated group [161]. Inmates were still mixed in terms of gender, social status and needs for security, as distinctions according to these parameters appeared later, in 1818, in Schleswig, Denmark. These corresponded to symmetrical arrangements, the introduction of single and double or triple cells and semi-circular development at the rear of the building [236]. These central European and English developments were still compact volumes, unlike the French pavilions. However, all models, whether pavilions or not, had cells that permitted control over the interactions between inmates, and supervision started to play an important part in the design of psychiatric buildings.

Moving over to France, the 18th century was the starting point for psychiatry, as a new discipline of medicine. It supported the idea of a therapeutic relationship with the patient and the belief in the possibility of cure, using scientific tools of observation and experimentation [11], [161]. Pinel, influenced by Rousseau and the French Revolution's ideas, supported the viewpoint of the ill person as a subject and the illness as alienation. Improvements in treatment and revised public opinion about the sufferers stemmed from this new understanding of "madness"[236]. Yet, the political liberation of the insane led them to homelessness and starvation because their "freedom" was not accompanied by a discharge policy, similarly to the recent closure of the large psychiatric institutions in Italy and America.

In the 1790s the Quaker W. Tuke established the York Retreat. Religious and moral principles emphasised a family-like hierarchy, tranquillity and physical labour, while every form of restraint was considered inappropriate [236]. Foucault interpreted the emphasis on these old principles as a protective agent against social evolution and labelled the asylum an obsolete environment (1964). The setting resembled a farm, with views, and the exterior of the Retreat looked like a home [161]. The floor plan, with rooms on both sides of a long corridor, is symmetrical and an easy environment in which to orientate oneself. The plan seems not far from many of today's psychiatric wards in terms of scale and spatial arrangement: the rooms, some common rooms and the staff rooms, are all arranged on both sides of a corridor for easy supervision and accessibility.

Pinel's and Tuke's opposition towards violence emerged from a new, better understanding of the illness, looking more closely at the person than interpreting external factors [11], [236]. These first attempts at psychotherapy are known as "moral theory". The French part of moral theory was more medically oriented. By contrast, the Quaker approach was under religious influence and Tuke's business-oriented background gave a more practical flavour to it. Somatic treatment approaches were replaced by the new "psychological" concept that temporarily set aside the physician's key role: the practitioner gradually specialising as alienist and later as psychiatrist [161]. Yet, Foucault was skeptical about the diagnostic and therapeutic intentions [101]. The clinical procedures that required observation and analysis of the symptoms led gradually to increasing isolation of the ill. The controlled environment of the hospital became the new home for the patient, with 'family' values and relationships.

In the mid-19th century, the moral treatment principles in the US framework led to the Kirkbride model at the hospital of Pennsylvania. The architect Samuel Sloan translated this into a linear building with rooms arranged on both sides of a long corridor, providing adequate daylight and ventilation, expandability and ability to separate some parts easily. Groups of 15 patients were formed according to their condition (gravity and need for security). Single rooms were used to increase safety and security. Hotel and hospital facilities were in accordance with patients' social status.

Progress throughout history tends not to follow linearity and psychiatry could not be exception to that rule. The large number of paupers in the psychiatric institutions soon put financial and social pressures on this model. In order therefore, to lower the overall costs of the institutions the limit of patients in them rose above 250 patients, decreasing the ratio of medical and nursing staff per patient [65]. However, moral theory did plant seeds for the development of psychiatry, despite the financial constraints. French physicians and the British Ellis and Conolly attempted to connect psychiatry to medical science. Again, there was some degree of variation between the two approaches: the French was fact-based theorisation (rationalism) and the English emphasised practical experience (empiricism) [81].

In France, Esquirol proposed the term asylum to counter the bad reputation of the French hospitals, used patients' isolation for therapeutic purposes and determined the relevant legal framework. Thus, in 1838 special institutions were introduced for the treatment of the mentally ill under the first law on public health, recognising the need for "real" hospitals [11], [81]. Architects and 'alienists', co-operated to design modular buildings that were repeated according to the service user categories and followed the aesthetics of other contemporary public buildings, and more precisely the neo-classical ideal [149]. The new framework aimed at patients' protection, therapy and care [56]. Among the new ideas introduced was the principle of Sectorisation, with the establishment of an asylum per each geographical departement (equiv. of province). Another pioneering development was the regulation of admissions by doctors, family and the State. The law aimed at protecting social order and safety as well as creating the conditions for therapy [11]. For that, staff acquired both juridical and medical responsibilities by guarding personal freedom and protecting against abuse for the former, and by being responsible for diagnosis, admissions and therapy for the latter [56]. Some of these principles sound very familiar and very modern today, in that safety and security are two of the main purposes of modern acute units and in that even though the service user is not considered immature, the "sectioning" is there to ensure public protection. Moreover, the principle of sectorisation has been recently re-introduced as a community psychiatry value.

Architecturally, Esquirol emphasised the importance of the plan as an instrument for cure. Esquirol's plan for the ideal asylum is characterised by its geometrical layout and is closer to the pavilion- campus model with pavilions varying according to needs. He introduced smaller scale accommodation to replace dormitories and made important proposals for the wellbeing of the inmates, stressing issues of hygiene and welfare. His colleague, Parchape, proposed aspects of "patient clarification" and determined the size of the units around 200-400 patients. These were the optimal figures for economy of scale [10], [81].

In alignment with French law, the 1845 Lunacy Act in England obliged the Counties to build asylums, and introduced the Commissioners in Lunacy, responsible for the control, the inspection of building projects and the arrangement of design standards. Previous legislation (1808 Act) permitted the building of asylums for the care and support of the mentally ill that were among the socially excluded groups of the pauper or the criminal. However, only 17 asylums were built under that law. During that period, at Hanwell asylum, William Ellis introduced occupation therapy techniques and John Connolly removed mechanical restraints [229]. His radical book "Treatment of the insane without mechanical restraint" enabled more elaborate forms of treatment [197]. Of the asylums that were built after the 1838 law, Maison de Charenton was the first and the one that influenced the rest. This was developed by Esquirol under his theory for 'madness', comprising "broad separation, provision of dormitories, categories, further degree of flexibility within, in the single rooms or other individual facilities" [171].

Regarding the architecture of the building, care was taken at all levels of design decisions, from the exterior to the interior and from large- scale to details that the building would be in accordance with the therapeutic aims. Regarding the location of the buildings, the optimum placement was amid nature, as country life was a contributor to mental health. Internal courtyards with trees were also in accordance with this. For the exterior, architect Gilbert employed classical aesthetics to promote calmness. As to the interior of the building, the proposed spatial arrangements were clear and direct, but variety and complexity characterised the smaller scale, since differentiation of the units occurred according to the user category. For the interior design, the principles of hygiene, environmental comfort and the sense of a less threatening environment implied cross-ventilation, central heating and detailing such as unobtrusive window-grilles and rounded edges [171].

At about the same period in England, in regard to Hanwell, Connolly expressed his opinion on the exterior of the asylum: "more cheerful than imposing surrounded by gardens or a farm" [229]. The day spaces were gradually introduced. What is particularly striking about this is that around 200 years later, the late 1990s built "John Connolly" mental health unit in the campus of Ealing Hospital was considered by some staff to be a boring building with institutional fittings and a rather clinical organisation that does not even have some essential safety and security features. Staff working in the acute unit described the nearby old and vacated Hanwell building as a friendlier place to be.

The last of the asylums built under the influence of the ideas of the 18th century was the new Hotel Dieu, built by Diet between 1861 and 1978. Pevsner [197] characterised the use of pavilions at the Hotel Dieu, as progressive. A strong element of French "positivist" thought was the belief that architecture could act as a control factor that could contribute to a more ordered and rational society [171]. Pevsner emphasises the move towards a massive and forbidding image that was employed to impose order. Some of these austere buildings, such as St Ann's and St Pancras Hospitals in London, reached the new Millennium providing still their services for the English NHS, giving a dimension of timeliness to this history review.

2.3. The transition from the "second Age of Confinement" to social psychiatry

In 1815-16, when the House of Commons faced the need for a greater labour force, they expected psychiatry to help the mentally ill, so that they could contribute to society [81]. In this way, they regarded the mentally ill as a potentially active part of society, a concept very far removed from previous 'out of sight, out of mind' ideas. Yet, this approach did not last long, as new social forces prevailed.

Edwards [84] perceives the hundred years between 1850 and 1950 in England as showing the least possible concern for the mentally ill. This backward movement had financial and political origins. Between 1850 and 1950 the confinement was 30 times greater than the Great Confinement of Foucault [11]. In England, the Lunatics Asylum Act (1845) generated the establishment of asylums all over the country, in accordance with Victorian values. It was an expression of philanthropic intentions to provide care to a wider part of the population, with "deliberate mass institutionalisation" of the pauper classes during the Industrial Revolution [32].

This overcrowding combined with the scarcity of means and staff increased the custodial character of the 19th century institutions and led to a series of expansions that resulted in complicated forms [236], [161]. Categories of patients became more elaborate. Galleries and day rooms were differentiated in accordance with classification principles [161]. The design aimed at providing the maximum amount of sunshine and southern orientation, leading to the development of the "broad arrow plan" and at the same time symmetrical plan and monumental appearance generated easily supervised, prison-like solutions, giving administration a focal point [10], [229].

Additionally, there were special institutions for "idiots" and, after 1860, special buildings for "criminal lunatics". The State Criminal Asylum Broadmoor (figure 8), was built by a military engineer [229]. When the fieldwork was conducted Broadmoor was still the major high-security psychiatric prison in England. The mention of this building here is not irrelevant: some of the service users that participated in the main research, had a past history of long hospitalisation and one participating service user was discharged from Broadmoor.

Figure 8. Broadmoor High Security Psychiatric Hospital. Old parts coexist with recent, surrounded by impenetrable walls.

That period showed elements of legalism with three different laws enacted: the Lunacy Regulation Act 1853, the Lunacy Act 1853 and the Lunatic Asylums Act - deal with different classes of lunatics: the ones so found by inquisition, private lunatics and pauper lunatics, under the Poor Law and judges' decisions about admissions [60]. The three acts became one only after the 1890 Lunacy Act [84].

At the end of the 19th century, as a result of the influence of the Enlightenment, the concept of asylum was questioned again [236]. In 1858 Lord Shaftsbury commented on the grievous prevailing asylum system [197]. In the 1870s a medical superintendent designed a horseshoe type, for the Lancashire County Asylum, with recreation, dining and services located centrally. During the next two decades substantial buildings (for over 1000 patients), with centralised and extensive circulation spaces prevailed [229].

At the beginning of the 20th century, E. Toulouse in France transformed the asylum into a hospital through the creation of hospital spaces as well as family spaces. The newly named "mentally ill" had the option of outpatient services and free admission. Toulouse talked about prevention, introduced mental hygiene and expressed his opposition to the "total irresponsibility" of the mental patient [11]. In Russia, after the Revolution, the Soviet Government built small community projects in Moscow, and in 1932 the Russians established an equivalent of what would nowadays be called a day hospital [154], [243]. At about the same time, in 1929, the Germans started using occupational therapy as a means for the mentally ill to recuperate [243]. In the meantime, the Maudsley Hospital in South London was built after World War I. It was a teaching and research hospital, in which the need for medical and moral treatment was stressed. Gradually hospitals for acute service users emerged in the old asylum campuses [229]. In the US, the Movement for Mental Health in the Community was formed, setting the ground for de-institutionalisation [65].

In the aftermath of World War I, the need for the treatment of "shell shock" in 1917 initiated social psychiatry as a new field of medicine, responsible for the provision of social services [154]. Methods of social and vocational rehabilitation were introduced, together with concerns regarding institutional behaviour due to long- term sojourns [243]. Between the 1920s and 1930s, UK legislation tried to provide for mental health as part of its public healthcare programme [32]. The 1930s also saw advances in medicine [84]. Meantime, in private clinics in the US and Berlin, Germany, psychoanalysis was a newly emerging influence. However, nothing changed in public institutions [65]. Architecturally, the twentieth century followed the general architectural trends. According to Pevsner, apart from the monumental chapel of the Steinhof Asylum, Vienna, by Otto Wagner, at the beginning of the century, no other building deserves special mention [197].

2.4. Social psychiatry and the return of the mentally ill into the community

The Second World War was a turning point as far as disability was concerned. During the war, in the UK military psychiatrists conducted research, while in France, a lot of the asylum population died of hardships. Yet, as it is expected, the numbers of mentally ill increased after the war ended, creating poor conditions in the existing facilities [79]. The numbers of war victims generated a more sympathetic mentality in regard to the integration of the poor and the disabled into society, initiating the concept of rehabilitation. However, it took 20 years for the US to include the mentally ill in rehabilitation procedures and forty years for Europe to follow suit [77].

Social re-adaptation of the mentally ill targeted the return of the hospital population to the community and, if possible, to employment [241]. In France, Sivadon pioneered in the field with the establishment of the Treatment and Social Re-adaptation Centre. This Centre gradually led to the creation of the association Elan Retrouve in Paris, in 1948.

The social and economic changes of the aftermath of WW II promoted the acknowledgement of social psychiatry and the re-invention of the psychiatric profession. In 1953, the discovery of tranquillizers was a turning point in the history of psychiatry [32]. They enabled the exit of a great number of chronic patients back to the community, the re-evaluation of the role of the psychiatric hospital, and the creation of psychiatric departments in General Hospitals leading to the medicalisation of mental health [60], [65]. New treatments such as electro-convulsive therapy and encephalography became available [84].

All those developments cast doubt as to the role of the hospital as a provider of long term care. Barton proposed the term "institutional neurosis" to describe the difficulty in coping with everyday life activities acquired by long-term service users during their hospitalisation [192]. A timely discharge was the new target [243]. Complementary to that, in the UK the "therapeutic community" movement considered a stay in hospital as a step in the treatment, targeting recovery and a subsequent return to the community. It aimed at increasing service users' "daily living skills" and valued the role of psychotherapy [45], [218].

The model introduced some revolutionary ideas, such as the disuse of uniforms and the promotion of self-government for service users, as well as the use of first names for service users and doctors [57]. Additionally, it supported the involvement of non-medical staff, such as therapists and psychologists and emphasised service users' well-being. The concept of the "therapeutic community" was opposed to the medical model, which favoured the use of drugs and ECT [57]. However, service user empowerment began when the service users acquired the right to participate in the administration [45].

In 1944, former hospital inmates had set up in New York the WANA (We Are Not Alone), a self-support group. In 1958, WANA members hired a social worker, J Beard, who designed the Clubhouse [69] (figures 9, 10). This was a club that prepared people for life after hospital, prevented members' isolation in the community and restored their self-esteem. The members ran the facility and hired staff [34]. Gradually, its members provided training for more such projects to open and eventually clubhouses operated in several locations in the western world, including the UK.

Figure 9. Facade the Mosaic Clubhouse   **Figure 10.** The interior of the Mosaic Clubhouse

The 1950s proved to be a period with important developments regarding legislation both in the UK and France towards de-institutionalisation. In 1951 the French legislation included prevention and social re-integration of the mentally ill in its framework [56]. In the ensuing years more countries included community care in their formal policies and legislation. In the UK, the Royal Commission on the Law Relating to Mental Illness and Mental Deficiency in 1957, known as the Percy Commission, established the medical character of mental illness, even without evidence, and doctors took over from magistrates [60]. Subsequently, the Mental Health Act of 1959, transferred mental health issues from jurisdiction to doctors and enabled informal admission, where patients were deemed to be visiting mental hospital as if it were the same as any other medical institution [84], [60], [188]. That Act reflected the "optimism" about the potential of therapy and the increasing status of the medical profession. It remained the main body of the UK legislation for mental health until 1983 and influenced the legislation of other countries as well, as in the case of the Greek legislation of 1973 on mental health [60], [189].

Baldwin interpreted the Mental Health Act of 1959, which enabled the relocation of the mentally ill to the community, as a way of cutting down public expenses. Indeed, the UK Hospital Plan in 1962 among other measures proposed financial cuts [32]. However, it was backed by the concept that the asylum was a dying institution, that psychosocial theories such as the "therapeutic community" would help eliminate chronic conditions and that occupational re-integration was considered as the necessary next step [241]. There was also political and social pressure exerted for attention to neglected and deprived groups and the re-arrangement of NHS resources [231].

From a legal point of view, the 1959 Act was the butt of criticism that it sustained an impression that the community needed to be protected from the mentally ill (Deirdre et al 1996). That dual character of mental health services was not helpful in eliminating the stigma of mental illness or the full acceptance of the mentally ill by the community and is an issue that since the new Millennium has reappeared on the agenda of the UK government.

In 1960, from the UK and France, doctors A Baker and P Sivadon and architect RL Davies collaborated on the WHO publication "Psychiatric services and architecture". They proposed a system of psychiatric care, with the psychiatric hospital occupying a central role within an extensive network of community facilities. The hospital attended to those cases where hospitalisation was necessary, for as long as it was therapeutically appropriate. The hospital should no longer resemble a prison but be as close to a domestic setting as possible. The community structures they proposed were the dispensary and "early treatment centre", the day hospital, protected workshops, after-care at home and in the working community. They also emphasised the proximity of all services to the community they served. Their system incorporated and offered continuity of care. For the new hospitals they proposed the model of the village, where the space should help therapeutic staff restore service users' health. The services, i.e., service user accommodation, therapeutic workshops, social centre, medical centre, and administration, should be in distinctive blocks to avoid long corridors and large- scale buildings. Additionally, through the composition of spaces and architectural details such as colours, lighting and heating, they aimed at the social re-education of the service users and suggested that the size of the village should be approximately 280 beds [31].

For the existing hospitals, the team disapproved of complexes larger than 1000 beds and proposed an upper limit of 300 beds, explaining the extensive changes that they considered necessary for their modernization. They proposed a continuous system, included the family as an informed participant in the process and incorporated psychosocial theories into the design of the units. The theoretical context that combined psychosocial theories and architecture with therapeutic intentions became known as "psychiatric architecture".

Despite WHO recommendations for the size of a psychiatric hospital at around 250-1000 beds and research suggesting that the financially optimum solution was for about 400 beds, the reality was harsher [248], [236]. The psychiatric wards of that period could reach numbers of 80 service users, featuring small openings, locks, padded cells and immobile or very heavy furniture. Yet, the return of mental health to the general body of healthcare was underlined by the gradual introduction of diagnostic and therapeutic services into the psychiatric department of the general hospital [236]. The psychiatric department was initially a ward following the rest of the hospital layout, physically integrated to the hospital complex, using the hospital facilities and enabling economy of resources. The psychiatric department removed the "out of sight, out of mind" approach of asylums. The hospital campus and the shorter stays served the elimination of stigma [163], [236]. The short period of stay in the general hospital generated peripheral facilities. Initially, community services such as the day hospital that was introduced in the UK in 1948 to keep service users close to their physical and social environment, covered prevention as well as primary care and, in a few cases, secondary care [153].

The movement of community care was introduced in the 1960s, was a derivative of medical and psychiatric influences and lasted until to the late 1980s. It helped demedicalise services, promoted the role of other disciplines in the provision of mental health by showing the limitations of the medical model and advocated prevention as a factor that can reduce hospital admissions [32]. As a result of the opening of the services to non-medical environments, the 1960s also saw a growth in social services [84].

Nevertheless, the motives behind community care were sometimes driven by a lack of resources or a need to cut down on expenditure, rather than scientific evidence. The possibility of "the new chronic mentally ill" and the "revolving door syndrome", i.e., the frequent re-admissions of service users mostly because they lived in poor conditions in the community or there was no follow-up, had not yet become apparent. Baldwin recognised the medical concept and ethos behind community care, but insisted that, politically, it facilitated the under-funding of mental health. This was the case in Italy and the US but was even earlier the case in the part-time hospitalisation introduced in the USSR before WWII as a means to counteract the lack of psychiatric beds [62], [157].

In the US, the Kennedy policy, the war in Vietnam and the social pathology of urban life played a leading role in the recognition of social psychiatry [154]. Prevention and early treatment to prevent more serious disturbances were among the aims of the American system [26]. President Kennedy proclaimed mental health and learning difficulties as the nation's major health problems and established the Community Mental Health Centres (CMHCs) [233].

The CMHCs received governmental funding in 1963 [241]. They were located in a variety of settings such as storefronts, office buildings, former private homes or even self-contained luxurious clinics and provided in-patient and out-patient care, partial hospitalisation, covered for emergencies and provided such services as education and consultation [26], [237]. In the subsequent fifteen years, 700 CMHCs began operations and many of the hospitals were either closed or renovated to assume a new purpose [159].

The CMHCs served the population of specific catchment areas and attempted to build a close relationship with local communities [26], [237]. Nevertheless, the local community was often opposed to them and it was then that the infamous slogan "Not In My Backyard" (NIMBY) was first pronounced. A possible contribution to this was the wave of homeless mentally ill people that followed the closure of many psychiatric hospitals [168]. Many former hospital inmates lacked the skills to survive and support themselves in the community and the existing community facilities had not been adequately planned or co-ordinated to prevent this [6], [77]. Additionally, there was a lack of affordable and accessible housing for them to go to and inappropriately premature discharges added to the families' burden [180], [132], [134]. Even later, in the 1970s and 1980s, the absence of high quality services in the community, in the US context, kept the levels of the revolving door syndrome high [241].

Gradually, psychiatry was the target of criticism for its inability to cater alone for the needs of the mentally ill. The notion that the wellbeing of the latter and the "effective reduction of disability" were equally important gained ground and have since remained as focal points of the therapeutic elements of care [61], [185]. The lessons gained from the US experience influenced European policies, and the social services provision for the mentally ill in Europe became more comprehensive [77]. Here, pressure to acknowledge the rights of the mentally ill brought about the opening of the gates of the mental institutions. Yet, in real life there were still wards of 60 beds, lack of privacy and inadequate sanitary facilities: a situation that demanded a change [227].

The events of May 1968, played a significant role in the Italian de-institutionalisation [154], [241]. Italy moved large numbers of service users from hospitals into community based services. In the context of these new policy ideas, it should be mentioned here that in France in 1960, the sectorisation principle came on the agenda. Nevertheless, it took twenty five years for it to be implemented. According to the sectors policy, local multidisciplinary teams co-ordinate care and prevention efforts in the locality [242].

Among the options for life in the community, the "hospital house" model was rediscovered in the early 1960s in the UK, for stays of between six months to a year. For more independent service users, there were the group homes [1]. These were run mainly by service users after their discharge from hospital, with visiting psychiatrists spending some time there during the day. The homes were ordinary houses on lease, for about five to six residents, or twelve in the case of group-home mansions [150].

During the same decade in Scandinavia, the seeds for "normalisation theory" were sown. Normalisation theory stood at the opposite side of institutionalisation, attempting to bring everyday-life practices to people with disabilities. The theory was initially concerned with people with learning difficulties but gradually received a more generic character and nowadays it aims at the social re-integration of vulnerable groups and advocates that their lifestyle should be as similar as possible to that of "non-disabled citizens" [192]. Normalisation greatly influenced the design of environments for disability, with an emphasis on "homelike" solutions and played an important part in the theoretical framework of this dissertation.

Returning to mental health and the psychosocial theories in France, Professor Sivadon identified a therapeutic element in space itself. Among other solutions, he created spatial situations, for instance alternating between secure and insecure areas, to trigger service users' emotions for therapeutic purposes [219]. The Institut Marcel Riviere was designed in accordance with Sivadon's principles. Design details should convey hidden messages to users. For example, he proposed relatively wide hallways to avoid a feeling of captivity and considered the use of diamond-shaped steps or arches to impose "therapeutic" insecurity [219]. Later, those designs would feed the bipolar elements concept of Amiel [10], "a village where he feels secure and fulfils his need for dependency, a social centre, where he finds satisfaction for his stomach and mind but in an environment where he is exposed to the danger of encounter. And between these two poles, both attractive for opposite reasons, is an insecurity spatial obstacle" [219].

In 1961, in Salt Lake City, an interdisciplinary conference stressed the lack of systematic information on buildings for psychotics. With that in mind, a project was put into effect in Topeka State Hospital, Kansas, to address the problem in practice. The psychosocial needs of service users constituted the main concerns of the programme, under the slogan "architectural modification to meet functional change" and space aimed at the maximisation of service users' assets and the minimisation of disabling factors. The project focused on the modification of an existing women's ward, which typologically belonged to the "Kirkbride" type, a model based on moral theory and first designed for the Philadelphia Hospital. About fifteen rooms were arranged on both sides of a double-loaded corridor, each room occupying the largest possible space that would ensure single-room occupancy [108].

Similar to Professor Sivadon's theories, Good, Siegel and Bay manipulated the environment for therapeutic purposes. More specifically, the ego integration and the social integration of the individual comprised the psychosocial dimensions of the study. For the establishment of identity, they employed "cultural familiarity, unambiguous surroundings, consistent environmental cues, access to the experience of one's identity via for example mirrors, calendars, clocks; and daily and weekly newspapers for orientation to time" [108]. Staff imposed less control when the service user was progressing. For the social integration, the team added interaction among the therapeutic tools. For instance, chairs and sofas in communal areas were arranged in small groupings, instead of being placed against the walls.

This was a broader study compared to Baker, Davies and Sivadon's. It covered a wider range of facilities and included cases where both modifications and new constructions had taken place. On the other hand, it did not reach the depth of Good et al. to include detailed plans of furnishings and "unit systems", neither did it follow detailed mapping of the ward activities as they took place before the renovation. The European team was closer to a psychoanalytic approach, while in the second team we can identify the experimental nature of the project. The team aimed at a "scientific" approach, oriented towards environmental psychology. To build on the experience of the project, a conference was held two years later. Methodology was discussed extensively during the conference, and in general terms there was optimism about experimental studies, especially if they focused on small details [108].

In the 1970s, de-institutionalisation became more concrete in Europe, albeit in a variety of ways. Belgium, a country with a tradition in the humane treatment of the mentally ill, made its transition from the asylum model to the psychiatric centre in the 1970s and transferred acute beds from psychiatric hospitals to general hospitals in the 1980s [97]. Additionally, the decree of 1975 established fully equipped multi-disciplinary teams, including psychiatrists, nurses, psychologists, social workers and work therapists [99]. Psychiatric wards co-operated with community services. In Flanders, the tradition of foster families was revived and 1100 service users, most of them with an additional form of learning disability, lived in half-way homes and were served by a 250 bed hospital in Gheel, mostly as out-patients [62]. However, although there were no reported cases of discrimination, anthropological research indicated that those people "were kept at arms-length socially" [206].

In the UK, community mental health started to gain public support, yet there was still prejudice and mental health was still a politically "embarrassing" issue [3]. Steps towards de-institutionalisation were more cautious than in the US. Hospital beds were reduced to 80-120, and the concept of the hostel for 20-30 residents with learning disabilities gradually moved to mental health [32]. Staffed hostels were similar to the group homes but served a younger service user group with no or limited previous hospital experience. Additionally, the number of hospital service users declined due to deaths of chronic mentally ill inmates who had reached old age, and the development of new types of facilities [103]. One of these was the hospital-hostel, which was created for the "new long stay" group, i.e. service users who had spent between one to five years in a psychiatric hospital [103], [200]. Later on, the "core and cluster" model, with residential, "satellite" units and a group-home (6-12 residents) were favoured [32].

Italy on the contrary, following left wing party political pressure and under the influence of anti-psychiatry and the tenets of Basaglia, stopped hospital admissions from 1978 [62], [241]. Out-patient departments treated all new patients, and in-patients gradually moved to accommodation in the community, including flats and their own homes [62].

In France, Professor Amiel revisited the term asylum to restore its original meaning as a haven, and advocated the vital role of the hospital [62]. He envisaged the hospital as one instrument among all the therapeutic tools the psychiatrist had and used the term "topotherapy" to emphasise the therapeutic properties of three-dimensional space. According to topotherapy, spatial relationships could aid the restoration of personality [10]. This was based on the concept that space and time were axes upon which personality was developed, and on theories proposing that spatial relationships appeared genetically earlier and were simpler than the temporal ones. Furthering Sivadon's earlier concept on proximity and distance to trigger behavioural responses, Amiel [10] presented five bipolar pairs that the therapist could use:

- Solititude vs communal life
- Small vs large group
- Relaxation vs activity
- Dependence vs independence
- Security vs insecurity

The role of the designer was to address a mass of other pairs, e.g. open vs closed or dark vs light, based on the previous five, and to create a space that would facilitate a return to the community. Amiel rejected the appearance of both the public buildings and the house as a model to achieve this purpose, and found the residential hotel style as the preferred option.

H. Goodman, Chief Architect of the British Ministry of Health took a stand contrary to Amiel's theories and became actively involved with hospital projects. Goodman [109] speculated that the building served clinical purposes by providing a normal environment, with respect to clinical needs. According to him, staff and service user involvement was essential and integration of the facility to the locality should be above architectural gestures. Cost effectiveness and the social problems of the mentally ill were the first priorities, compared to architectural issues. Regarding the exterior design, he favoured the "small residential college", in a domestic style, which blended in with its surroundings. He accepted brick walls and sloping tiled roofs, "if this is vernacular" [109]. For interior design, he insisted on normal furniture and carpeting. When faced with the dilemma between a normal environment and security, the balance favoured the first, as a more "traditional" approach to providing special measures for physical security, and averting suicide was increasingly being regarded as unnecessary and self-defeating [109].

As community care progressed, the results from the fragmented systems and the gaps in the services started to show. The role of the facilities had not been clearly defined. Uncertainties concerning the transitory versus permanent character of types of accommodation such as group homes could create confusion over their exact role [230]. There was also a growing realisation that service users in mental health care, be it a hospital or a community setting, could gain only a certain degree of independence [102]. At the same time, the policy of abandoning the old hospitals and substituting to them with the medical environment of the general hospital was criticised by some [62]. There were even those who warned that the psychiatric hospitals were resistant to change, and that more than hard work and experience were needed in order to modernise the social environment of the hospital [45]. Experiments by Rosenham in psychiatric hospitals indicated the limitations of psychiatrists to distinguish between "real" and "pseudo" service users in the hospital environment, shedding more doubt on the whether this type of environment was the right one [35]. These experiments were clearly influenced by anti-psychiatry ideas, and have fairly often been used by the advocates of community care to discredit the hospital setting.

Yet despite this criticism of the hospital, experience in the community showed that reality was not black or white. Professionals started to caution against the hasty adoption of a community care model. Practice had shown that institutional behaviour was not necessarily a trait of the hospital environment. Community facilities cultivate institutional behaviours too [62], [231]. The next step was not so much with a view to creating new, revolutionary facilities but to evaluate the efforts so far and to try to make the most out of them.

2.5. The rationalisation of mental health care under the managerial perspective and the involvement of social services

As the historical review of the second half of the century indicated, several care models appeared around the world, differing as to the place of the hospital in their systems. During the 1980s, all three options co-existed [227]:

- Total community care, translated into ordinary housing for all
- Community care driven by pragmatism, i.e., care in the community but in co-operation with a hospital or small- scale asylum
- Radical approach to hospital care, which proposed that modernised hospital care provided a community network in its own right

These approaches should, however, be set in the broader context of the main developments in different parts of the world. The US, for example, is at one end of a spectrum in which the hospital, at least in the public sector, was replaced by a diverse array of community projects under the Community Support System (CSS) despite the serious problems stemming from the under- funding of its public mental health sector [232]. Yet, starting from the 1980s, they regarded mental health as a condition rather than an illness. The CSS, that influenced the UK system, comprised ten areas of service provision: crisis response, mental health treatment, service user identification and outreach, rights protection and advocacy, rehabilitation, family and community support, peer support, income support and entitlements, and housing, as well as general health care [233]. The private sector of the country, however, was driven by market policies and that also reflected on the buildings.

In Europe, the mental health care picture varied according to the context. The UK is again located among the countries that kept a more critical eye on the hospital issue, while France and Belgium will present two models that retain the hospital. France presented an extensive network of community projects, with the hospital keeping responsibility for the acute part. Belgium developed three types of care: the intramural, the transmural and the extramural. The first consisted of several types of hospital settings including large psychiatric hospitals, like the 672 bed Bethanienhuis, and psychiatric departments of general hospitals. The second type comprised nursing homes and various degrees of sheltered living, the third provided ambulatory care and there was also the foster family program. In Belgium many of the rehabilitation functions took place in hospitals or in village-like hospital campuses (figures 11) and reintegration was a major part of the therapeutic mission of the hospital, where day or night hospitalisation were available [97].

Figure 11. Psychiatric units in Belgium with high quality environment, coupled to the use of art and other service user oriented approaches. Yet, they were located on the sites of former asylums. However, their outreach policy and the independence of their units retained the therapeutic balance.

Finally, Greece took the big step towards de-institutionalisation, passing the 815/84 law under European Union pressure and is one of the countries that could benefit from the discussion but also the country where psychiatry was born. Greek psychiatric care was centralised and a co-ordinating and supervisory mechanism was absent [225]. The programme to be followed included four parameters: the introduction of CMHCs, an increase in the number of GH psychiatric wards, improvement of the conditions of psychiatric hospitals and the movement of people back to the community. Of those measures, Ramon (1996)[206] recognised that only the second target had been dealt with seriously. Inspectors, whose power was limited, were imposed to supervise the program, but who described the psychiatric hospitals in gloomy colours [82].

In the section regarding new community projects, ECITE [168], mentioned new facilities such as hostels and therapeutic apartments, in new buildings, but located within the walls of the old institutions (figures 12) or on the island of Leros.

Figure 12. The psychiatric unit in Stavroupolis, Greece

These facilities operated chaotically or antagonistically to one another, and absorbed the "easy" cases, while in the psychiatric hospitals medication continued to provide the major therapeutic instrument [164]. Nevertheless, although the 815/84 Regulation was fragmentally realised and lacked the planning and inspection mechanisms to safeguard its effectiveness, it provided Greece with the opportunity and the funding to start the Psychiatric Revolution and to modernize its services [215]. The new facilities have made an important contribution, despite inadequacies in information, mismanagement and lack of organised programmes [143]. Studies so far reported service user satisfaction with the new community projects [137], [234]. However, in the last few years no major changes in the service occurred, and the financial state of the country took its toll on the quality of the services.

2.6. Community Care in the UK and France from the Eighties on

In what follows, developments in the UK and France are presented in greater detail, due to their selection as locations for the empirical part of the research that follows the theory part. In the UK, in the 1980s, mental health, together with other public health fields, experienced the influence of managers in the system as the NHS was undergoing a financial crisis [126]. Planners, managers and administrators were employed to run the system under the new "business management" [32]. Principles from the running of other public-use facilities, hotels for instance, were brought up for discussion, questioning the extent of medical authority. Mental health and social services co-operated in terms of the way in which residential settings were being involved in the NHS care program, with emphasis on the planning of the service and not on the actual facilities [233]. The DoE encouraged experimentation in housing provision for the mentally ill and for people with learning difficulties, emphasising the 'core and cluster' model, and urged for more involvement by housing associations [194].

Influenced by normalisation principles, this co-operation translated into the belief that ordinary housing should become accessible to the mentally ill [103]. The House of Commons proposed a move towards local over distant networks, small over large schemes, and home over institution [245]. Additionally, comments on the role of primary care in early treatment and prevention were borrowed from the US experience [193]. The debate included the involvement of GPs in long-term follow-up and re-curing episodes, provided that GPs acquired new skills [224].

The joint work by the NHS and social services, as Turner-Crowson pointed out, lacked coherence. Organisational and financial inadequacies of the service followed the restructuring of the system, characterised by massive hospital closures [55], [144]. Moreover, institutional solutions could still find their way into the new reality. For instance, a common community setting, the day hospital, was mainly situated in hospital sites [211].

Thirty years on, the mental health sector of NHS suffers from tight budgets and limited political initiatives. Yet, the British reforms of the 1980s have been recognised later on by countries like Italy, which was advanced in clinical terms but neglected the managerial aspects of the service [72]. They could even provide a model for Greece to consider, since the country is trying to modernise its mental health care sector and could benefit from more structured approaches and some questioning of medical authority. Moreover, they could act as a reminder of these years, when a strong questionmark was placed on all aspects of institutions. That would be very valuable these days, where the unweighted importance on everything that takes away the "burden" of responsibility regarding risk, even if this compromises other choices or aspects of care threatens with the formation of new institutional environments.

In the second half of the 1980s, proposals came up regarding the use of ordinary accommodation for all service user groups. [217] had foreseen the greater use of existing housing for hostels, mainly because of its cost-effectiveness. Brandon proposed the solution of ordinary housing that operated flexibly in relation to staff levels, from full time to unstaffed, according to service users' needs , and there was also the proposal for the Haven Community, of Frien Hospital [103], [176]. The Haven Community aimed to revisit the concept of the asylum with its initial meaning as a haven, which would be able to provide specialised care and develop ties and interaction with the community [103]. It comprised four houses for those most in need of specialised care in the hospital. Other houses and flats on the campus or locally, provided various degrees of supervision. The hospital had plans to include functions and to share facilities with the local community, to encourage the latter in the campus.

Organisationally-wise, according to Ramon [206], in Britain there were three ideas about mental health provision that were not entirely compatible amongst themselves. First, there were those who favoured more profit-oriented approaches in which professional interventions became a costly option. Second, normalisation and "social role valorisation", which translated to service user participation, opposite to the aforementioned centrality-oriented model. Last, there was the rehabilitation approach, according to each service user's capabilities.

The services were patchy and unevenly developed among the health authorities, with considerable inequalities among facilities that performed a similar function [138], [214]. Tomlinson [231], described group homes with high standards in the UK but also mentioned places in a poor physical state, that were unhygienic, neglected and dangerous for staff and service users alike. Thus, at the beginning of the new millennium, there were areas such as East Ham, London, where the hospital was still the major provider of care, or the psychiatric unit in the campus of Ealing Hospital, London, which totaled over 400 beds, and areas like Northern Birmingham, where home treatment teams and a network of Community Mental Health Centres, that included small acute wards, which had replaced the hospital. Yet, both professionals and the general public became more interested in the quality of the facilities provided in the community than in issues of hospital treatment and detention [130].

Nevertheless, psychiatric advances, both in treatment and in community care, did not eliminate the need for specialised facilities providing intensive treatment and support, even if these were community based. There were warnings against the reduction of acute psychiatric beds, mainly because of the rising numbers of service users under section and the lack of consideration from the community-based facilities for violent service users [148], [214], [76]. As a result, ward occupancy rates reached in certain cases as high as 127%, which translated into compromises in admissions [214].

At the beginning of the millennium, the UK government issued the National Service Framework, a ten-year plan that set the general policy, together with standards and performance indicators. The plan focused on severe mental illness and suicide rate reduction. Additionally, it incorporated funding provision for around the clock staffed accommodation, secure beds, assertive outreach and home treatment [111]. The framework aimed to unify the provision of care around the country and moved forward the trend to include social services and the voluntary sector in the care and treatment of mentally ill people. Moreover, it promulgated an increase in forensic beds and incorporated a strong tendency towards single-sex accommodation. According to Gournay, the increased role of social services and agencies might move acute care towards more residential settings, instead of the psychiatric ward of the general hospital (2000) (figures 13-16).

Figure 13. Woodgreen Mental Health Centre (I)   **Figure 14.** Woodgreen Mental Health Centre (II)   **Figure 15.** Artwork in dining room of hostel for homeless mentally ill   **Figure 16.** Living room in hostel for homeless mentally ill

In France, sectorisation legislation was finally established in 1985 and the care provision was even greater than in the UK. The country was divided into approximately 825 psychiatric sectors, each with an initial population of 60,000, though there were variations in size and many of them exceeded this number [160], [242]. The objectives of the psychiatric sector comprised the better treatment of in-patients, treatment closer to home and the promotion of prevention and aftercare [241]. The sector referred mainly to the needs of the chronic population and the hospital concentrated on the provision of diagnosis and acute care [160]. Also, the sectorisation concept permitted access to care for all population groups, facilitated continuity of care and brought the carer closer to the recipient of the service [242].

As in other countries at end of the century, France witnessed an evolution in its services, and their growth within the national health services network. Despite the fact that the hospital remained the main provider for acute cases, 60% of service users would never have an experience of the hospital [241]. The Decree of 14 March 1986 regulated the alternatives to hospitalisation, and four years later legislation confirmed voluntary hospitalisation as the main form of hospitalisation [56].

Although France retained the hospital for acute care, it transferred many of the other functions to the community. In acute cases, service users could initially refer to crisis centres for a short-term stay to assess if hospitalisation was necessary. There was separation between full time and part time hospitalisation. Occupation, accommodation and hospitalisation were covered by different facilities [198]. The hospital service for 25-100 bed capacity was situated in the psychiatric hospital under the new name of Centre Hospitalier Specialise (Specialised Hospital Centre) and was supported by a wide of spectrum of facilities in the community [160]. The sojourn in the hospital was short, until service users were able to move into 24-hour staffed facilities in the community.

A variety of community facilities for after-care, chronic service user accommodation, rehabilitation and occupational reintegration, together with involvement of the community and combination of pharmacological treatment and therapies targeted individual needs [201]. Briefly, the 1990 circular established the following types of community services: the dispensary, which focused on prevention, the day hospital, the night hospital, the CAT (Centre for Assisted Occupation), and the therapeutic apartments [198]. Other types of facilities included the CMP (Medico-Psychological Centre), the CATP (Part time Centre for Therapeutic Activities), the Day Centre, the Crisis Centres, the Foyer de Post Cure (after care hostel) and re-adaptation organisations [160].

Hospitalisation beds were reduced in cases of combined use of night hospitalisation and CAT. Thus, service users could retain a job or an external activity, limiting the effects of exclusion, and this enhanced the quality of their lives [116]. The combined use of the night hospital and CAT targeted rehabilitation, prepared service users for autonomy and enabled people to work whilst undergoing treatment [198]. This combination of alternatives to in-patient care maximised independence and service users learned new skills in a more realistic environment. By the year 1993 there was great demand for the CAT and similar services, e.g. the fayer de vie, and growing concerns about the long waiting lists [152].

Night time hospitalisation, combined with the use of day centres, is a model that has not been used in the UK, where there have been no night hospitals and where according to Muijen [178] there was inadequate use of day centres. Muijen supported the view that night hospitalisation could be more beneficial than day hospitalisation because it had more social advantages and also provided treatment at night, when the risk factor for service users is generally higher. Even during the exploratory visits within the UK in connection with this thesis, only one night centre was identified. Yet, it operated like a crisis cafe, a place for a chat, with no specialised staff.

Communal houses targeted more autonomous service users who still needed 24-hour care and support from teams similar to those of the hospital, until they were ready for the next level of independence, usually therapeutic apartments. [145], [152]. Therapeutic apartments provided accommodation for service users past the acute stage but still in need of 24-hour medical and nursing care [145]. When service users who followed a social re-integration programme in the communal houses or the apartments relapsed, they moved back to hospital [152]. More autonomous service users moved to individual lodgings, alone or in pairs [152].

Alternatively, the French adopted the foster family model from Belgium, for short- or medium- term care aiming at the social re-education and re-integration of service users [117]. Another innovative project was the three weeks' holidays planned by service users, accompanied by staff or that could even be taken alone their stage of independence permit [196]. That took place in some of the French case studies observed in this research.

However, there has also been criticism about inequalities that existed between the sectors and the limited growth of out-hospital care [242]. The size of sectors, the percentage of out-hospital care, the types and the quality of the facilities and their buildings, which in some cases were in very poor condition, varied considerably around the country [160], [202], [238] (figures 17-20).

Figure 17. French psychiatric unit (I)   **Figure 18.** French psychiatric unit (II)   **Figure 19.** French psychiatric unit (III)   **Figure 20.** French psychiatric unit (IV)

2.7. Key messages regarding Community Care

The previous century witnessed some doubt arising about the role of the hospital, an initial optimism about community care and, later, increased insight into the realisation of the persistent character of mental illness. At present, there is no question of returning to the traditional psychiatric hospital model or a system that does not include community care, as alternatives to hospitalisation can prove to be at least as effective as hospitals [200], [241], [178], [248]. Many studies confirm the beneficial role of smaller units for service users' progress, autonomy and initiative [174], [120]. However, critical implementation of community care and careful planning is essential for its success. Inadequate funding or service users' exclusion from the decision making lead to inadequacies and underlying planning problems in the provision of care, even if the required standards for community care were higher than the hospital care model [133], [178], [96], [238]. In that respect and in a more comprehensive approach, 'quality of life' was also advocated as an alternative to 'quality of care' [32], [89].

An important factor for the implementation of the community care model is the attention to the needs of the new long-stay service users. The lack of alternatives creates either a blockage of acute beds or inadequate support for the service users, who might be deprived of therapeutic intervention and lead isolated lives [181], [245]. This unavailability of services may be impairing both the service user and the service [148].

Inequalities and uneven implementation of the model needs to be addressed. According to Nigel Crisp, then Chief Executive of the NHS, in 2002 10% of inpatient beds in the UK were still provided in Victorian asylums. Similar inequalities of provision also exist in France and were observed among the case studies for this thesis. In each country, there were projects of high architectural quality as well as units that were old, shabby and dirty. This was partly because institutional practice was very resistant to change. About thirty years ago in Fulbourne mental hospital in London, every morning, staff performed the humiliating task for service users of false teeth distribution: a nurse would try sets of teeth on older mentally ill people until they found which fitted [70]. Such anecdotal practices were not isolated cases. They were, for instance, reported in Leros in Greece in the late eighties [137]. The author, also, witnessed practices such as the morning distribution of cigarettes in various facilities in the UK, in France and in Greece.

Regarding the medical and organisational approaches for the two countries forming the basis for the fieldwork presented in the second part of this book, so as to summarise, the UK had a public service for all, under the NHS umbrella, while France operated in a quasi-market way [131]. For the UK, community care followed the service user in all steps of the mental health experience, including the dramatic experience of the acute episode. In France, on the other hand, the hospital provided acute care and the service user could return to the community once he/she was in a more stable condition. In that case, the step relevant to the research was the type of community care facility for service users closer to the acute stage of the illness. Under these circumstances, it is understandable that there could be no exact overlapping of the service user group or the service provision.

It is also understandable that in a discussion about domesticity, cultural issues and differences between the countries may arise, since healthcare is related to the cultural background of the people it caters for [190]. Differences in mental health can be found both in the theoretical background, i.e., Cartesian versus Empirical school, as well as in diagnostic tendencies, where loss of control symptoms were overemphasised in the UK, and lack of energy and loss of normal interests overemphasised in France [190]. Helman [127] confirmed that there is a relation to culture and normality, and therefore culture and mental illness, and specified differences in diagnosis of schizophrenics influenced by the Anglo-Saxon and French rationalism respectively.

Chapter 3

My view: the SCP model

During the last four decades, small units that could more closely adhere to the new psychiatric theories, replaced many of the old asylums. Ironically, some of the old asylums in UK territory have been refurbished, made in one word into expensive housing or, as in the case of the Georgian Grade 2 listed buildings of St' Bernard's, London, were transformed into a secure unit, as published in the architectural press [73], [246]. However, many of those new units were not up to expectations, indicating that it takes more than bricks and mortar to create a therapeutic, client-friendly environment. A MIND study revealed that it was some of the new units that received most negative criticism from clients [49]. There was criticism that some of the attractive architectural qualities of the old asylums, such as large spaces and open grounds, were replaced by new units with inadequate common areas and inaccessible external areas, while negative traits, for instance inadequate lavatories and having to live in confined spaces with strangers remained [59]. This is not to question the new community-based buildings, but rather to emphasize the importance of quality of their environment.

Many authors speculated that quality of environment was crucial for the self-esteem of theusers, the efficiency of staff and the reassurance of visitors, or that it indicated to users, i.e., staff, clients and visitors, that the institution showed the respect due to them [54], [107], [138], [158], [163], [246]. The American architectural literature, treating the subject of a market policy in health care, suggested that a friendly environment helped relatives to decide to admit a person, encouraged relatives and friends to visit more often and increased the possibility that clinicians would visit. Staff recruitment and retention tends to be difficult in mental health, so that a pleasant working environment could be a means to attract staff. Furthermore, the quality of finishes and money spent on the building indicated managerial respect for the facility.

Other research connected the environment with users' well-being. Research by Lipper in 1971 and Trites in 1970 showed that hospital design could have a significant impact on staff and patients' well-being [37]. Lawton, in 1987, established that design of the buildings had an impact on their users and Taira in 1990 stressed that "the environment has the greatest effect on the person with the least capacity" [162]. Satisfactory furnishings and facilities in residential care contributed to clients' happiness [192].

On the other hand, an inappropriate environment could undermine the process of therapeutic intervention. Basic amenities that might sound like luxuries when dealing with tough budgets, such as private accommodation or preparation of food in the unit, might comprise therapeutic and psychotherapeutic elements, whilst ignoring them might have implications for clients' treatment [73]. Absconding or early discharges could result from a frightening environment or poor living conditions in the institution [214].

Stainbrook in 1966 and Spivack, in 1984, speculated that clients and staff received messages from the environment as to their expected behaviour [114],[158]. In other words, details such as hard uncomfortable furniture, seatless toilets or bars on windows indicated to patients what staff expected from them and they responded accordingly [114]. Tough budgets and occasional lack of consideration for the therapeutic qualities of the environment among those responsible for the facility's provision led to a neglect of the physical settings of mental health care [163]. And despite a specific piece of research suggesting that aesthetics in outpatient rooms did not influence clients' mood and psychiatrists' perceptions [139], we should not generalise for inpatient care, which covers a greater spectrum of activities and interaction.

3.1. Opposing frameworks for the planning of mental health services

Consultant psychiatrist J Fisk underlined two major concepts for the planning of psychiatric facilities: that of the specialists and that of the generalists. The first concept referred to providing special care for a particular client group. The second major concept came from the field of learning difficulties and was based on normalisation theory. The theory advocated that a normal society, and therefore a normal setting, was more therapeutic than specialised care. Next follows a presentation of specialists' concepts in terms of staff and environmental organisation, with normalisation theory and its criticism following after that.

3.1.1. Specialists' concepts

As far as it concerned human resources, under the specialists' concept, mental health environments are run by skilled staff with the relevant background on the treatment and care of mentally ill people. Since mental illness was considered an illness, as opposed to mental disability, nursing and medical staff should constitute the main body of the teams that treated and cared for the clients [180]. There were even warnings against inadequate levels of medical staff participation in those teams [193]. In the UK, acute wards clients interacted mainly with psychiatrists and nurses, while psychologists and occupational therapists were not always part of the team [214]. Yet, their contribution was often cited as important to inpatient care and there were teams that expanded their professional base to include therapists on home maintenance or arts, transactional analysts etc [193], [249] Research and mental health professionals agreed on the importance of multi- disciplinary teams for inpatient care [214], [193], [249].

Over the years since the onset of community psychiatry, there have been developments in the recommended skill mix. More community support workers, with useful personality traits instead of formal qualifications in health care, participated in care delivery teams, especially outreach [166]. During fieldwork visits undertaken as part of this thesis in the UK, staff belonged to this particular group. There were also facilities employing resident medical students, like in the Sick Bay project taking care of homeless mentally ill [88], and in Foyer de Post Cure Elan Retrouve in Paris, serving as emergency night staff.

Environmentally, specialised care translated to an environment tailored to the needs of a particular client group, for example dementia sufferers, and was piloted in Airedale General Hospital [94]. An adequately designed environment, tailored to the needs and pathology of clients, could also alleviate staff burnout. Indicatively on that, staff working with clients who suffered from more difficult clinical conditions rated the wards' physical environment less favourably than colleagues who cared for less challenging populations [220].

Specialised environments do not necessarily have to be hospital-like. An interesting concept was in late seventies the "sanctuary". It used both specialist care and domestic elements and derived from holistic approaches and the concept of wellness, which has been a growing concept in the USA. It included physical fitness, education and mental health, and was often related to non-hospital places [43]. Under that concept, the whole person was treated in a community-like setting, though not in the actual community as in normalisation theory. There, environment played an important role and emphasis was placed on qualities like serenity, privacy, security and social interaction [43]. One could say that this concept revisits the ideal of the asylum as the Quakers defined it, where ideal environments could be created for therapeutic purposes.

Alternatively, manager C Kirk [142] proposed a range of outpatient services complemented by inpatient provision only when this was unavoidable. In the latter case, in "small hotel models" the District General hospital was recommended for short-term admission and the intensive rehabilitation hostel for a longer stay [142]. This follows a general trend in hospital architecture where modern hotel-like interiors provide inspiration for health care architects and planners in terms of comfort, cosiness and aesthetics [93], [49]. Yet, mental health disorders affect mentally ill people's lives longer than a stay in general hospital.

The relocation of large numbers of mentally ill from hospital sites to the community generated a need to consider the framework for the 'new' life in the community of the long-term mentally ill. Among the health care professionals there were those who advocated that the normalisation theory model could be transferred to mental health.

3.1.2. Normalisation theory

Normalisation theory aimed at strengthening the social role and value of mentally ill persons, a group targeted by social exclusion and stigma. Its therapeutic aim was to reintegrate those people in society and give them back their principal role as "people" instead of "mentally ill". Under that prism, environmental restriction and protection were kept to a minimum [58], [192]. Instead, the aim shifted towards social and personal interaction and the new role of the resettlement worker, who aimed to comprehend clients' lifestyles [58]. Participation in ordinary life was important and therapeutic procedures tried to increase the skills that enabled gradual integration until clients reached independence.

As in ordinary life, as Carling and Ridgway put it, accommodation was provided in ordinary housing, and programmes for treatment, support and rehabilitation were on offer separately and according to individual needs [176]. On that small scale, ordinary housing and the existing community provision networks were ideal, but both housing types and provision varied among the different organisations involved [222]. Therefore, in practice, accommodation could be anything from 24-occupant hostels, to the MIND core and cluster model, i.e., ordinary housing spread around the community and served by separate administration units, to ordinary houses, preferably adapted to individual clients' needs when residents moved in [222].

Normalisation theory was client-focused in terms of clients' preferences and priorities. According to research, clients valued independent accommodation more than shared

Figure 21. Domestic-looking accommodation for the mentally ill.

psychiatric settings, regardless of symptom severity, level of functioning and demographics [187]. More analytically, the most preferable solution was one's own home, followed
by subsidised housing and boarding homes, whilst more structured settings like psychiatric group homes, long-term hospitalisation and crisis accommodation comprised the
least preferred options together with homelessness.

In practice, it could be argued that British mental health care provision was influenced by some of the normalisation principles. Community Care, as it has been advocated by the DoH, aimed at transferring services to the client where feasible, involving
treatment and support as close to home or in "homely surroundings", as the DoE phrased
it, with the client's own home being the optimum solution [113]. Clients' preferences,
practicability and cost effectiveness were the reasons behind the initiative.

Environmentally, the concept of normalisation was related to that of homelikeness
(fig. 21). Remen [209], interpreting Bettleheim, related homelikeness with client-centred
approaches. Under that concept, homelike did not denote a mere resemblance to domestic surroundings, but had clearly to do with freedom of choice, clarity and comfort. Architecturally, it translated into domestic scale, non-institutional furnishings and normal
space, sequence and configuration [209]. To Remen [209], homelike environments bore a
positive symbolic meaning even to people with troubled family histories. Accordingly, he
opposed the earlier "topotherapy" model, which used architectural features as symbolic
references that could have therapeutic extensions, and Amiel's intentions for the therapeutic use of space. More analytically, Remen called the "medical potency" of architecture an "exaggeration", emphasising the distress that the mentally ill faced because of
their condition. In short, a risky design did not guarantee effectiveness. If design proved
wrong it would be too costly to abandon, and residents would have to live in an environment that could augment their anxiety. Under the same spirit, organisationally, psychiatrists supported the view that the facility should be formed like a normal house. It should
include bedrooms, bathrooms and common areas, e.g., kitchen, dining room and lounge,
yet, alternatively, it could resemble a small institution with sub-facilities, such as bedrooms, therapeutic areas or catering, which could be separated from one another [208].

The perception of what is homelike is relevant to an individual's culture (Fig. 22a,
22b). What appears homelike in one country might appear institutional in another. For
example, carpeted floors have been used in UK facilities for the sake of domesticity, although they are impractical where human fluids might leak (Fig. 23). Carpet would not
be appreciated in a South European context, where other floorings, such as natural stone,

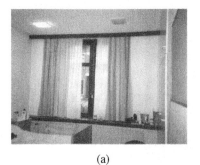
(a)

(b)

Figure 22. Domesticity in a mental health facility in Belgium.

Figure 23. Domesticity in a mental health facility in the UK.

Figure 24. Domesticity in a Greek mental health facility.

(a)

(b)

Figure 25. Unit for elderly mentally ill.

porcelain tiles or wood, are associated with domestic environments (Fig. 24). Phippen [199], comparing the UK with France, expressed the national character of homelikeness and mentioned the British association with domestic environments with the use of carpeting and the French preference for hard, tiled flooring for the same purpose. He added that the French prefer domestic environments to be large, brightly-lit spaces.

For some, normalisation theory constituted a useful tool but was not a panacea and could not airily be applied to all cases. Morris [176] recognised the effectiveness of normalisation for secondary disabilities, i.e, competence and social integration, but questioned its effects on the psychiatric symptomatology and cure. In other words, normalisation could not replace care treatment and ignored the specialists' contribution to severe and persistent cases. Ekdawi and Conning [85] recognised the positive value of normali-

Figure 26. Maap Architects Little Bromwich Birmingham, older adult assessment unit.

sation but retained some concerns that it might place much pressure on clients to reintegrate. They recommended that clients should be able to live in a degree of normality that
is comfortable for them.

For others, normalisation lacked consideration of specific needs. Although a normal setting had the local culture as a basis, it resulted in strong heterogeneity because it
gathered people with very different needs [94] (Fig. 25a, 25b). Thornicroft criticised the
concept of a normal life in a group home as unrealistic, since most clients were dependent on drugs and professional support [230]. Other criticism described normalisation as
a pessimistic theory, as it involved seeking for acceptance rather than emphasising the
respect that individuals receive when they participate creatively in society [24]. A similar
approach interpreted caring as a form of control, in the sense that the individual accepted
illness and asked for support, and consequently, normalisation that was based on support
in the community, was underpinned by coercion. Precisely, Davies named loneliness as
the by-products of that attitude and advocated that community care was based on the
assumption that the community "cared" [71]. Instead, the community could prove in-
sensitive in issues related to mentally ill, with NIMBYism to include the voices of the
people suffering from various forms of disabilities and the revival of specialised institutions (fig. 26). Here, it is necessary to address the social and personal issues of people in
such facilities, such as loneliness, boredom, and having a say, including expressing their
dissatisfaction.

3.1.3. Social exclusion in the community

Life in the community did not guarantee the actual return to its social structures and the
inclusion to its life. Loneliness has been related to a hasty return of clients to the community, as the history of de-institutionalisation demonstrated. Similarly to isolation, it
could affect both clients and staff involved in community care settings. It should be mentioned here that loneliness is a subjective concept. Yet, it could be described as being the
opposite of social support or the subjective equivalent of social isolation, which could
be measured by counting weekly total social interactions, activities etc [239]. Community units have been accused of contributing to the social isolation of clients. Tomlinson
[231] commented on some clients who found fewer opportunities for social interaction
in group homes than in hospitals, and linked this with the lack of support facilities for

Figure 27. Horticulture in the activity room of an acute mental health facility in London.

leisure, work, refuge etc., together with the way group homes function as institutions. Regarding resettled clients who lived in group homes and attended day centres, Ramon [206] proposed that although they conducted more satisfactory lives than before and had more choice and freedom, the majority tended to contact only service providers.

Isolation of staff in small residential units in the community was mentioned among the problems that staff faced in residential settings, with implications in clients' options as will shortly be discussed [200]. This could happen in all contexts. For example, staff of CMPs (Centres Medico-Psychologiques) in France that were located far from the sector and the hospital, felt isolation and a sense of being cut off from the rest of the service [202]. According to researchers in the field of community psychiatry, projects should be integrated with the existing health and social care system, co-ordinate their programmes to meet clients' needs and be co-ordinated between themselves for efficiency purposes [120]. Interaction between several mental health services, in terms of multiple use of areas and physical overlapping could be a possible solution as it increased client interaction [28]. Structure in the life of the units would encourage clients to leave their bedrooms, or engagement in activity inside the units or in the community could push clients to communicate with other people or prepare them for social interaction. However, as our fieldwork suggested, lack of staff to escort clients, seriously compromised the latter. Additionally scarcity of resources could increase the feeling of boredom and the passivity of clients. On top, there were more problems that inpatients faced with the use of day centres, related to institutionalised practices, subjects of activities, accessibility and inflexible opening times [211].

Further, excessive passivity could be damaging to mental health, even though overstimulation could trigger relapse [177]. The Sainsbury Centre [214] suggested that activity should follow clients' varying needs and that recreational activity should be available throughout the day and during the weekends. Muijen [178] supported the therapeutic effects of structure or controlled pressure and balanced levels of stimulation for schizophrenic clients as opposed to inactivity. However, the Sainsbury Centre highlighted the importance of organised activity in the wards and warned that disorganised and unpredictable activity could increase violence. In this direction of activity as a means to counter institutional behaviours such as passivity, research recognised the importance of intensive rehabilitation in hospital, possibly in rehab flats as Benians [38] suggested, before resettlement in the community, for clients with increased re-admission rates like young, new long-stay clients [146].

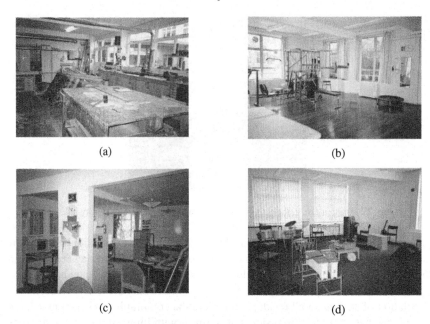

(a)   (b)

(c)   (d)

Figure 28. Organized activity room St Anne's hospital London.

Figure 29. Organized activity room.

In practice, a survey of UK wards came up with very low activity rates. 40% of participants were not engaged in any social or recreational activity and 30% did not participate in any activity at all, while therapeutic interventions were absent from the schedule of some of the participating wards [214]. The same study revealed that activities did not always follow a formal schedule but depended on nurses' workloads. Yet, activity could include even minor occupations (Fig. 27) such as meal preparation.

Davis and others [73] considered the occasional participation of acute clients in food preparation as therapeutic for the following two reasons. First, it obliged them to cope with daily living activities that they might find problematic. Second, it was an exercise in the division of labour and co-operation. However, ready meals were considered necessary for higher dependency residential clients, and comprised an important option for medium dependency clients [208]. Staff could use meals as opportunities for socialising with clients [73]. Staff and client interaction in acute wards were related to ward effectiveness [214].

3.1.4. From exclusion to social valorisation

All this discussion on specialised or normal environments, reveals that mental health care provision is not based on mere 'survival' but is related to clients' gradual return to their optimum possible function in the society and the improvement of their quality of life. Loneliness, for example is but one result of their social exclusion and an indication of a poor quality of life. Client satisfaction is gradually becoming one of the up-coming priorities for the health services (Fig. 28a-d, 29). Benians [38] included high client satisfaction among the criteria for the provision of community care. Kunze argued that care in the community could become institutional, and to prevent that, he proposed that new facilities should look more closely at clients' needs [243]. Ryan agreed that provision needed to be needs-led and client focused [213]. Perceived autonomy in lifestyle, greater autonomy and positive self-concept had a direct and significant relation to the quality of life of chronic mentally ill clients [253]. Hafner and An der Heiden [119] proposed the following components for the measurement of quality in community mental health care:

- Client's location within the community, in terms of access to facilities such as leisure, shops, education and employment
- Relationships
- Choice in decisions, from small everyday things to major decisions and the exercise of rights
- Competence (enabling of full participation in everyday activities)
- Respect, which required fulfilment of all the previous components

In the above measurement components of quality of life there is no immediate connection to space, but to the one the measurement concerning the location of the facility. Yet, design could facilitate the rest as well, as many authors have indicated the advantages of psychosocial design on patients' health [235], [163], [80] and in particular in clients of mental health services [67], [110], [66]. Under this concept, Scher [216] categorised client-focused environments according to their experiences with respect to the following five issues:

- spaciousness
- privacy
- comfort
- variety
- communication

From the client perspective, psychiatric wards tended to be unpopular with clients, with the lack of freedom and the rigid regimes being the commonest reasons for dissatisfaction, followed by nursing staff's attitude and unavailability. Environmental issues, such as lack of space and cleanliness, as well as boredom, were found to be less of a problem in the same survey, although 22% of one survey in acute wards were not satisfied with the cleanliness of their ward. What clients valued most in the wards were safety and the opportunity to get away from problems [214]. Food was also related to residents' happiness in a Social Services Survey on residential care [192]. More than one third of inpatients participating in a survey did not find meals pleasant and enjoyable, while 28% did not like the food [214]. Representation in the planning and design process could be an important measure for clients to participate in decision making and bring up their needs. Especially since quality of care is directly linked with patients' health [78].

Multi-disciplinary teamwork at the planning stage was acknowledged by professionals and people involved in the planning and design of mental health facilities [73], [159], [249]. Gutkowski and others stressed this co-operation in interventions at a later stage [118]. In general, this co-operation could bring forward the complexity and the variety of issues that arise in the microcosm of mental health care. A multidisciplinary team at the planning stage might also help clarify any misunderstandings that arise from the "jargon barrier". This is very important when terms such as friendly or domestic tend to be subjective [90]. A similar lack of clear definition could occur in describing any type of mental health facility. Symons [227] remarked that facilities with the same "name" might differ considerably, and different names could be attributed to the same type of facility, increasing the need for the architect to demand clarification to understand the use.

Similarly, views, needs and even the term "user" depended on individual perspectives. So, in studies regarding the quality of life in mental health care, views varied between professionals and those responsible for public policies, clients' views varied from those of professionals, and individuals' opinions varied among their peer groups [98]. Perception of needs might differ too. In a study by the Sainsbury Centre clients rated their needs slightly higher than staff across all categories but their health, and the lack of information was a major source of complaint (45%) from the clients' perspective [214].

Finally, the term "user" does not always describe the same group. There have been cases where, by the term "user" involvement, planners meant therapeutic staff or neighbours and "excluded" the clients of the services. This could happen in cases where there was opposition from the neighbouring community related to the development of a mental health project in their vicinity. Here, we refer to three distinct groups of users. One is the neighbouring community, another group involves the professionals, i.e., staff working in the facilities and last but not least the clients of the services.

In the UK, NAHA (National Association for Health Authorities) [180] proposed that neighbours should be consulted and involved in community projects, especially since opposition to new facilities was a common occurrence. Local people's involvement from the early stages of Community Mental Health Centres planning has been proposed by Goldie and others [107]. The acceptance of the local population was crucial for the running of the programme and the social re- integration of clients back to the community [120]. The architect, by contacting local leaders, inviting their approval, and involving neighbours in the design, could diminish local opposition [43]. An example of this practice was the Arbour Hospital in Boston: the architects prevented costly litigation procedures by inviting local people to a direct participation in the design process [24]. Besides, the better co-operation of the locals with a mental health facility through formal or informal interaction with the neighbouring community was considered beneficial for clients who belonged to ethnic minorities [41]. Also some flexibility was necessary to incorporate their lifestyle and their cultural and religious requirements [41].

Involving all levels of staff in the planning process not only generated ideas and solutions, it also increased staff co-operation towards the final project and their willingness to adapt to the final design [73]. Several authors [159],[28], [14] advocated input from nurses throughout the design process. Nursing staff played an important role in clients' treatment and nurses have come up with design solutions [159]. Other authors insisted on co-operation between architects and psychiatrists [118]. Yet, Gainsborough and Gainsborough [105] advised architects to take into account doctors' and nurses' "hidden" roles, occasionally patronizing, as well as their sensitivity to clients' criticism.

Part of client-focused design in health care environments required client involvement during the various stages of the process. In general development projects, (i.e., not only mental health), residents d participation in the planning process may prevent them from feeling powerless and frustrated [122]. In mental health, user involvement could no be taken for granted. As history taught us, the family and the carer's role in decision-making until very recently, proved to be more powerful than the client's. Lately, clients' voice gets stronger day by day. However, this does not happen in all countries and there is still a long way to go even in a European and definitely, in a global level.

The absence of clients from the planning process raised concerns about the lack of expression of the voice of the "anonymous" client, as opposed to "user representatives" or even voluntary organisations, which advocate on behalf of the mentally ill. Research pointed out the importance of getting client focus groups to participate in decision making and the possibility that their priorities might differ from those of the carers or "proxy" users [191].

In practice, dialogue with users could be a challenging procedure. In a survey by a client advocacy organisation, clients expressed their criticism but nearly a third of them did not make any suggestions. Moreover, some issues raised contradictory opinions within the client group [214]. Nevertheless, by knowing the different expectations the designer might be able to incorporate elements from several approaches into the project [159]. The same need for plurality derived from studies in quality of life [98]. Moreover, interviews with users could form a part of the therapeutic procedure. Clients' involvement with the problem could help them get accustomed to the change that a new unit will bring to their lives, since mentally ill people have difficulties in coping with change, and would allow the cultivation of a bond between the centre and the clients [159].

Equality and respect are presuppositions for any dialogue. Payne and O'Gorman [191] pointed out the ethical approach of an honest approach of a dialogue between all users in terms of equality. Abatzoglou [11] stated that occasionally carers adopted dominant behaviour, ignored clients' wishes and thoughts or clients could find themselves in the position of being treated like an object. To Abatzoglou, these two positions could affect chronicity. Practice indicated that clients were often consulted late in the process or not taken seriously enough and most often they were not reimbursed for their time [49]. However, user involvement needed legislative interventions, especially in respect to consumers' rights and staff training [111].

3.1.5. What lies between the asylum and the misinterpretation of domesticity: the need for a new paradigm

Under the influence of normalisation theory, domesticity has been a growing concept in psychiatric care, yet in most real cases it has not based on normal family housing. Facilities ranged between normal housing and a clinical environment with "touches of normality", like the scale or the materials or the furniture (figures 30-32). Yet, domestic was the term that has been predominantly used, as opposed to other accommodation forms such as student accommodation or hotels that appeared quite often as positive building stereotypes in health-care architecture in general. This could be the case even for facilities with more functions than accommodation, which combined residential and communal use [17]. In that sense one could argue about the accuracy of the term "domesticity" and the possibility that if it is used one-dimensionally it could lead to oversimplifica-

Figure 30. Domesticity   **Figure 31.** Domesticity   **Figure 32.** Domesticity

tions that could even result in buildings that obscure instead of promoting the therapeutic procedures. It is important, therefore, to examine the adequacy of normalisation theory and the extent that domestic elements could be used in community psychiatric facilities, taking in to account the limitations that derive from the therapeutic milieu.

Historically, the fear of mental illness resulted in an architecture with coercive elements. The need for safety and security, however, appears to be no longer connected with exclusion. Community psychiatry theories aimed at spaces that were integrated within society, even if they were specialized. Still, these facilities had to be able to deal with the loneliness that sectioned people or those living away from home might feel, and the boredom that stemmed from spending a considerable amount of time inside the premises of relatively small institutions with not much choice of activities. In short, the question was what were the mentally ill able to do in community-based settings that were as close to normal life as possible, without underestimating their competence or without having to suffer too much stress by carrying out tasks they are not ready to undertake? Moreover, to what extent and in which ways should they participate in the life and the environment of the facilities to allow their social inclusion, even during their stay? Taking into account the three - at times contradictory – aspects behind the treatment and care of mental health: the idea of dangerousness that includes the danger of harm and self-harm, the idea of disability that occurs as a result of the illness itself or as an effect of institutionalization and last but not least the idea of social reintegration as it is expressed by clients reclaiming their role in decision making. These three aspects of mental health care could be translated as three dimensions of a model for evaluating and defining the therapeutic environment of the facilities, which will highlight any limitations regarding the domestic character of those environments. Those dimensions/parameters suggested here that architects and planners have to take into account to avoid oversimplifications of what domesticity might mean in psychiatric environments, were safety and security, those of competence and of personalisation and choice.

There are obvious contradictions between some of the principles involved in the design of mental health facilities, i.e., safety and privacy, so trade-offs have to be made. Moreover, these principles have not always received equal attention. Priorities among the principles have changed historically, e.g., custodial or security issues have gradually weakened over time. The client group in terms of pathology or severity could also shift priorities. Additionally, the point of view could influence the order of those principles. For example in the nursing literature security was a serious issue, while the architectural press valued privacy and aesthetics considerably more.

From the foregoing it became clear that the general talk about user involvement, or consultation on behalf of the users evolved to demand users' realistic inclusion in the decision process or dialogue. Providing information in a way that was relevant to the users and also empowerment were necessary to achieve user involvement [138]. Moreover, the new UK National Service Framework included users, i.e., various staff representatives as well as client and carer representatives, to form focus groups [111]. Occasionally, staff and, in some cases, clients were consulted about the planning of facilities. Sevenacres in the Isle of White and Meadowfield in Worthing included clients at the planning stage, and staff made field trips around the country to learn from the experiences of other projects [86].

Both Sevenacres and Meadowfield examples of projects that resulted from the need to replace relatively new-built units, where things went "wrong".

3.1.6. Safety and security

Safety and security in psychiatric environments are not solely architectural issues, since people and policies are important contributors thereto. The views among mental health professionals and architects have concentrated on two distinct positions. There were those on the one hand who supported the view that organisations could not rely on staff to "do their job" all the time and proposed that architecture could play a preventive role, particularly important in times of staff shortages and financial restrictions such as this period. By contrast, there have been those who feared the repetition of institutional solutions, such as heavy or fixed furniture, that lately has a strong come back in UK facilities and even padded cells. However, in the aftermath of the introduction of anti-psychotic drugs, confidence in the effectiveness of drugs cast doubt on the need for safety to be the architects' concern.

In the last fifteen years though, security has become more and more of a concern in UK literature and architectural practice, especially after tragic incidents that received extensive media coverage. West London Health Estates [249] advocated that safety, and an environment that was and felt safe, were equally important for both clients and staff. A case in point is Sevenacres in the Isle of Wight, where a new unit had to be replaced after staff's concerns on inadequate safety of the existing unit [183]. However, this concern about increased security in the UK appears lately even in initiatives such as the Better Bedroom by DINM feature anti-ligature solutions even without clear definition of the exact need for security, giving to safety and security a new gravity, perhaps contradictory to aims of the psychiatric revolution.

Nevertheless, despite the growing concerns about safety and security in psychiatric buildings, the briefing terminology occasionally differed among, or even within trusts, which could confuse architects with no prior experience as well as those who had previously worked with other trusts. This resulted in new facilities frequently being refurbished soon after opening, to enhance safety and security levels [208]. Answering to the uncertainty and confusion about the need for security, WLHE [249] recommend that planning should "err on the side of the eventuality of more disturbance than currently experienced", as facilities could admit or retain people because of gaps in the provision of domestic care and the lack of alternatives. Therefore, the designer should be able to incorporate the safety requirements in a residential ambience [158].

Justifying point made by psychiatrists on safety, suicide concern formed one of the priorities of the new British National Service Framework. The country experienced about 200 suicides per year, a third of which took place in wards [16]. Areas of potential danger could be as predictable as window-openings on upper floors [70] or architectural features designed to create more interesting spaces, such as a 20cm deep fishpond in an acute ward in Haugesund Norway that triggered a suicide attempt [39]. This factor of "unpredictability" makes the design of safe mental health areas an architectural challenge.

Addressing the need for safety due to clients' dangerousness, the Royal College of Psychiatrists attributed to the hospital the role of detaining clients and, for community settings, recommended more loose, yet secure provisions. These concentrated on medication storage areas and anti- ligature windows. Concerns also regarded the possibility of theft and the necessity for staff to be able to enter/unlock all rooms at any time with half-spindle locks or removable doors to prevent barricading, as well as the importance of explicit policies and staff training [249], [208].

Cox and Groves [68] considered restricted opening on upper floor windows but other details such as toughened glass or plastic and fixed furniture should be applied according to needs. Other considerations included unbreakable glass, collapsible towel hangers and curtains and attention to sources of extreme temperatures, such as radiator surfaces, hot-water taps and avoidance of details such as a cache space where clients could hide objects, or toxic materials [73], [158]. Malkin also recommended the use of furniture that was "too heavy to throw", without sharp corners or removable hardware and that anything tall should be fixed on walls to prevent door blockage. In general, Malkin followed a strong safety direction and some recommendations would appear institutional compared with the reality of many European acute wards. For example, she "secured" artwork, "housed" stereos and TVs out of reach, and recommended unbreakable containers and fixed or built-in bedroom furniture. In Belgium for example, these considerations would be met with in more secure environments than an acute ward, such as "SGA"-pavilion, a type of facility for clients with challenging behaviour who were also self-mutilative and suicidal and whose pathology resisted drug treatments, [97]. In other European countries such as the Netherlands, observation panels might be considered for example obsolete, as preventing staff from being in closer contact with the clients. Similar concerns about the increased safety measures over the therapeutic aspects of care in the US and the UK and the influence of this practice in the European Union have been raised by initiators of the community psychiatry movement in Europe, such as Megaloikonomou [167]. In: Psychiatry department of AUTH (Aristotle University of Thessaloniki) , Society and medical health conference. Thessaloniki, Greece, 20-21 October 2007.

Clients with challenging behaviour form a special part of mental health services users and, with the presupposition that there is a comprehensive network of facilities, they receive care in environments tailored to their specific needs. And although clients with challenging behaviour differed from our target group, there is a point in mentioning the two different approaches to dealing with violence in psychiatric care, as those approaches might be found more and more, sometimes even as an expression of prejudice, in environments for mental health that accommodate more stabilised clients. An exploratory work such as this research should therefore take them into account. The first approach incorporates opportunities for controlled destruction through the availability of a sacrificial layer and the second eliminates the possibilities of damage and leaves very few opportunities for destruction.

A "sacrificial design layer with objects easy to destroy but equally easy to replace", such as Velcro curtain rails could be employed, and at the same time spaces could be designed in such a way as to reduce territorial conflicts, such as broad corridors and bathrooms clearly related to certain rooms [179]. Alternatively, damage resistance could be an important criterion for furniture selection [73], [158]. Highlighting the prevention factor, research showed that although soft furniture was positively rated, there were some critical remarks from staff members and occasional requests to remove upholstered seating in favour of vinyl-covered solutions in a psychiatric ward [220].

One of the means to manage violent behaviour temporarily and therefore reduce the risk of harm and self-harm has been seclusion. This was in the past connected with punishment, but research by Teicher on children and adolescents indicated that there could be therapeutic benefits from the use of a specially designed seclusion room [158]. However, there were a lot of acute wards with no seclusion room and constant observation was a more common practice, indicating the ambivalence on what best practice for crisis situations could be [214]. Also its use varied considerably among the wards [214]. Alternatively, there was guidance for provision of designated intensive care in acute units [249].

Figure 33. Seclusion room (I)   **Figure 34.** Seclusion room (II)   **Figure 35.** Seclusion room (III)

In visits to hospitals and community facilities in Europe, the seclusion room usually contained a fixed bed with an exposed mattress or just the mattress, a soft seat, which was made from foam and occasionally a clock and a WC (fig. 33-35). The considerations comprised suicide prevention, maintenance and observation. Malkin recommended the use of soothing colours, the avoidance of carpet for an odour- free environment and cushions with Velcro closures to enable environmental manipulation from the client [158]. For observation purposes, she mentions, as being in common practice, the placement of the room close to the nursing station, the presence of a Lexan window and the occasional, camouflaged placement of CCTV. In the facilities visited in Europe, a curved mirror provided a view round blind corners.

One of the trickiest issues under the safety prism is fire safety regulations and needs. Fire safety is a generic concern, yet its interpretation in mental health required special attention because of residents' self-destructive behaviour or neglect and because of the need to contain and "guard" residents in the buildings. The latter requires careful thinking through of the evacuation scenario. For fire safety and access to dangerous items, recommendations concentrated on operational policies as well as panic situations and fire alarm use, and not on architectural features [249], [208]. Cox and Groves [68] highlighted the need for fire safety in psychiatric environments but with escape routes being monitored. Having said that, fire regulations and the Act for Residences for Persons in Care could be criticised for promoting institutional environments, such as the fixing of official notices on walls or use of special rooms for the laundry, instead of using the kitchen [222].

Another important element for safety is observability. Observability and visibility could be of paramount importance for the prevention of suicidal or violent behaviour. Amiel [10] proposed that fear increased agitation and aggressiveness, whilst reassurance and a sense of security could come from sufficient and direct staff presence. Yet, observability is contradictory to privacy. The nursing station and visual intrusion into more private areas as well as electronic monitoring devices lie at the interface of the two (fig. 36-37).

The nursing station constituted an important feature of the design of psychiatric wards but lately its effectiveness and therapeutic value have been questioned. Medical Architecture Research Unit, a UK based academic institution that specialises on healthcare architecture planning management and design known as MARU [163] criticised their effectiveness in single-room accommodation; since psychiatric patients were usually peripatetic. Recently, to design a friendlier environment, the nursing station was omitted or it comprised a bay without a glass screen, which, for Amiel [10] blocked the contact between staff and clients. A glass-free nursing station was designed in Woodgreen Mental Health Centre, in North London, but staff later added a glass screen for privacy and noise reduction. In some cases the nursing station was replaced by staff offices, usually close to the entrance. WLHE [249] described spaciousness, unobstructed view and clear observation from the nursing office as fundamental for safety in acute units. Poor visibility in Newcroft hospital was blamed for the increasing attacks on staff from clients, reaching the number of 13 incidents in a month [86]. The unit was replaced and the nursing station of the new unit was placed centrally, where the wards met, to control client movement [183].

On the subject of safety and observability, there is a fine line of distinction between private areas and the risk of harm. Watch panels, with or without curtains, and doors that

Figure 36. Nursing bay in Belgium

Figure 37. Nursing bay in Belgium

staff could open even if locked, affect the way staff can carry out their work and on the other hand affect clients' privacy, especially at night where light and noise obstruct sleep. Amiel [10] criticised the use of torches for night time observation, still a continuing practice, and instead proposed diffused floor lighting.

Moreover, on safety and observability, the use of electronic devices such as CCTVs raised opposing views among health care professionals. In the past, the literature was opposed to the use of cameras as they were believed to be a medium for increasing distress [10]. Other guidance thought reconsidered the use of CCTVs in non-clinical areas in acute facilities and questioned their custodial references, especially since they have become more common in public places [249].

A final issue that does not appear directly related to the need for safety and mental health is maintenance. This stems from two facts related to the illness: the violence that exists in mental health facilities and the possible distortion of clients' olfactory sense. Regarding the former, there is an obvious relation of violent behaviour as a result of clients' pathology and therefore heavy wear and tear of mental health buildings, which implies that maintenance should receive detailed consideration in acute units [249]. The literature has pointed out that maintenance should be considered at the briefing stage. To "minimise the impact of such (i.e. aggressive, violent) behaviour" in a mental health project, the design team could interview staff on clients' expected behavioural patterns [123]. Staff has been reported to recognise that one way to cope with tough NHS budgets was to incorporate maintenance among the design principles [40]. Second, to respond to changes and hypersensitivity of the olfactory sense, the proposed solutions included properly functioning ventilation and sufficient toilet facilities [186]. WLHE [249] proposed detailed consideration of ventilation in acute settings. Also, for a clutter-free interior, adequate storage areas were necessary for the smooth running of the facility and often did not suffice [249]. Building recommendations outlined that service areas should be self-contained and plant rooms accessible from outside [208].

In short on safety and security, it is important to deal with the issue of dangerousness but there is a fine line between safety and institutionalization that stems from the sense of incarceration references and the sensitive issue of observation vs privacy retention. Yet, in compliance with the professional recommendations, for many years architects have attempted to avoid introducing coercive elements into the building by means of design [21]. Even in the literature about high security buildings, the message conveyed was about creating better conditions and avoiding coercive elements. Efforts concentrated on transforming technical security elements into architectural gestures, such as creating a clear layout that minimised the use of observation systems, or a shape of the building to reduce the length of the security fence [254] (fig. 38).

An example of a clinical-secure environment with normal details, is the Three Bridges Medium Secure Unit, Middlesex UK. Devereux Architects included a clinical input in a concealed way, whilst trying to emphasise normal elements [246]. Firstly, they piloted the Medium Secure Unit Guide and separated the admission beds from five intensive care beds to cater for different stages of the illness. To achieve the second goal, they created spacious and light areas, introducing a variety of privacy levels, of different shapes and sizes. Moreover, they used high quality materials with a domestic touch, for example brick (fig. 39), and they strategically placed institutional elements, for example the security fence, in less obvious ways. These examples demonstrate the possibility that acknowledgement of the needs for safety that each type of facility requires together with

Figure 38. Avoidance of coercive elements via design: the security fence in this high security courtyard in Belgium has been replaced by a curved finish on the upper part of the wall that clients could not possibly climb.

Figure 39. Three Bridges Medium Secure Unit, Middlesex UK. Devereux architects has a domestic looking appearance, without visual hints for its function as a mental health facility.

investment in design might be a way to create non- institutional environments that are and feel safe.

3.1.7. Competence

The disabling effects stemming from mental illness can affect clients' independent functioning. There can furthermore be an additional burden on clients' autonomous functioning, which is the result of institutionalisation. Yet, it has proved difficult to eliminate the latter even in community settings. Davis's list on deficiencies stemming from mental health, already presented in the opening chapter of the present thesis, includes difficulties in dealing with oneself, in dealing with others and forming interpersonal relationships as well as engaging oneself to a wide spectrum of activities from personal hygiene, to occupation. To those must be added the traumatising experience of institutionalisation and the damage to self-esteem due to their inability to cope [73].

The fact that under the mental health umbrella lies a variety of diseases, such as depression, bi-polar syndromes and various forms of psychoses creates a diversity in needs and expected behaviours, especially for their classification in community settings , and has more to do with the acuteness of the episode rather than the diagnosis of the type of illness. The unpredictability of the development of the illness and the possibilities of relapse episodes complicate the picture further, as the gravity of the symptoms during clients' stay in the facilities does not necessarily follows linear progress. Here under the term competence, we discuss the issues of physical competence, and activity performance, including simple everyday activities and concentrates on the diversity of needs that affect the level of functioning and the implications of this diversity in service provision and spatial design. As a solution to this problem of diversity of needs, appears the core and cluster model for the developing of mental health facilities.

Regarding physical competence, the mentally ill tend to be more able than people with physical disability problems as, to a great extent, they are peripatetic. Yet, design for physical accessibility was often mentioned among the requirements of mental health care projects [249], [107]. Consideration for physical disability, in the sense of accessibility, has been integrated in the design of public architecture in the UK since the implementation of Part 3 of the Disability Discrimination Act in the mid-1990s (DDA, 1995). Peace [192] categorised factors that related to access in a care environment according to organisation or design, to time, to control over space and to responsibility or accountability. Scher [216] speculated that access and way finding affected the communication experience in health care facilities.

Yet, despite the fact that the mentally ill are physically mobile, they might face motivation issues, sometimes encouraged by institutional forms of care. During the author's visits in about 200 mental health facilities in Europe, staff often reported that clients might avoid touching or washing body parts as a result of their hallucinations or mental connections relating to those parts, as in the case of a psychotic client who would not touch and wash her left side as she associated it with "Judas". However, apart, from that specific case, staff needed to wash clients as their personal hygiene as motivation could be limited. The same applied to housekeeping and laundry [72]. Low motivation as a result of symptomatology as well as of the drug treatment, might affect everyday activities. Thus, clients have difficulties with preparing food, which could also relate to their difficulty in co-operation with others that the production of meals might imply. Here must be taken into account the issues of dangerousness that may be related to the use of cookers and sharp objects.

Activity, including meal preparation, is mainly connected with mental health rehabilitation, yet boredom is a common problem faced by clients in the facilities, especially if they are wardbound. Scher [216] states variety as basic component of a positive experience in health care environments, which could include activity. Health care professionals supported the view that client satisfaction with their therapeutic intervention was associated with client participation in the procedure [234]. During art sessions for elderly clients, the use of lavatories decreased [173]. In mental health, art therapy was more needed than works of art, together with employing various types of artists, including writers, musicians and dancers, according to the project's requirements [172] (figure 34).

Being an heterogeneous group, clients have diverse needs. Contrary to other forms of neurological or psychiatric conditions, dementia for example, where architecture can compensate for dysfunction [136], there is an unclear picture of expected behaviours and disabling effects. Remarks on the changing needs of inpatient resources, and the need for flexible solutions, were also reported by Davis et al [73] and Manoleas [159]. The build-

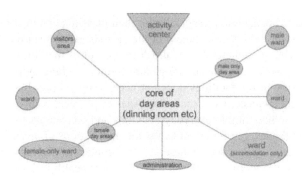

Figure 40. Possible types of the core and cluster model

ing should then be able to adapt to epidemiological changes, policy changes such as the UK's recently introduced single-gender policy, treatment changes or even changes in the characteristics of a certain client group. Most of the UK acute settings were designed for a different care regime from what is happening more recently, including the increasing numbers of acute cases [138].

To deal with the diversity of needs could translate to variety in service provision and as buildings are an expensive investment, they are consequently supposed to last. Symons proposed conversions over purpose-built units as a more flexible solution [227]. MARU [163] criticised the practice of taking into account the possibility of an entirely different use than for mental health in the future, especially if doing so translated into compromises with respect to mental health requirements. Under that prism, the flexibility of a unit should focus on its ability to adapt to future changing needs in therapy or in a target group. Gutkowski and others [118] advocated the importance of continuous, minor architectural changes in existing units.

As far as it concerned the co-existence of different types of diseases and therefore different needs for calmness and stimulation, Davis and others [73] proposed environmental design that permitted outbursts from agitated clients, while at the same time stimulated the withdrawn clients. Yet, to manage instances of increased disturbance, WLHE [249] recommended the inclusion of a more secure and suitably staffed area within acute units. These designated intensive care areas could either consist of one or two rooms with special characteristics such as vision panels or sound containment, as NBN 35 proposed, or comprise one ward in a unit designated for that purpose. Arguably, allocating specific self-contained wards for individuals of increased dependency raised issues of the diagnostic predictability of those case. Alternatively, as in the District Mental Health Centre, Yardley Green, Birmingham, the service could accommodate the evolving needs of the clients, instead of moving the clients [163]. This was achieved by providing various levels of support in the same building and with easily distinguishable zones, where clients could move about. Finally, Malkin [158] proposed the solution of placing flexible areas between open and closed wards to add beds according to needs. A similar type of flexibility was seen in some UK units between female and male wards.

One way to cater for clients' changing needs was the core and cluster model in a psychiatric campus or a hospital campus, or in the form of a Community Centre. For staffed homes that replaced hospitals and accommodated a wide spectrum of pathologies, multidisciplinary research concluded that it was preferable for those homes to be grouped in a 'core and cluster' arrangements (fig. 40) [146]. Thus various types of accommodation could be located at the periphery of a central facility for structured activity, administration or clinical facilities, such as ECT if it was provided. In this way economy derived from multi-use, clients moved up one stage towards independence, gradually, and the environment appeared more normal with accommodation being separated from certain clinical functions and therapies.

An interesting example of the core and cluster model is Vista Hill Hospital, in San Diego, a project that rejected the asylum concept of the past and proposed a more unusual interpretation of normality. The aim of the environment was to prepare for a return to normal life, and the setting was a medical campus, a concept familiar, as we have seen, in American health care provision. Accommodation was provided in separate buildings from therapy or administration and landscape played an important role in the whole project. Yet, at this time, normality and healing, an idea which is often cited in American health care literature, were usually expressed through references to a "suburban educational campus or business park" [87].

WLHE [249] stressed the clinical priority of acute environments' design without ignoring regulations, yet recognised the beneficial role of some "domestic" elements, such as small size. The core and cluster model enabled that parameter, by emphasising either domestic or clinical elements according to needs or by having the possibility to break down the volume of a large facility into a village-like concept. It could still be argued that despite its breakdown into smaller units, the core and cluster model, because of the accumulation of wards and activity or medical areas, tends to be larger spatially than a self-contained domestic unit offering less options.

To ease the possibility of co-operation, HBN 35 guidance focused on the ease of movement between day centres and wards, stating that few clients needed to stay in the ward throughout the day. Since its introduction, it has been found that the core and cluster model decreased staff isolation and could provide extra staff support in crisis. Additionally, clients could benefit from a central facility for structured activity, where they could move flexibly according to their progress [146]. Yet, even in that case, inadequate staffing would considerably limit the opportunities for clients to leave the wards, if clients needed to be escorted or required supervision. This could happen even in units that were physically adjacent to a day centre, and the separate management and funds allocation between the wards and the centre could increase the inflexibility further [163].

3.1.8. Personalisation and choice

The last of the three parameters, personalisation and choice, refers to the psychosocial aspect of the model. In that respect it concentrates on aspects related to clients' psychological resumption, wellbeing and social interaction. It is not about protection from oneself or from others as the first parameter implied or handling the disability as the second parameter implied but a step closer to psychosocial valorisation. Choice and control are associated with comfort in health care environments [216] and personalising space allows the expression of self-identity [192]. The components of this third parameter, that aims to give back to the individual the choice and control of his/hers decisions will be presented shortly and include privacy, territoriality and socialisation. There could be an overlapping between the second and third parameter regarding socialisation, as the lack of it is part of the disability concomitant with mental illness, but since the emphasis here is not only on dealing with the symptoms but exploring a more integrated approach to the restoration of health, socialisation will be discussed in this section as that will attribute to it the element of contributing to health (psychosocial approach) rather than dealing with it as a symptom of the illness (medical approach).

Privacy and dignity were growing concepts in the vocabulary relating to mental health buildings and central to the principle of personalisation and choice. Ittelson and others [135] related a personal sense of privacy to the "range of choice open to the individual" and vice versa and Peace defined privacy on the basis "of who has access to space and the activity undertaken within it" [192]. Under Ittelson's interpretation privacy is directly related to personalisation and choice parameter, whilst under Peaces' definition it is related to control and therefore indirectly related to choice (in the sense that the choice of access might or might not be available).

Alternatives of private, semi-private and public spaces could serve the various and changing needs of people with mental illness and allow them to select for themselves the most desirable level of social interaction at any particular time [147], [159]. Single room accommodation could be a way to tackle clients' need for retreat. There has been talk in favour of single room accommodation as far back as the 1950s, but this has usually been accompanied by considerable controversy about the benefits and limitations of single room accommodation. The debate has been further fuelled by disagreements about the most appropriate number of occupants for rooms containing more than one person. For some, single room accommodation, especially if the rooms were large, increased the chances for clients "to make their room their own" [39]. Here it should be mentioned that Bergsland is an architect in which case his opinion does not derive from health care professional knowledge and might carry a degree of prejudice.

Amiel [10] expressed his reserve about allocating single rooms to lonely clients and considered that in three or four-bed rooms clients could form opposing groups, raising the safe number of beds to five or six combined with the use of cubicles and individual, lockable storage space and individual shelves would help increase independence [10]. Amiel [10] and Osmond [186] expressed concerns about the hidden messages that double bedrooms might convey. Health Building Note 35 argued that observation was easier in dormitories and even tough rigid partitions or curtains could compromise observability [163].

Osmond [186] recognised the need for a private place and supported single room accommodation for the severely mentally ill but objected to single room accommodation for people who were bedridden, to reduce loneliness, unless it was necessary. However, other research related single rooms, even if of smaller size, with wider freedom of choice than larger, multi-occupancy rooms, which were thought to cultivate passive behaviour [135]. Clients in private bedroom accommodation withdrew least in activity participation, and in cases of shared accommodation, there was an increased tendency for clients to isolate themselves or adopt passive behaviour in the room [135]. Additionally, staff could encourage clients to stay in public spaces, for observational purposes [192]. Moreover, the quality of stay in dormitories raised concerns [147], [214].

Regarding the organisation of the room, Williams [250] stressed the difference between the hospital room, which was organised around the bed, and a nurse's or student's bedsit, where a desk with a chair were additionally required and which allowed privacy for activities like reading. In the architectural literature there was the theory that small rooms would encourage clients to use other spaces [246]. Adequate room size could however be important in cases of violence.

More processes that favoured privacy, were proposed by the National Institute of Social Work and those were lockable bedrooms where appropriate, the right of users to spend time alone in their rooms, respect for the right to privacy from visitors, staff and other clients, and finally, the opportunity to use the phone without being overheard [192]. A soundproof environment and confidentiality was also advocated by NHS Executive in 1995, Scher in 1996 and West London Health Estates in 1997. Clients reported problems with noise in a MIND survey [214]. Especially for converted buildings, Goldie and others [107] highlighted the need for particular attention to noise reduction. Amiel stressed the importance of noise reduction for undisturbed sleep, mentioning corridor insulation and non-disturbing doors [10]. For disturbances of an auditory nature the avoidance of echoes in corridor design were proposed by Osmond in 1970 and Manoleas in 1991. Osmond proposed the avoidance of auditory peculiarities, as echoes and other sound distortions could undermine a therapeutic session or consultation, so that consultation or interview rooms should be designed to provide clarity of sound [73]. Speaking about distortions of sound and hallucinations, it should be mentioned here that there is once more an overlapping between the parameters, as in this case privacy under the personalisation and choice umbrella, overlaps with safety issues: triggering of hallucinations might induce a relapse episode or a client's crisis episode could negatively affect the rest of the facility.

The need for retreat has been mentioned in the medical and psychological literature [186], [159]. Especially in a crisis, it was described as a prerequisite for the creation of a therapeutic climate [44]. Bonnet also recognised the importance of "vital space". Physical withdrawal could prevent clinical regression [159]. Ronco in 1972 supported the view that hospital design was mostly tuned according to staff needs and patients could experience loss of privacy and control [37]. Privacy versus surveillance was a common dilemma that architects were asked to solve [221]. A great deal yet remains to be done in that direction. In a survey conducted in acute wards, one fifth of the clients felt that washing facilities lacked privacy [214]. The same survey indicated that 71% of clients did not have a secure place to lock their belongings [214]. Women tended to express more concern for lockers and private washing facilities [214]. Yet, as it appears, women's privacy needs tend to be more complex in order to preserve the separation of the genders for modesty and decency.

An important issue connected to privacy is gender segregation. In the UK, mixed gender wards constituted the vast majority of the provision [214]. As long ago as 1976, Thornicroft found that clients in single gender group homes or in those with only one member of the opposite gender, acted more independently as a group and got on better amongst themselves than in mixed group homes [230]. Research has focused on the needs of women in secure settings [138]. The Royal College of Psychiatrists' paper "Not Just Bricks and Mortar" has also expressed the beneficial role of single, en-suite facilities for women. Perhaps as a response to these finding, the NSF tried to implement a single gender policy in psychiatric wards around the country [49].

The reasons behind those initiatives ranged from increasing respect for individuals to responding to ethnic minority traumatic experiences, as these have been on the increase in recent years and have coincided with the implementation of a 'diversity and equality' agenda across all government departments. Since 1995 the NHS executive has therefore advocated a single gender policy in all healthcare facilities with respect to groups with strong beliefs against the mixing of genders. These included Muslims, and women who might have suffered from mental illness because of past abuse by men. It was recognised

Figure 41. Mott House, West London

that inappropriate relationships and offensive behaviour could occur even in the most organised units [182]. Women seemed to be more concerned about safety issues than men and staff reported problems of sexual harassment, some of them serious, on more than half the wards in the Mental Health Act Commission census [169].

On the other hand, there were those who expressed caution about single gender policies as obsolete and artificial. We should bear in mind that gender segregation dated back to the asylum era and was associated, in psychiatric terms, with the prejudice "that any sexual feeling would lead to mental disorder" [94]. Even in the UK, where the separate wards issue occurred, there were people among the nursing and the medical staff who found gender segregation institutional, and in the case of recovering clients destructive, as part of the rehabilitation process includes mixing with people of the opposite gender [246].

In practice, the implementation of a single gender policy, however, could increase the bed problem that the country already faced, due to a shortage of 24hour supported accommodation [76]. Yet, the NHS considered that cost effectiveness should take into account clients' wellbeing and staff's time and activity [182]. In order to resolve this contradiction, Sevenacres, Isle of Wight, and Mott House, West London (fig. 41) Acute Mental Health Units tried to implement this compromise between privacy, in terms of single gender accommodation, and normality, as expressed in gender mix by having single gender wards with mixed common areas between them, and that could therefore inform design guidelines on the subject. Both have combined separate sleeping areas and a female lounge with mixed common and therapy areas. West London Health Estates and the Sainsbury Centre [214] advocated the provision of safe space for women. Other possible arrangements included the presence of a female-only lounge [249]. To recapitulate the gender segregation debate, one point that should be made clear should be the motive behind it: it should aim at clients' wellbeing, under the prism of the reduction of traumatic experiences, respect of individuals' culture, ethics and dignity and the elimination of possibility of harassment, and not of isolative institutional practices. For that purpose the possibility of choice of the desired level of co-presence could be something to be further investigated.

Another important psychosocial factor related to the personalisation of space and the choice available to clients in it is territoriality, in the sense of clients controlling and protecting their desired level of personal space. Research has produced interesting results concerning mentally ill people and their relation to personal space. Various studies, mentioned by Bechtel [35], showed that mentally ill people of various pathologies kept greater personal distances, and other studies indicated that those distances were related to the type of illness. Mentally ill people kept "inappropriate distances to the situation" from other people, causing discomfort, especially schizophrenics, who formed a significant part of the sample group of this thesis, who kept greater personal distances and felt more comfortable with greater space [35].

For perception of own body disturbances Osmond [186] recommended spacious and congenial surroundings. Both indoors and outdoors, spaciousness helped prevent tensions in mental health facilities [249]. Researchers and professionals from the disciplines of medicine and psychology recommend against overcrowding and over-concentration of clients in wards [186]. Scher [216] agreed that minimum standards did not provide patient-focused architecture. Sloan Devlin's research on psychiatric wards [220] suggested that staff should be advised on the amount of furniture on a ward since too much furniture increased crowding, blocked space and limited accessibility, especially for wheelchair users.

Research in care homes also showed that territoriality related to chairs affected clients' identity positively and allowed them some control [33]. Gubrium in 1975 explored the marking of chairs as "private spaces within public spaces" [192]. Regarding territoriality, staff needs too have to be taken into account, as their wellbeing is important for their performance and the life of the facilities. One has to take into account areas where they can retreat, perform tasks away from clients or even rest. Staff needed some space in the unit to withdraw and rest away from clients since "burn out" was a common problem [252]. Yet, quite often rest areas for staff were underestimated at the planning stage [249]. Practice indicated that if such an area was not available, staff would allocate some space for that purpose [73].

Staff areas were related to clients' dependency. Higher levels of support translated to greater appreciation of hygiene, work and rest spaces for staff, especially when they stayed overnight. As long ago as the 1970s, it was found that staff areas that were designed with the elimination of authoritative behaviour in mind were positively valued by staff, in a post occupancy evaluation [28]. In higher dependency residential services, an office that could host meetings, interview rooms and a changing room with a shower were considered essential [208].

Apart from the choice to withdraw and be private and the control of a comfortable level of personal space as expressed by territoriality, there is also the need to interact with other people from the ward or from the community. Social interaction is seriously damaged by the illness, as isolation, damaged self-esteem and passive behaviour are part of the symptomatology. Socialisation describes the process whereby clients interact and communicate with other people. Those could be other clients, visitors or people outside the ward. However, regarding clients, socialisation is a complex procedure that, because of illness and its 'attack' on clients' self esteem and interpersonal relationships and the isolative culture of the institutions, needs a lot of input from the therapeutic team. Yet, space could play its encouraging or discouraging part as will shortly be presented.

Spatially, socialisation could depend on:

- the layout of the building, the provision and arrangements of common areas,
- the visitor's areas;

(a) Sociofriendly   (b) Sociofugal

Figure 42. Example of furniture arrangement in psychiatric common rooms.

- the amenities that connect the ward with the rest of the world such as telephones or the web;
- the opportunities that enabled client interaction, such as ward activities for instance, or interaction with other people, through organised outings.

Regarding the layout of the facilities, visual contact between areas and people, as well as relatively small distances between areas allowed user interaction in Norwood CMHC, US [28]. Choice of day areas was considered a significant issue for acute facilities [249].

Research by Olsen in 1978 and Taylor in 1979 in hospitals, showed that visitors and patients had limited choice and control, encouraging patients to adopt passive behaviours [37]. Yet, environments providing options and spatial complexity could lead to "more positive emotional responses" [37].

Discussion on socialisation extended to furniture arrangements and their flexibility (fig. 42a, b). One early study on this topic found that sociopetal furniture arrangements, i.e., arrangements that enhanced social interaction, in a geriatric ward more than doubled the number of conversations between clients, compared to the previous, sociofugal one, i.e., arrangements that hinder social interaction, according to research by Sommer and Ross [114].

Sommer talked also about clients' using the room according to furniture arrangement and about their reluctance to alter the furniture arrangement as a result of passivity and of the notion that it was up to staff to cater for clients' needs [158]. Malkin commented that shorter lengths of stay, i.e., two weeks-long on average, could prevent this passivity. Contrary to Sommer, Davis et al. in 1979 claimed that single pieces of light furniture that could be combined into groups of three or four, would help staff draw conclusions on clients' mental health state according to their furniture use. So, signs of progress could be indicated if withdrawn clients lifted a chair to form part of a group. Furthermore, for manic or aggressive clients, staff could observe their response to the limits via their behaviour towards chairs.

Visits formed an important part of clients' social life, as did connection with the community. Visitor policy, in terms of the welcome factor, visiting hours and entertainment facilities could affect clients' happiness in residential care [192]. Yet, despite the fact that the majority of clients in acute settings had at least one visit during their stay, in nearly half of the cases there was no quiet area to receive visitors [214], compromising both their and the rest of the residents' privacy. For residential settings recommendations about visitors varied according to the dependency level. Particularly for medium dependency, psychiatrists suggested separate/dedicated sitting rooms whilst higher dependency solutions should allow auditory insulation, yet permit visual observation [208]. Finally, on socialisation, infrastructure provision, i.e., telephone and information technology was mentioned among guidance for the planning of acute units [249]. Yet issues of privacy arise in respect of the location of those facilities in the ward and in the need of staff to control clients' access to such amenities as mail and calls.

3.2. The physical milieu of the psychiatric units

3.2.1. The interface with the community: location, scale and external appearance

An initial approach about a healthcare building could be the facilities' interface with the community. This could mainly include the placement of the facility in relation to the hospital campus or the community, the scale of the facility, as determined by the functions it accommodates and finally the external appearance, and more precisely to what extent the facility is integrated to the surroundings.

The main concerns regarding the location of the facility stem from needs regarding clients' safety, and the controlled access of clients to sources of danger or stress, and their need for participation, according to their competence, within the community. WLHE [249] advised that acute units should be located away from areas that could facilitate suicidal attempts, such as railway lines or canals, or that could aggravate drinking problems, i.e., off-licences, or even too close to families, since families could sometimes be the source of clients' trouble. Health Building Note 35 delegated responsibility to the providers to decide on the location of facilities, recognising the relation of the facilities to the community they served and the possible interaction with the hospital. West London Health Estates [249] acknowledged the controversy on the issue, but preferred the hospital campus site, with the presupposition that the acute unit was stand-alone, having its own entrance and "within "trolley range" of the acute services". Medical staff advised on the separate entity of the psychiatric unit in the hospital campus, preferably surrounded by greenery [147]. Weller [245] expressed concerns about the growing placement of mental health facilities close to the city centre, because of the increased pressure of urban life. Yet, for residential units of more settled groups, the Royal College of Psychiatrists proposed community networks with facilities [like here yes, in the sense of 'similar to'] shops and leisure centres. Public transport seemed important [107], [208].

Normal housing accommodation, located directly in the community, was more often used in rehabilitation or housing projects for the mentally ill requiring long- term care, as in the group home cases. The co-operation of health authorities and housing associations permitted health care projects to be integrated with general housing schemes. For example, in Mother's Square development in Hackney, East London, six forms of housing, including a nursing home for the mentally ill, were so integrated that association flats for residents that did not have any relationship with the mental health system were placed on top of a project for elderly mentally confused [223]. Additionally, a general housing scheme in Clapton, East London, also incorporated sheltered housing for older people as well as adult mentally ill people discharged from Friern and Claybury Hospitals and a day centre for confused mentally ill [51]. All accommodation elevations followed the symmetrical pattern of the facades.

In Tasman House in Hillington, North London three houses for eight short-stay people with developmental disabilities formed part of a "normal" housing estate. These mental health units were separated in several adjacent houses and administration and therapy areas were situated in an adjacent section. Anecdotal evidence suggested that the unit was fully integrated socially to the estate due to its external similarity, which discouraged initial perception of its purpose and subsequently, any adverse initial reaction [207]. The model of the adjacent houses was proposed for economy of scale [142].

Regarding the scale of mental health facilities, approaches varied from organised village-like forms, offering more opportunities for activity to community integrated "houses" closer to normality, yet with limited choice for wardbound clients. Psychiatric hospitals, which normally developed on a larger scale and in outer city areas, could afford to follow a domestic scale and low densities and gather smaller, dissimilar buildings that "formed" villages [68]. We will briefly present two interesting examples, both in the USA where market economics determined the need of those facilities to be appealing to the potential clients as they were choosing where they wanted to stay and the fees were paid by private insurances: the Meninger Foundation and Rock Creek. In that sense, their large scale did not bear reference to the old large institutions based on economy of scale and functioning as 'storage' of people but aim at the idea of the wellness centre or the sanctuary. Architecture played an important role in removing architectural references to the stereotype of large scale institution by investing in decoration and introducing domestic references. It should also be mentioned here, that this US type of facilities is not exactly community-based, in the integrated sense as it is in Europe, they rather form communities of themselves.

The Meninger Foundation in Topeka, Kansas was a complex of 18 new and seven re-used buildings for various pathologies and an average stay of about a year. The designers intended a homelike environment with a village- like campus [18]. Domesticity focused on decoration and provision of normal spaces such as a kitchen in each ward, despite the existence of a central dining area. Yet, there was a significant number of shared rooms and the wards accommodated 24 clients. According to critics, the Meninger Foundation was closer to the concept of wellness, since it re-introduced the meaning of community and incorporated it into the therapeutic process, giving importance to the whole of the individual [43].

Another example of a psychiatric campus that created a community with its rules and values was the Rock Creek Centre in Chicago. Its vision was borrowed from the sanctuary, where the sense of community was reinforced with procedures that included staff dining with clientsand campus-wide staff and client meetings [52]. To achieve the idea of the village, the architects emphasised the homelike design of the accommodation buildings. Because of the campus's sanctuary character, restraints such as locked doors and seclusion rooms were avoided [52].

It can be inferred from this, that apart from scale, mental health building facades constitute an important message-conveyor from the facility to the exterior world. The building can either be disguised as a residential facility, a public health care building or a building with a strong architectural presence. Facilities with the external appearance of family homes could serve a larger population than an ordinary family and include therapeutic activities in their regime, in an effort to protect clients' privacy through integration [250]. Occasionally, even buildings without residential accommodation aimed at domestic-looking elevations, like Woodgreen CMHC, North London, which combined

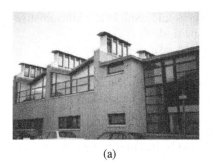
(a)

(b)

Figure 43. Woodgreen CMHC, North London.

the clinical spaces of an acute day hospital and a day centre (fig. 43a, b). The building followed the "rhythm" of terraced housing and incorporated the use of warm materials such as timber and bricks. This solution opted for both the de-stigmatisation of mental health care and the creation of a welcoming, and therefore more accessible environment for clients [47].

Cullinan attributed domestic appearance to an attempt to conceal the function of the facility, rather like Davies [71], who interpreted "neo-vernacular" medical architecture as a way of disguising doctors' power and saw in architecture a chance for social critique, rather than neutrality. The motive, though, in strong architectural gestures and costly construction could be described as society-focused, conveying the message of the superiority of a society that allocated extra funds for suffering populations [212].

3.2.2. Outdoor areas

Focusing more closely on the facility, one has to deal with its interface between the society and the protected interior, i.e. its outdoor areas. Outdoor areas in health care are related to therapeutic, psychological and socio-financial benefits. Research found that views to trees speeded surgical patients' recovery, which translated into cost savings [50], [172]. Uzzel and Lewand [235] pointed out that research demonstrated the therapeutic benefits from outdoor areas design, but more research was needed on particular groups of patients and environments. Pollock [205] mentioned the therapeutic implications of landscaping for dementia sufferers. Several projects for the elderly mentally ill used outdoor areas to enhance safety, comfort or the identity of the units, even in small, restricted spaces [14], [95].

Landscaped external areas could have practical benefits for the facility. Strategically planned green spaces could reduce energy costs in healthcare, and landscaping enhanced the facility's public image [50], [95]. Moreover, the use of art could enhance the value of the property and decrease the misuse that public buildings were susceptible to [228]. This would apply particularly to mental health facilities since they have become targets for vandalism.

Well-designed outdoor areas could affect clients' interaction with space. To Hagedorn, a formal, frequently geometric garden design might invite people to look but not touch, which could be used to prevent access for the sake of safety, and a backyard-like approach might, with the help of a therapist, promote client participation in the activity and subsequent feelings of ownership, increasing their personalisation of space. Involvement of the landscape designer at the briefing stage would result in more imaginative and versatile solutions rather than just an area for some fresh air [121].

All activity-related decisions, however, should take into account clients' competence. Stoneham [226] commented, on garden design for people with disabilities that there was a tendency to expect them to be "keener (gardeners) than able-bodied people". According to occupational therapists, gardening activity was limited in acute wards, even though a courtyard, depending on its design, would provide relaxation, a space for interaction, and if possible a barbecue to enhance the variety in the life of the unit [121]. However, in longer-stay accommodation gardening could be included in the activity schedule [172].

Stoneham [226] made a list of elements of good design applicable to mental health, since inpatients might moreover have movement restrictions, or have a lot of spare time and face boredom. Mentally ill people had also limited motivation for active behaviour. Stoneham's list included:

- Access
- Views that were interesting to watch (bus stops, e.g.), to be retained
- Points of interest close to the building
- Seasonality
- Domestic/ Intimate design
- Seating
- Security
- Wildlife
- Maintenance

Of those elements, some might seem more obviously relevant to our discussion so far, for example domestic design or security. Yet, interest closer to the building could be useful for clients that were in higher observation levels. Small "events", views, say, or events related to seasonality or wildlife, could add variety and interest in a restricted environment. Seasonality could provide connection to time, as illustrated by anecdotal evidence from Leros Asylum, Greece, where chronic clients within the walls of a courtyard planted only with eucalyptus trees, ignored the seasons and the fact that leaves fall in autumn [137].

Yet, despite the well-documented benefits of providing outdoor areas, in the UK new units might lack direct access to open spaces [49]. Architects with experience of secure environments stressed garden accessibility as a major aspect in the design of mental health facilities [183]. In order not to ignore the needs for safety and to include wardbound clients, secure and protected external areas should be available [208].

3.2.3. Internal organisation of facilities

Moving from the exterior of the building to the interior, one of the first decisions a unit has to deal with regards the capacity of the facility, i.e, clients' beds. This is not relevant to scale, as scale can be very much determined by the functions hosted. For example, a facility with few clients in spacious single room accommodation but with many activity and therapy areas or even with units such as a day centre or an ECT facility or even facilities for external clients too, might be on a much larger scale than a facility that provides shared accommodation only and has little communal areas. Here, in the number of beds, the discussion is not about square footage but the co-presence of people in the facility. The HBN 35 on acute provision set a lower limit for the size of the units, of two wards and a day hospital, with the ward capacity being between 10-25 clients. The Note did not however set a clear upper limit. Kirk [142], from the managerial perspective, proposed an average of twenty beds for acute admissions. WLHE [249] proposed the number of 15 beds as a maximum in acute wards, downsizing to ten for intensive observation. According to the same guidance, a stand- alone unit should range between three to five wards based on calculations about availability of trained staff in a crisis and a resident doctor, unless a separate entry point was provided for more wards [249].

MARU [163] supported the view that small units enhanced accessibility, taking into consideration the multi-ethnic minority, inner city clientele of urban environments as in London or Birmingham or towns such as St Albans and considered small units as the flexible answer to the underused large wards of the 1970s, yet without defining "small". An unpublished study by the University of Kent, mentioned by Pilling [200] concluded that small, i.e., less than 8 clients, residential units "have serious problems in managing challenging behaviours", increasing the chances for hospital re-admissions. Cox and Groves [68] located the size of hostels for the mentally ill by rule of thumb; i.e. as the smallest that could satisfy three parameters: clients' need for privacy, need for society and staff availability. Recapitulating on unit capacity, there was no agreement on the exact number of wards or clients, but there were suggestions on the dynamics that should be taken into account, comprising safety, provision for activity (competence), and choice between privacy and socialisation.

Regarding the internal organisation of the building, the discussion will open with internal communication. Something that is of particular interest in mental health facilities is the security of the entry points, both avoiding absconds in closed units or for sectioned people as well as for the protection of the facility, which could be a target of vandalism or of thefts, or the ever- present matter of issue of drugs from or to the unit. Apart from recommendations for the use of CCTV that has already been mentioned, for acute units WLHE [249] recommended the use of security staff or a reception that overlooked the entrance, which ideally should be the only entry point to the building. For community residential settings, psychiatrists outlined the need to observe the entrance from an office or reception area [208]. It should however be borne in mind that apart the observation of the movement inside and outside the ward, there is the need to observe what happens inside the ward. There therefore appears to be a need for decision where the emphasis should be regarding the placement of the staff base, be it an office or a nursing station, especially since mental health matters have always suffered from tight budgets.

Probing in more depth into the internal organisation of the building, the discussion will shift to circulation. Hospital wards developed around double-loaded corridors to cut down on distances and increase nursing staff effectiveness. Psychiatric wards in general hospitals tended to follow the hospital layout. Those were strongly questioned when researchers and practitioners stressed the importance of avoiding dead ends in corridors and the importance of views and alternative routes, to avoid a sense of entrapment or captivity [28], [68], [249].

As far as the length of the corridors is concerned, there was diversity of opinions between those that saw institutional references to them and those that saw the corridor as an important area for physical release of wardbound clients and social interaction. WLHE [249] and Cox and Groves [68] advised the avoidance of long corridors. Spivack concluded that the character of long, seemingly endless corridors in psychiatric hospitals was anti-therapeutic [114]. On the opposite side, there were those who advocated that hospital corridors were usually not enough for clients to walk about in, as opposed to old institutions with large open grounds [147]. Anderson and others [28] supported the importance of corridors and circulation areas for movement and interaction. To facilitate this interaction, in the publication "Not Just Bricks and Mortar", which referred to community residential settings, psychiatrists recommended the use of articulated corridors as a more friendly option [208]. Groves and Cox [68] proposed the facilitating of social interaction or withdrawal in ward corridors, with alcoves, bays or in combination with day areas. Close to those principles, MAAP architects used single loaded corridors, combined with internal courtyards, in various acute units they designed. As a result, they provided internal spaces for clients to walk, integrated the inside with the outside and enabled external areas to be easily observed [221]. This connection to the exterior eased orientation as well. Alternatively, for the latter psychiatrists have advised on the use of colour for orientation and stated that colours influence behaviour [43]. For way-finding, colour has been used on corridors, or doors, or even on doorknobs to indicate different levels of accessibility or use [75]. However, research on dementia clients questioned the effectiveness of the latter and approved bolder colour statements [36].

As far as the rest of the organisation is concerned of the remaining social areas of the wards, there was not much research or even architectural discussion so far. As we have seen, the main topics under discussion on community psychiatric buildings regarded issues relevant to the stigma, thus concentrating on the external appearance, issues concerning safety, with much emphasis on observability and as earlier discussion in this chapter indicated, issues concerning staff areas and activity, but with still many issues on the latter untouched. There was as a result no information on day areas, or therapy areas, their types and their spatial relations inside the facility. There was only one interesting interpretation by Aldo Van Eyck of psychiatric environment as an entity of its own, as a "building which cannot be left or entered" [23] pp.76-77). In a clinic in the Netherlands he expressed the need to focus on the open spaces within the perimeter and to reduce the prison-like feeling. Visual connections between spaces and enclosed spaces, as well as placing importance on the design of windows, were among the means for that purpose [23].

3.2.4. Decoration of facilities

To compensate for the inability of a considerable number of clients to leave the premises, the design has to be able to alleviate the isolation they face and yet appear as least institutional as possible and at the same time be and feel safe. The literature on mental health interior decorations concentrated on avoidance of optical illusions, through light and patterns as well as on suggestions regarding lighting, colours and the furniture of the wards as the means for that purpose and they need to be selected in order to provide a domestic feel that does not trigger clients' pathology.

3.2.5. Patterns

A serious concern for the decoration of the facilities is safety and avoiding that they should trigger hallucinations or optical delusions through suitable light and patterns.

Clinicians and environmental psychologists have advised architects on perceptual disturbances in the mentally ill [186],[159]. In their opinion, space should discourage hallucinations, which could vary in nature. Malkin [158] mentioned the sensitivity of schizophrenics to too much stimulation and advised on window treatment because of the sensitivity to light and sunburns that they might suffer from, as a side effect of medication. To prevent visual hallucinations, Osmond [186] proposed small, reassuring, easily encompassed spaces. In the architectural literature, Malkin [158] mentioned possible behavioural patterns of schizophrenics such as visual hallucinations including distortions of size and image, the "passion for order and symmetry", the tendency to attribute magical qualities to common objects and the identification of symbolic meaning that could lead to performing rituals, as factors to take account of in design. She also cited Spivack's studies on optical illusions produced by glare and reflections on shiny surfaces and lighting, as well as studies on paradoxical images and ornate materials that could be deceiving. Manoleas [159] mentioned the need to avoid light patterns, "especially refracted and prismic light from certain window designs". Contrasting carpets or vinyl border designs might cause difficulty to clients with compulsive behaviour disorders who do not wish to step on lines or inside frames [158]. Amorphous art might lead to connections with Rorschach tests or trigger images [158].

3.2.6. Colour

Colour was often proposed in the architectural literature as a means to create a client-friendly service, though the use of colour seemed to be subjective, as colour is associated with mood but no one-to-one relationship to emotions has been identified [83]. In the Horton Mental Health Unit UK, Nightingale Architects had instructions from the Trust to specify a stimulating use of colour [246]. Their decision to choose bold, yet co- ordinated colours, was estimation-based. Another way of attempting stimulation and structure through colour derived from the association of colour with functions, i.e., green for areas with lots of activity, blue for rooms and rust for areas with moderate amounts of activity [73]. Alternatively, consideration for both client groups, those who needed stimulation and those for whom a calm environment was more appropriate, could be incorporated in the colour decision, in the form of a balance between neutral and "cheerful" colour [73].

Despite the voluminous suggestions on colour, Frisk, after scrutinising papers on the impact of colour or lighting in mental illness, noticed that they lacked firm documentation, since they had not controlled the experimental conditions. The positive effects mentioned could come from the change per se [100]. Malkin [158] expressed similar caution on tests about the colour preferences and responses to colour of the mentally ill, which often yielded conflicting results. Her recommendations on the use of colour in psychiatric environments followed laws of perception rather than evidence for the preferences within the particular client group. Among others, she recommended the use of colour in areas or furniture according to what staff wanted to "bring out" or to "conceal", and the use of colour as a way-finding tool. She made a specific recommendation only about the association of the colour red with blood, which occurred in one of our pilot study interviews but for one particular object only, while according to the research evidence base, yellow was a colour that schizophrenics disliked [158].

3.2.7. Light

Apart from the aforementioned advice on avoidance of hallucinations the literature addressed light as an element of wellbeing. In practice, lighting has been used to differentiate functional areas [73]. In Ingalls Memorial Hospital, the US alcoholic and psychiatric treatment pavilion, the architectural team co-operated with a psychiatric consultant to provide a solution that would promote therapy. With the use of daylight as the main tool, they arrived at a setting that combined "the reassuring elements of both hospital and home" ([18], p 98-101). Alternatively, daylight could help counteract institutional feelings and a sense of enclosure [19], [123].

3.2.8. Furniture and fittings

Additionally, as to decoration, there were mentions in the literature regarding furniture, carpets and clocks. More analytically, besides the discussion on light or heavy furniture and its relation to safety, there were additional suggestions about its forms. Amiel [10] used the creative antithesis of his bipolar pairs to produce guidelines for furniture design. He used the circle, a shape he connected with the body and movement, and the rectangle, the frame of movement, to induce behavioural responses. Diamond shapes and spirals furthered the sense of disorientation [10] . There was lack of scientific backing for those statements and there have been contradictions by other writers. For example, he suggested that round tables in rectangular rooms were particularly reassuring, but according to Malkin [158] round tables lacked clear boundaries for some mentally ill people.

Carpets were extensively used in mental health facilities in the US and the UK, even in clients' bedrooms. The reasons behind this preference included aesthetics, noise reduction, and the creation of a more relaxed atmosphere. Additionally, carpeting was preferred because it encouraged people to "sit and talk on the floor" [73]. Lee reported noise reduction that followed carpet installation in a psychiatric environment [114]. On the other hand, there were drawbacks regarding carpet use. Damage or dirt from fluids, spillage and flooding in en-suite rooms were common problems in mental health facilities. Yet, architectural solutions have been employed occasionally to minimise those effects. In an assessment and treatment unit, to counteract the damage from flooding from taps that were left running, architects constructed a discreet drainage channel into the carpet, instead of avoiding carpet use in bedrooms [123]. Malkin [158] recommended carpeting in bedrooms, but advised against its use in the seclusion room. Lately, there is an increased concern about the use of carpet in UK facilities by infection control staff, yet, there is no justification behind these concerns and mental health problems.

For time-sense troubles, tools that remind of real time, like clocks, calendars and newspapers were proposed [186]. Malkin [158] considered the dayroom as an area suitable for such a "reality check", including information about place as well.

3.2.9. Dealing with tough budgets: small changes

Finally, something that concerned people involved in the design of mental health facilities was dealing with tough budgets. This could of course not be discussed as a panacea or excuse to obscure serious safety issues or lack of activity area provision etc., but rather to encourage small, low-budget interventions when means prove really tight. Renovation of common rooms towards a more appealing design not only increased the use of the room, but also affected the whole ward with a redistribution of activity [135]. Simple environmental improvements, i.e. plants, brighter lighting, new day hall furniture, wallpaper and paint, were related to a significant decrease of stereotypical behaviour among clients and an increased use of the day-hall in a psychiatric ward. Plants were particularly welcomed, and it was remarked that "even more were needed" and in this respect Sloan Devlin cited research from Kaplan on the importance of plants for "human wellbeing" [220].

3.3. Need for research

Despite that there is half a century since what is called now community care started, one should expect that we would be much more knowledgable on the subject of designing for mental health. However, there are still many contradictions and gaps in this knowledge and often architectural decisions, as on the therapeutic use of colour, were based on speculations. This gap has been pinpointed by researchers, architects and professionals working on mental health facilities. This gap is even more important in periods where decisions are taken for larger scale interventions (such as the UK P21), or fragmented initiatives such the several "better bedroom" initiatives around the county that cannot by any means fill the gaps of solid scientific research.

In 1969 Griffin and others, after their extensive review of the environment and behaviour findings on mental health-care, realised that the research findings at that time referred to isolated aspects of space and could not provide the psychiatrist with the necessary knowledge to use the environment for therapeutic purposes. The findings of those studies had limited applicability, since they looked at one environmental variable at a time and in isolation, and could not address the interaction of variables and the results of their combination [114]. More recently, Bechtel [35] has testified to the change in the field, which involved interdisciplinary research to a greater extent than most social science. However, he as well as Groat [115] still considered the lack of any coherence or synthesised view as a major problem of the discipline. Bell and others [37], too, recognised the difficulty of generalising from the results.

Malkin [158] warned that superficial, anecdotal research was often taken too seriously by architects. She recognised the difficulty of conducting experimental architectural research in natural conditions and recommended building on experience. Postoccupancy evaluation, in other words, could reveal both failures and successes from past projects. In similar terms, Frisk insisted on the importance of evidence from everyday practice in the wards, in this way encouraging the collaboration of the architect with users, i.e., staff and clients [100].

According to the director of nursing of West London Health NHS Trust, buildings could be clinically unfit either when there was no clinical input, or were based on obsolete clinical models. In both cases teamwork among architects experienced in health care architecture and healthcare staff might have eliminated those possibilities [246]. In the meantime, the trust recognised the importance of environment for clients and its contribution to attracting "high quality staff" [246].

At a recent conference on mental health architecture, the NHS chief executive recognised that "more evaluation" was necessary and leading architect Mungo Smith admit-

	Design elements	Model		
		Safety & security	Competence	personalization & choice
Safety and security oriented design	Anti-ligature elements	+	0	-
	Medication storage	+	0	0
	Room locks (operable by staff)	+	+	+
	Fixed heavy furniture	+	-	-
	Unbreakable glass	+	0	0
	Nonweight-bearing fixtures	+	0	0
	Safe radiator surfaces	+	0	0
	Sacrificial design layers)	+	0	+
	Seclusion room	+	-	-
	Observability	+	0	-
Competence oriented design	Flexibility	_	+	+
	Core and cluster model	+	+	+
	Physical accessibility means	+	+	0
	Activity areas	0	+	+
Personalisation/ choice oriented design	Privacy	-	0	+
	Single room accommodation	0	+	+
	Soundproofing	0	+	+
	Private washing facilities	0	0	+
	Lockers (private)	-	+	+
	Single gender	+	0	-
	Single gender ward parts	+	0	+
	Territoriality	+	+	+
	Socialization opportunities	0	+	+
	Variety of common areas	0	+	+
	Visitors areas	0	+	+
	Telephones/internet	-	+	+
	Flexible, lightweight furniture	-	+	+

Table 1.: Evaluation of design elements according to the three parameter models as they derived from the literature. A plus sign means that the element is significant for that particular parameter, with the degree of importance denoted by the number of plus signs. Likewise, a minus sign shows a potential adverse impact from the element on that parameter. A zero sign suggests that the element has no impact on that parameter. It should be noted that many elements are contended, and have both positive and negative implications.

	The physical milieu	Model		
		Safety & security	*Competence*	*Personalization & choice*
The physical milieu	Location	++	+	0
	Facility Scale	0	++	++
	Facade style	0	0	+
	Landscape	++	++	+
	Facility/Ward capacity[1] (Service users)	++	+	++
	Entrance	++	0	0
	Layout/Corridor design	+++	++	+
	Decoration	++	++	++

Table 2.: Priorities for the design of the facility according to the three parameter model. The plus, minus and zero signs should be read as described for table 1, above.

ted that during 13 years of experience on mental health design he did not acquire any solid knowledge of the field [70]. Dr Garnietta Rands, consultant psychiatrist in a NHS trust, was surprised by the lack of architectural "follow up" in the buildings architects designed, even in cases of serious accidents [70].

However, there were exceptions to the practice of terminating any involvement in a project once it has been occupied, and some architects have adopted an "anthropological" approach to obtain a better understanding of life in care. For example, architect Knut Bergsland faked a 24 hour admission in one of his projects in Norway to enhance his evidence about post-occupancy evaluation. Characteristically, apart from achieving a better sense of the place, he noticed that he "got better information from staff… because they felt I was taking that seriously" [39]. He concluded that the designer should empathise with the clients when designing for psychiatry [39]. SOM Architects, prior to development work in a psychiatric hospital, lived inside the old unit for several days, to have a better understanding of the balance between private and public spaces [18].

A similar approach was adopted by W. Radysh, who designed many of the facilities for Camphill Trust, and reflected in his projects the Trust's approach of enhancing social understanding of mental disability [179]. He urged designers to live among mentally handicapped people, as he did, to achieve first-hand knowledge from observation.

Finally, as a suggestion before moving to the next part of the book, the SCP model presented earlier (named after the acronyms of the parameters) could serve as a grid for the classification of the design elements and the major architectural decision steps. This could form as a planning or evaluation tool or as a framework to raise possible research topics. As an indication of that, the topics addressed in this part have been summarized using its help.

Chapter 4

The physical context

In a discussion on domesticity, cultural issues may arise. To identify these cultural aspects, the focus will concentrate in two countries, France and the UK. Different approaches to mental health were found in their theoretical backgrounds, for example, Cartesian in France versus Empirical in the UK, and also in different diagnostic tendencies [190]. Helman [127] confirmed the relation to culture and socially constructed concepts of 'normality', and specified differences in diagnosis influenced by Anglo-Saxon empiricism, on the one hand, and French rationalism, on the other.

As well as evidencing entirely different theoretical contexts and different diagnostic tendencies, the two countries had different healthcare services, a different role for the hospital in the healthcare system and different community care structures, despite the physical proximity of the two countries to one another. Because of all those differences, any similarities found in the architectural design of facilities for mental health would be more likely to reveal generic issues related to the illness itself and make the design implications deriving from those commonalities more appropriate for global applications.

Since the nineteen eighties, the role of the hospital was ever more questioned. In the new millennium even in France, where there was more reluctance to close down the psychiatric hospitals, community based structures were gaining ground. The mental health care provision buildings chosen were those closer to the acute stage of illness as service users nearer to the acute stage would have a greater need for specialised medical care. Therefore, the discussion on the limits that should be placed on domesticity to prevent oversimplification would be of more importance. This decision was justified in due course, as gradually incidents of security failure in community mental health facilities began to reach the press headlines in a series of unfortunate incidents that sometimes involved members of the public. Yet, it is important to acknowledge that even community facilities could cultivate institutional behaviour patterns.

As service provision in the two countries differed, the first tier of community care facilities were specifically those that either, in the UK, replaced the hospital, or that were the first step after it in France, as in the latter case service users moved to community settings as soon as their condition stabilised. Due to those differences, the two countries could not be directly comparable. However, our focus still remained as close to the acute condition as each country's system allowed for community settings. Thus, the 'ward' in Community Mental Health Centres in the UK and the 'Foyer de Post Cure', in the case of France, provided the respective physical milieux for the comparison.

4.1. The selection of cases

To bridge a quite wide gap in architectural knowledge, a broad, exploratory approach to identify areas of key interest was essential. The lack of precise overlapping between the wards and the foyers, indicated an illuminating comparison of the major trends. The variations in the facilities within each country required a large enough sample. Contrary, the breadth of the issues of interest required a more manageable number of in- depth case studies. Thus, ten case studies, five in each country, were examined in architectural and policy terms, to enable a distinction to be made between local variations and global trends. They presented diversity, in terms of location, size, connections to the locality and wider social networks and care regimes. The buildings had been purpose built, in use for a sufficient period of time to allow any problems with the design to have surfaced and yet sufficiently contemporary to be relevant to a study of current good practice.

In order to examine the adequacy of health care premises, the participating five Foyer de Post Cure in France and five Acute Mental Health Wards in the UK provided the grounds for an international comparison of design variables and treatment regimes. Each group included facilities with differences in terms of location and sitting, scale and building layout, whilst being spread among different health authorities. Most important of all, all the participating facilities had to be 'visitable' and willing to permit both the physical fabric to be inspected and the staff and service users to be interviewed.

The criteria implied that the buildings were designed with a therapeutic regime and practice in mind. Also, enabled to see the outcome of diversity in terms of location and placement in the system, as well as to identify common factors in the country overall, irrespective of local policies. Moreover, they excluded all projects that were part of the internal organization of a hospital scheme. However, facilities located in hospital campuses but that did not belong to the same organisation as the hospital complied with the inclusion criteria. The final criterion ensured the service user- focused character of the study.

In France, service users could be admitted directly from psychiatric hospitals, psychiatric associations or psychiatrists directly. In any case, service users were closer to rehabilitation than those admitted in the Acute Mental Health Ward in the UK and all service users were voluntary. Acute Mental Health Wards, on the contrary received service users having an acute episode and referrals could even come directly from the police.

The French cases presented a great deal of diversity, concerning the number of service user, the policies, the services provided and the quality of the built environment. There, facilities were run by non-profit associations, which obtained funding from public insurance funds. By contrast, the UK cases were more uniform, as they were all under the NHS umbrella. Service users were there under section or voluntarily, and in all cases they could stay in the ward the entire day as their condition was closer to the acute state. That was not always possible in the Foyers, as the foyer service users were closer to independent living.

The number of service users in wards tended to be smaller in the UK, where a larger facility would usually be broken up into more than one ward and where service users would not easily mix between the wards. For that reason, in the UK the case studies concentrated on the wards if there was more than one ward in them. Service-wise, foyers could offer more rehabilitation functions and therapies, while in the UK the wards could be connected with more clinical functions such as ECTs. In general, the UK wards could be stand alone or in health care premises, whereas in France all Foyers were directly placed in the community. The final selection of cases was made after having visited over 120 mental health projects in the UK across the whole spectrum of care, and 40 in France in order to ensure that the ten cases were typical of the broader spectrum of the provision in each country.

4.2. The SCP model': towards a critical scoping of the concept of Domesticity

In the late nineteen-nineties there was deemed to be a connection between architecture and therapy, leading to a generally-held view that a health care building could promote or obstruct therapy. According to the precepts of normalisation theory, buildings with institutional references were considered to prohibit therapeutic intervention, whilst environments with domestic references could enhance the therapeutic efforts of staff. 'Domestic' as dealt within the mental health literature, was mainly addressed as the opposite of institutional, and was used even in cases where the similarities were in fact closer to hotel or student bedsit accommodation than an actual family home. Yet, as normalisation theory was quite influential, domestic was the dominant term used for solutions that favoured treatment. Everyone had their own idea about what it meant, but no one was able to define it explicitly. There was agreement that a clinical environment should be abandoned in favour of domesticity, though again the idea of a therapeutic environment was ill-defined.

The best that could be said was that in the course of the late 1990s and early 2000s, a domestic environment in mental health provision was not regarded as equivalent to being at home, but it was seen as just one step away from living at home. Thus, it was both extremely vague as a concept, and whilst it was not always accepted unquestioningly, an environment that looked something like an ordinary home was widely regarded as offering the most efficacious solution. As a result, an integrated dynamic model was necessary to address the complex issue of domesticity in a critical way, preventing the oversimplifications of accepting domesticity as the panacea for mental health care.

The domesticity versus institutional concept suffered from a number of problems, stemming mainly from its linearity. However, it is not the aim here to offer a critique of the linear model, but rather to contrast it with our three-dimensional model (used in the sense of being a hypothetical description of a complex entity or process). This model has made use of three parameters, namely:

- safety and security
- competence, and
- personalization and choice.

Each of these variables comprises one dimension of a cubic problem space occupied by three axes (x, y and z) where safety and security implies an opposite pole where the building is unsafe and insecure, where dependency is fostered in the service user, and where no personalization and choice is allowed. Individual buildings might vary in their capacity to provide safety and security, encourage competence and allow personalization and choice, thus each could theoretically occupy a unique position in the three-dimensional problem space of the model, which is therefore both more sensitive and more specific than the polar opposition between domesticity and institutionalization. The dimension of safety and security (and its polar opposite) was derived mainly from the medical-jurisprudence literature; that of competence (or otherwise) from the literature on nursing; and the dimension of personalisation and choice (and its inverse) was derived from the psychosocial literature.

In this respect, it was too simplistic to assume that everything that appeared domestic about a building was good for the service users and staff, and everything institutional about a building was bad. However, because so little was known about what actually worked well in practice, it is important to know what could be the right amount of domesticity for the service user group, and how this might afford them the appropriate amounts of safety, competence and choice.

4.3. The design of the user-centred questionnaires

The biggest innovation of our approach was that it monitored service user' perception of their needs and recognised their voices for the first time, rather than using doctors as advocates. Providing them with a valid saying allowed their contribution in the design process. To serve this principle, two questionnaires were prepared for the interviews: one for the service users and another for the staff. Each comprised three sets of questions. Each set corresponded to one of the three parameters of the SCP model. The questions mainly arose from topics mentioned in the literature with emphasis to opposing opinions.

To test the questionnaires a pilot study was conducted, in Laffan Ward of the Huntley Centre, an acute mental health unit in St Pancras Hospital, London. Laffan Ward did not participate in the main study, since the building did not fulfil the other requirements of the study. The aim at this stage was not to draw conclusions about the spatial preferences of the users, but to check the questionnaires in order to revise the final ones. In general terms, the reaction to the questionnaire was good and any problems that occurred were not serious enough to drop the service user questionnaire and work only with health care professionals. The vast majority of the users involved were willing to help, came up with interesting ideas and displayed a good knowledge of the situation and their needs.

4.4. The conduct of the fieldwork

In view of the need for the least possible disruption in the facilities and the realisation that ward life and balance was very sensitive, time spent there had to be the absolute minimum. Incidents from prior visits and the pilot study had shown that the tranquillity of the wards was very fragile and direct observation of activity in the residential spaces could trigger pathological conditions among service user. The primary purpose of the study was to evaluate environments using an integrated approach involving the people who spent a considerable amount of time in them, i.e. service users and staff. Understanding of the policies for service delivery, and of users' perception of them and of the environment in which they lived or worked, came from the interviews conducted with service users and staff.

Within each Unit, the questionnaires were administered according to the availability of private spaces, in staff offices or quiet or interview rooms when available, to common rooms and even in the case of bedridden service user, in bedrooms. 50 members of staff from diverse backgrounds were recruited according to their availability. 65 service users were recruited according to their willingness to participate. They were at liberty to withdraw at any time, but this did not happen.

Due to the serious and unpredictable nature of the service user' mental state, it was not possible to select those who participated in a randomised manner. Pathologies varied according to current admissions policy. As an instance, people with learning difficulties might suffer from mental illness too, but mental illness cannot result in learning disabilities, unless after a serious brain injury [180]. Service users with learning difficulties were not recruited.

Overall, it became possible to triangulate the relationship between the spatial organisation and the therapeutic aims of the building, and the extent to which that perception was validated by the users, be they service users or staff. Priorities were thus viewed under a new perspective. For example, conditions that architects might have considered institutional might have increased people's sense of safety in the building or alternatively architectural interventions, such as elaborate corridors, might compromise the sense of safety. Subsequently, the architectural perspective was tested by care professionals who strongly interacted with service user, but who again might have had their own motives, and by service users who also had their limitations, for instance lack of motivation to participate or the possibility that they might not give honest replies, as they might be unwilling to reveal their problems. That might stem from the fear that their replies might be revealed to staff or by the wish to appear more competent or healthy than they actually were.

In the past, the views of service users had been underestimated and their voices silenced. It was only as a consequence of the relatively recent anti-psychiatry model - which itself is regarded as contentious - that questions began to be raised about the nature of mental illness itself and the mentally ill were given the first opportunity to acquire a voice that has been strengthened with the thinking about service user involvement.

4.5. The need for an architectural checklist

Healthcare buildings have been considered by Marcus [161] as a means to retain the prevailing system - in this case the medical model, as even in the era of community psychiatry doctors still dominate healthcare provision - and in that sense it was very important to examine the buildings in respect to the care regimes and the prevailing expressions of healthcare policies. This was even more important in the case of residential accommodation, as the idea of one's home is connected with autonomy and increased power related to oneself, whilst the idea of institution is connected with service user' powerlessness (in case of total institutions) as the history review has indicated. Under that concept, the more domestic a building was (as opposed to institutional), the larger degree of autonomy service users should experience.

Yet, is that what was really sought? Are service users still under the influence of an acute episode ready for the experience autonomy or is the latter incapacitating them as unsuitable to their needs (inadequate safety, too demanding in terms of competence or insufficient/'wrong' type of choice)? In other words, are the buildings enabling service users to return from the institution, especially those with past history of hospitalisation, back to autonomous life in the community or do they function as a more local, community-based 'storage' of mentally ill people furthering their social exclusion?

It was important to investigate the sample of buildings physically in terms of their facilities and environmental attributes, to see to what extent they met the objective of domesticity. This was achieved by a qualitative evaluation of the buildings, in connection with the care regime they implemented. The initial approach to recording the facilities included the collection of data about functions, services, care regimes, the connections to the community and staff and service user demographics. Then, it became necessary to design a more objective instrument that could begin to provide answers to emerging problems with the concept of domesticity itself.

It has already been suggested that one idea dominated the architectural discourse about how best to design residential accommodation for people with mental health problems. This was that the building should be designed so as to appear and function as much like an ordinary home as it was possible to achieve by architectural means, given the programmatic constraints of the building and the specific needs of the service user group. The idea of creating as domestic a setting as possible was intended to contrast with the appearance, form and layout of the institutional buildings in which the service user group had previously been accommodated, which, under the influence of normalization theory, now appeared to be outmoded, inappropriate or dysfunctional. The architectural discourse was therefore dominated by a one-dimensional, linear concept that set domestic architecture at one pole and institutional architecture at the other. A successful solution should come as close to the domestic end of the axis as it was possible to achieve by architectural means.

This idea was supported by a small corpus of research [210] that set out to list and evaluate all the significant design features of accommodation designed for people with learning difficulties, so that architects could consult the resultant checklist at the design stage to ensure that they had not inadvertently specified features that could be regarded as unnecessarily institutional solutions. Likewise, facilities managers could evaluate their existing buildings using the same criteria, in order to improve their performance from the point of view of their appropriateness to the domestic environment required by their service users. Robinson's approach was adapted for this project in order to assess the architectural character of each building, including its domestic or institutional characteristics.

To quantify further, and place the participating projects on a scale from Institutional to Domestic according to purely architectural and spatial characteristics, a checklist was therefore constructed in a similar manner to that of Robinson. This more quantitative method of an architectural checklist was specifically designed to address the domesticity of the buildings, to add weight to the qualitative, descriptive approach previously described. The outcome from both these approaches contributed to an overall assessment of the degree of domesticity represented by each of the case studies. However, it should be borne in mind that the result was still not able to evaluate whether that domesticity was for the benefit of the therapeutic aim of the facilities or if it was in practice, and despite the claims of normalisation theory, a source of trouble. At this point the users' opinions also had a part to play, through the interviews, as the means not only for studying the physical, designed environment as it relates to therapeutic processes, but also how this environment impacted on people's lives.

4.6. The detailed design of the Checklist

The checklist comprised 215 features relevant to the building, the building's setting and its detailed design. For each feature the phenomena were rated that would render it institutional, as opposed to domestic. Elements that were similar to what one could see or what existed in the nearby housing were considered to be domestic. For example, if a building had a similar window size to the neighbouring dwellings this would be considered domestic, as would a situation in which each residential unit had its own kitchen as opposed to none or to more than one.

Institutional elements could be elements that were associated with public building architecture, such as the existence of a reception or front desk at the entry point, or the presence of medical or therapy functions, such as an ECT room or an arts and crafts room. Fixtures and fittings associated with public buildings were also rated as institutional, for example professional laundry equipment or a wall-mounted hand drying machine. Additionally, features that an individual would not encounter at home, such as sharing a bedroom with a complete stranger, would be considered institutional. Each building was then scored on each feature as either institutional (I) or Domestic (D).

The 215 features were grouped in three domains according to the Robinson Checklist, and under that grouping, 22 features referred to Site and Context, 40 features to Building and the remaining 152 to Space and Room. Site and Context dealt with issues regarding the surroundings and the exterior of the facility. These covered questions about the location, the relation of the building to the neighbouring architecture and the organisation of the facade and the access point. The aim was to identify the integration of the facility to the local community, the accessibility that residents had to local amenities and the degree to which the building stood out as an institution by its appearance. The emphasis of the Building section was on corridors, as they formed a vital part of the life in psychiatric facilities, bearing a resemblance to the streets of city life, for the connections they enabled and the opportunity for physical release they provided. Both this section and the following one were more detailed than the one relating to the exterior of the building, as psychiatric facilities tended to be introverted. Especially when most service users were sectioned the facility operated like a micro-cosmos, with very limited external interaction for service user. Space and Room the vast majority of features and recorded all the public and private amenities that a unit included. 'Public' referred here to psychiatric, therapy, administration and hotel related areas or facilities, and 'private' to bedrooms and WCs, from their general organisation to decoration details.

In order to identify the basis of what might be considered essential requirements in mental health buildings in practise, the checklist features were then classified according the frequency with which each was met in the case studies. Moreover, features characteristic of each country and therefore the differences between the acute mental health wards and the foyers, in relation to the building features, were also identified. All those features were related to the 'SCP model', in order to identify their origin in respect of the domesticity versus institutionalisation discussion. Thus, the features owing their origin to jurisdictional and medical reasons were classified and discussed under the safety and security perspective. Those introduced for nursing and caring purposes were related to the competence parameter. Finally, those related to the psychosocial model were discussed as related to the personalisation and choice parameter perspective. In this way, it became possible to see from which thinking process the institutional features that appeared in the facilities stemmed, and if that was because of necessity or because of remnants of past thinking. The interviews with the two user groups would then add their insight on that particular subject.

Each facility or country received an overall score according to its degree of domesticity, and this could then be juxtaposed with the users' view or the initial design aims.

Thus, if a unit was found to be relatively institutional compared to the rest, the next step was to see if that was because of increased safety measures, or low personalisation opportunities or because it did not allow service user' skills to develop, which again could be correlated to the relevant topics from the service user and staff interviews.

4.7. Advantages and limitations of the methodology

It is very difficult to compare such varying buildings. Yet, the reality of mental health facilities is interrelated with this variety. On the other hand, the inclusion of so many different methodologies and topics kept case studies sample short, yet indicative. This practice raised topics that would never have come up if only the staff and service users were involved or if there was only a checklist of the buildings, or even if the sample of the buildings was smaller, as important points met in only one building might have been lost. That justified the exploratory nature of this project.

The checklist could be used in future as a research tool, or a way to evaluate and improve an existing building or to criticise a proposal at the design stage. However, it was not possible to relate the checklist to measurable therapeutic outcomes, as this would have entailed a more intensive, longitudinal study of service user' progress. When using the checklist it should be borne in mind that not everything that is 'domestic' in nature is necessarily 'good' for the occupants of the building. Thus, while it is helpful to know whether each building is 'domestic' or 'institutional', the intention here was to stimulate informed, evidence based debate among all the professionals involved in delivering the service, that takes into account the needs of service users and staff, on the question of which features need to be domestic or institutional in their design in order to serve the needs of the particular service user group and therapeutic regime that the building is intended to serve.

As expected, the Checklist had its limitations. One possible limitation of the current checklist is that the same weighting has been given to each point. Thus it equalised the weight of individual features that did not necessarily have the same impact on service user' lives. A further refinement, based on more in-depth studies of its features, might allow the gravity of each variable to be weighted differently, according to its impact on the users' experience of the building. Second, the Non-Applicable parameter caused statistical problems, since it differentiated the N number of valid features for some units. This could not be avoided, since there was ambiguity about the functions hosted in such facilities, as the sectorisation principles and community psychiatry encouraged the lack of a common brief and promoted local interpretations of the therapeutic regime.

Chapter 5

The physical milieu of research: the unit buildings

5.1. The care regimes

As case studies we are going to present 5 Foyers de Post Cure in France and 5 Acute Mental Health Wards, in community settings in the UK. In general, they were spread around each country and varied in size and service user numbers, with more variations presented among the French sample. All the French facilities were independent in terms of administration and running, even in the case of Rene Capitant, which shared premises with a day centre. More precisely, service users of the foyer and most of the staff had to leave the premises, between 9.00-17.00 on weekdays, for the day centre to use the premises. Yet, there was no other connection, i.e., administrative, between the two projects. By contrast, in the UK, apart from Forest Lodge, all other in-patient facilities formed part of a broader health care scheme. However, despite their location in a health care scheme, their function and administration remained independent.

General Information			
Cs	Location	Connection	No. of Service users
France			
Bois (Bois St Joseph	La Crau, Var, Cote d' Azure d'Azur	Independent	81
Elan (Elan Retrouve)	Paris	Independent	25
FrT (Francois Tosquelles)	Bully- les- Mines, Pas de Calais	Independent	13
Ger (Geraniums)	Mouans- Sartoux, Provence	Independent	47
RenC (Rene Capitant)	Paris	Sharing premises with Day Centre	24
UK			
AlbL (Albany Lodge)	St Albans	Part of a CMHC	24
ForL (Forest Lodge)	Southampton	Independent	18
Lake (Lakeside)	Southall, Greater London	Part of CMHC	16
New (New Bridges)	East Hull	Part of CMHC	12 (Finch Ward)
SmH (Small Heath)	Birmingham	Part of CHC	14

Table 3.: Information regarding the location, the connection to other facilities and the capacity of the case studies. C(M)HC stands for Community (Mental) Health Centre.

Foyer/ ward	Gender	Age	Referrals from	Sectors	Status	Referrals to	Diagnosis
France							
Bois	Mix	17-35	Hospitals Clinics MH Associations	10 sectors (incl. Cote d'Azur /Provence	V	More independent Forms of accommodation	Mental health problems, mainly psychosis.
Elan	Mix	18-50	Psychiatric or general hospitals MH Associations Psychiatrists	Broader Paris	V	Protected apartments Best close to foyer	Mental health problems, mainly psychosis.
FrT	Mix	18-55	Psychiatric or general hospitals MH Associations Psychiatrists	Several sectors	V	More independent accommodation, like apartments	Mental health problems, mainly psychosis.
Ger	F	17+	Hospitals, psychiatrists	Alpes Maritimes + other sectors (Var, Paris)	V		Mental health problems, mainly psychosis.
RenC	M	18-65	Hospital/ university Hospital	Paris, mostly around the university	V	More independent accommodation	Mental health problems, mainly psychosis.
UK							
AlbL	Mix	18-65	Hospital wards, community services, A&Es		S/V	More independent accommodation	Acute mental health disorders
ForL	Mix (but a house at night)	18-65	Hospital or failed placement in less dependent accommodation		S/V	Homes, community places	Severe and enduring mental illness, (high dependency)
Lake	Mixed	18-65	A&Es or assessment in the community under Mental Health Act (GPs, CMHT, the police or courts)		S/V	Community places, homes	Acute mental illness, including psychotic disorders, schizophrenia and depression.
New	Mixed	18-65	Consultant psychiatrists via primary care and emergency teams		V/S	Mostly homes	Acute mental health problems, from minor to psychosis
SmH	Mixed to become single	18-65	home treatment teams		S/V	informal community places	Psychotic disorders

Table 4.: Service user admission and referral criteria.

As far as admission criteria and policies were concerned, the gender, age, origin of the referral, the diagnosis and the status of service users at that time have been summarised in Table 4.

In general, foyers tended to employ a larger number and more diverse paramedical staff, including psychologists, social workers, occupational therapists (OT) and occasionally pharmacists, than the UK facilities, whilst UK facilities relied mostly on nursing staff and non-qualified staff, such as care assistants, that were employed in all UK wards. Similarly, administration staff, such as secretaries or accountants, were employed in most French facilities, even as managers as the case of Bois St Joseph indicates, but in none of the UK cases, where administrative work was carried out by nurses. Chefs were employed in all facilities where food was freshly cooked on the premises, apart from one, where food was prepared by service users under staff supervision. All facilities relied on domestic staff for the cleaning of the facility.

Staff	Nurse	MD	Psycho-logist	Social worker	OT	Pharma cist	Care assistant	Trainee	Stu dent	Admin	Dome stic	chef
						Foyer/ward staff						
						France						
Bois	x	x	x	x	x	x				x	x	x
Elan	x	x	x	x					x	x	x	x
FrT	x				x					x		
Ger	x	x								x	x	x
RenC	x	x	x	x						x	x	
UK												
AlbL	x						x			x		
ForL	x				x		x			x		x
Lake	x	x	x				x			x		
New	x	x			x		x			x		x
SmH	x	x					x	x		x		

Table 5.: Staff specialization in the case studies

As expected, restrictions regarding time spent in and out of the facilities and access outside of them were more relaxed in the foyers. Yet even there, as a rule, service users were disciplined regarding outings. This was despite the fact that foyers were deemed to be 'open' facilities. In the UK, service users could only go out of the ward alone or escorted by staff, depending on their status, in one facility only. In the remaining facilities, sectioned service users could not leave the ward premises, and there were restrictions even in the use of the courtyards, as table 5 indicates. Visitors' policy was not related to the facility type, i.e, foyer or acute ward but was a decision of the administration and it therefore varied considerably among the case studies (table 5).

In all facilities, in both countries, access was restricted to staff offices and staff areas and the clinic. Access to the professional kitchen was allowed to service users only in one foyer and service users could not access the service user kitchenette at night in two UK wards to prevent coffee and tea consumption at night.

Night time observation involved staff checking in service users' bedrooms at night, apart from one foyer where a nurse slept in her bedroom and service users could wake her up in case of emergency. The frequency of checks varied according to service users' condition, with rounds being more frequent in the UK, where in some cases staff could check service users continuously, as Table 6 indicates. Nevertheless, in two of the UK units rounds were as frequent as in most French units, blurring the differences among acute wards and foyers. Moreover, in one of those there is a seclusion room and an intensive care section, even if the latter is not used as such.

Table 7 describes aspects of care regime relevant to everyday life activities such as room maintenance, meals and service users' schedules. In all facilities except one, staff were responsible for bedroom maintenance. Similarly, in only one foyer were service users allowed to participate in everyday meal preparation. In all the rest of the case studies food was either prepared by a chef or reheated by staff, and in one case this did not take place in the ward premises. As for meal times, they were fixed in all facilities. The medication timetable was stricter in acute wards. Activity times had fixed times in one foyer, on a schedule that was prepared with service users every Monday and in another service users had to follow their personal activity schedule. In acute wards, activity was more casual, for service users that were willing to attend.

Regarding available activity (table 8) there was no activity pattern for the foyers. In the two where service users left during day, activity did not actually take place in the wards. Yet, some form of casual activity related to the communal life, such as the editing of a journal or games could be available for whoever wished to participate. In the one

Operational policies				
Cs	Opening restrictions	Access	Night shift	Visitors
France				
Bois	Service users could leave the unit, keep the foyer key.	All areas but administration/ Offices/ clinic/ OT out of activity hours	2 staff, rounds on hour, check rooms	All common areas, garden, Rooms
Elan	Service users had to be out 9.00-16.00 (weekdays) And no later than 23.00 (0.30 Saturdays)	Common areas only (no student area, kitchen, offices, staff areas incl. WC and library)	1 nurse at her room, no rounds. 1 student on call	Only visitors room (outside main area)
FrT	Rooms locked between 9.30-17.00 but 30' for nap after lunch. Service users could leave the foyer between 17.00-19.00, escorted	No access to staff toilet, offices, clinic	5 rounds, entering rooms, checking outside	Not allowed except under special circumstances (common room)
Ger	Gate door open 24h, no security outside, yet service users not supposed to leave at night. Service users could go out alone (not late) with staff permission	No access to kitchen, offices, clinic	3 rounds by one staff member, checking in rooms. Internal call system for emergencies	Not allowed in bedrooms
RenC	9.00-17.00 weekdays, service users left and foyer functioned as day centre (for other service users too). Service users could lock bedrooms	Not access to foyer 9.00-17.00, staff areas, clinic	2-3 rounds at night, entering rooms	Entrance and ground floor common area (Rotonde)
UK				
AlbL	High security and observation levels. Service users only in fully enclosed courtyards.	No access to staff areas, kitchen and kitchenette at night, clinic	Continuous checks in rooms	Consultation rooms upon availability. Children at entrance outside ward
ForL	Service users could go to the garden and out of the centre, escorted or alone (depending on M.H. condition. Houses closed at night (1 staff per house).	No access to professional kitchen. Restricted access to offices, OT. No access outside their house at night. clinic.	2 rounds per night, entering rooms	All day areas, rooms
Lake	Access outside of ward (outdoor areas, including the enclosed courtyards, garden or the hospital campus) restricted for sectioned service users.	No access to kitchen, clinic, staff areas.	2 rounds per night, entering rooms	interview room or common room. Partner/ children: bedrooms
New	Service users could not leave, unless they were voluntary.	No access to kitchen, clinic, staff offices.	Depending on service user, from 15'-60' , entering rooms	Conservatory /children, into the building's main entrance
SmH	Service users had to leave the foyer to the day centre for lunch, dinner.	No access to office, linic, staff lockers, kitchen at night	Continuous checks in rooms (suicidals even every 5')	All day areas, corridor, bedrooms

Table 6.: Operational policies regarding opening and access restriction, night time observation and visits in the case studies

that during working hours service users could not enter their rooms, any activity that was taking place in the foyer was obligatory. On the contrary, a foyer with a strong rehabilitation character and provided a larger variety of activity on the premises, service users had choice in which activity to participate. Finally, there was a foyer with no opportunity for external activity, and a poor opportunity of internal. In the UK, apart from a ward that catered for more stable service users than the rest of the acute facilities, the rest of facilities offered little to nothing at all by way of activity provided inside the ward premises. On the occasions when there was organised activity in the premises of the MHCC or the CHC, it was up to staff availability or to service users' status to be able to attend.

cs	Room maintenance	Food preparation	Fixed meal times	Schedule
Facilities day function regime				
France				
Bois	Staff but service users could tidy up depending on condition	Reheated in kitchen By staff and service users	Yes	Meals, activities
Elan	Service users with help.	Prepared by chef	Yes	Meals, medical appointments.
FrT	Staff but service users could tidy up depending on condition	Prepared by service users	Yes	Wake up time, Meals, room closure, medication/ nap/ activities/ outings/ TV off/ bed time
Ger	Cleaning by staff, bedroom tidying up by service users	Prepared by staff	Yes	Meals
RenC	Cleaning by staff, bedroom tidying up by service users	Reheated by staff	Yes	Meal/medication times, foyer closure 9.00-17.00 and closure at night
UK				
AlbL	Cleaning by staff	Reheated by staff	Yes	Meals/ curfew time
ForL	Staff but service users could tidy up depending on condition	Prepared by chef	Yes	Meals/ wake up/ curfew times
Lake	Staff but service users could tidy up depending on condition	Reheated by staff	Yes	Medication, meals, curfew times, ward closure at 21.00
New	Cleaning by staff	Prepared by chef	Yes	Meals, medication
SmH	Cleaning by staff	Elsewhere	Yes	Meals, medication

Table 7.: Daily regime regarding cleanliness, meals and obligatory schedule in the case studies

Activity	Bois	FRT	ForL	Rene	New	Lake	Elan	Ger	SmH	Alb	Total
Games		x		x	x	x	x		x		6
Art	x	x	x		x	x					5
Gardening	x	x	x								3
Cookery	x	x				x	x				3
Patisserie											
Hotel services	x	x		x							3
Travels	x		x	x							3
Trips											
Pottery	x							x			2
Ironing	x	x									2
Sewing/ clothmaking	x	x									2
Music	x	x									2
Group therapy		x						x			2
IT	x		x								2
Laundry	x										1
Discussion		x									1
Make up		x									1
Journal				x							1
Maths	x										1
Language	x										1
Humanitarian work	x										1
Discovering nature		x									1
Wood workshop		x									1
Book reading			x								1
Relaxation					x						1
Total activity options	14	13	5	4	3	3	2	2	1	Not in the ward	
External activity options	Yes	No	Yes	Yes	Rare	Depends	Yes	No	Yes	Depends	

Table 8.: Activity options for service users in the case studies

5.2. Building descriptions

The focus will now shift from care regimes to the buildings. To make the account more immediate and animated, it will be narrated in the present tense, describing the design and layout of the facilities during the 'ethnographic present' when the fieldwork took place.

5.2.1. Bois St Joseph

Le Bois St Joseph has provided psychiatric Post-Cure in a Convalescent House in Var, Cote d' Azur since 1996. The unit is situated in La Crau, a village between Toulon and Hyeres. Le Bois St Joseph has access to train and bus services and local amenities in the village including a rehabilitation centre.

It is a three-storey building with a two-storey east elevation, the same height as nearby houses (Figures 44-45). The garden (figure 46) starts from the two external sides of the unit, the south and the east, gradually expanding to occupy the semi-enclosed courtyards, which result from the geometry of the building. The northern side and the remaining part of the western serve as a parking area for staff.

The foyer has a vertical separation of functions, with accommodation and normal day activities sheltered above organisational and therapeutic activities. The main administration, the medical offices, the day centre and general activity areas occupy the ground floor. The two upper floors are mainly for accommodation.

Figure 44. Eastelevation   **Figure 45.** The foyer's main en-   **Figure 46.** The main entrance/
                              trance   reception/ waiting area

Figure 47. The main lounge   **Figure 48.** The lounge's quiet recess

Figure 49. First floor terrace accessible to service users

Figure 50. The dishwashingarea

Figure 51. The painting studio in the unit's day centre

Figure 52. Bedrooms are en suite and designed as double. In this case the second bed has been removed

Figure 53. Bedroom area corridor

5.2.2. Elan Retrouve

The foyer is in the Centre of Paris, in the 13th compartment, near the French Library on a pedestrian street. It is very well served by public transport. There are plenty of facilities around for sports, cultural or educational activities.

The building has no yard and the only outdoor area is a patio on the first floor, used by service users. The foyer (figure 54) extends over three floors. The ground floor comprises storage, students' accommodation and visitors' room. On the first floor are the administration, the day spaces and some accommodation. The second floor is the main accommodation area for service users. The main entrance is separate from the entrance to the flats but serving the students' flats as well.

The patio has a central bed of plants, a grouping of small trees and a rose that was brought symbolically from the old foyer.

5.2.3. Francois Tosquelles

The Foyer Francois Tosquelles is in Bully Les Mines, a miners' village near Arras, Pas de Calais. The unit is at the end of the village, past the railway tracks and rather distant from shops or public amenities such as the post office and the library or the station. Service users can go to town by train or staff may give them a lift to go to the market.

The plot of land is large and surrounded by green space (figures 65, 66), divided into a front and back yard by a brick-wall. The foyer is located in the middle of the front half,

Figure 54. The foyer-part of the building has brickwork on the facade, different standardized windows and is enclosed by the L-shaped block containing normal housing

Figure 55. The main corridor

Figure 56. Service user bedroom

Figure 57. En suite shower

Figure 58. The main lounge

Figure 59. Dining room

Figure 60. The service user kitchenette

Figure 61. Each service user had a refrigerator shelf in which he/ she can lock food

which has trees and a lawn with a few borders of flowers and roses. By the entrance to the garden, there is a small workshop for carpentry, housed in a former garage (figure 67).

The building was a new unit. It is on two floors. The main volume is a long parallelepiped, with a pitched roof. The middle part of the front elevation is brought forward, curved, and then recessed in the middle, in that way situating the entrance and breaking

Figure 62. The study   **Figure 63.** The games area   **Figure 64.** Bedroom corridor

Figure 65. Francois Tosquelles. External view of the facility

Figure 66. Back yard view of the building

Figure 67. Francois Tosquelles. Main entrance lobby

Figure 68. Kitchen and food storage

the linearity of the volume. Two columns on both sides of the main door state the entry point even more clearly. Organisationally, the ground floor holds all public activity and administration. On the upper floor is service users' accommodation.

5.2.4. Geraniums

The Geraniums is a Maison (house) Post-Cure, a convalescent care unit. It is purpose built, dated early in the second half of the 20th century in Mouans Sartoux, a picturesque town about ten minutes' drive from Cannes, and about four kilometres from Grasse, surrounded by forest and orchards. The foyer is on the outskirts of the village (figure

Figure 69. Shared bedroom   **Figure 70.** Unit's first floor corridor   **Figure 71.** View from the street.

Figure 72. South elevation from the front garden   **Figure 73.** North view   **Figure 74.** The main entrance   **Figure 75.** Ground floor common room

Figure 76. Shared bedroom, with en suite facilities   **Figure 77.** First floor corridor view   **Figure 78.** View to service user room for three

Figure 79. The dining room   **Figure 80.** The kitchen   **Figure 81.** First floor common room

72). There is no other mental health facility there to provide activities and not much activity takes place in the town either. The foyer is not well served by transportation. A fifty-metres-long path leads to the facility, which is surrounded by the garden (figures 73).

The foyer consists mainly of two volumes, vertically placed one next to the other and with an 8.5m distance between them. The western volume develops from east to west, and expands on four levels. The eastern volume develops in a north to south direction and has two storeys. The two blocks are linked on the first floor level with one single-floor bridge. The first block "escalates", gradually: on the first floor level to create a large terrace, with beams running over part of the terrace on the second floor and to allow a gently sloping roof for part of it on the third floor level. The second block follows the clear geometry of the parallelepiped.

The entrance of the foyer is at the rear, and one has to pass under the "bridge" (figure 74). Inside the foyer there is only a relative vertical separation of functions: common areas and administration tend to be on the lower floor and the upper floors are accommodation only. Bedrooms spread on all floors. The ground floor brings together administration, day spaces and accommodation. The first floor gathers accommodation, medical and paramedical offices and day spaces. The third and the fourth floor are accommodation only.

5.2.5. Rene Capitant

The Foyer Rene Capitant, in the heart of Paris near the Pantheon, is a community facility for young men recovering from an acute episode of mental illness. Rene Capitant is very close to the University and there are many students among the service user group. It is two minutes' walk from the Luxembourg Gardens, with sites for recreation, shops and markets, educational facilities, and mental health projects. The foyer is very well served by public transport.

The building is rather old but only the external walls have been kept. The interior was gutted and renovated in 1973. It is a terraced building, very long and narrow, developed over four stories and a basement (figure 82). There is also a second basement, not in use. The "co-habitation" with the day hospital involves the basement, the ground floor, the first and the fourth floor, whilst the rest of the floors belong to the foyer only. There are no outdoor spaces.

Figure 82. Rene Capitant from the street

Figure 83. Rene Capitant. The 'Bar' in the basement is equipped as a media room - I

Figure 84. Rene Capitant. The 'Bar' in the basement is equipped as a media room - II

Figure 85. The kitchen in the basement

Figure 86. The dining room in the basement

Figure 87. Part of the bar area

Figure 88. Main staircase

Figure 89. The TV room on the first floor

Figure 90. Service user's single bedroom

Figure 91. Triple room

Figure 92. The music room rarely used by the foyer

Figure 93. The art therapy room

There is a separation of functions in the foyer according to floors, yet the organisation of the building is not clear. The basement gathers communal areas. The ground and the first floor comprise mainly offices and administration. The second and third floor houses accommodation and the upper floor is used mainly for activities. Also, spaces change function during the 24 hour day. Areas sheltering an activity in the day hospital might have a different function in the foyer.

5.2.6. Albany Lodge

The unit is centrally located, in a residential area, part of St Albans Conservation Area. It is close to many services: post office, the high street, the market and the Cathedral and

Figure 94. The entrance, in the most private part of the building and accessible through the car park

Figure 95. Landscape design marking the entrance in a friendly, 'natural' way

Figure 96. The lobby

Figure 97. Fully enclosed courtyards

Figure 98. The hatch in the dining room

Figure 99. Non-smoking lounge

Figure 100. Internal courtyard, yet not fully enclosed by buildings

Figure 101. Bedroom

Figure 102. The bench at the module junction

adjacent to a park with a lake. It does not have any immediate neighbours, since it is next to a vehicle turning circle, used as a car park, and the park (figure 94).

Albany Lodge is a two storey building, consisting of four "arcades", which cross in order to form enclosed or semi-enclosed courtyards. The result is a volume with a square outline, yet quite light because of the internal atria. Pitched roofs shelter the "arcades". The entrance to the unit is "protected", accessible through the vehicle turning circle and close to the car park, yet marked with landscaping (figure 95).

Albany Lodge serves resident service users as well as service users from the community and other services. Internally, it is divided into two broad types of areas. The first is where service users visit or stay, comprising the ECT (electro convulsive therapy) and the CMHC. The ECT serves both the residents of the unit and service users from other services or the community. The CMHC is a space for therapeutic activities. Both are located on the ground floor. The consultants' offices are also on the ground floor, but resident service users rarely go there. The second type comprises the areas where the interaction with service users takes place: the administration and the office space for the teams (home-treatment and community treatment), both on the first floor. Here we focus on policies and areas immediately accessible to service users, which form the residential setting during their stay. Thus, the upper floor, which houses the mental health teams and the administration of the entire Centre, is not relevant since there is no interaction with the life of the unit. Additionally, consultants' offices and the ECT cover a bigger facility spectrum than the actual unit. All these areas are not integrated to the ward but have a degree of autonomy. They have therefore been excluded from our analysis.

There is a strong symmetry of the ground floor around the diagonal axis, concerning the perimeter of the building. These rules produce a module of two types, a cross and a T-shape, for the end corners and the junctions of the wings respectively. The cross comprises five or six bedrooms at the four limbs of a cross with three WCs in between. A corridor runs by two successive limbs, serving the whole area. The second case is an adaptation of the first.

The entire accommodation zone is a synthesis of these modules. The north corner of the building, as well as the west and its east end are formed by the cross type. Between the crosses, at the north-west and the north-east directions, the gaps are filled with T-shaped modules. In this way, the bedrooms are situated at the front of the unit, facing the two streets. The T-shaped modules constitute the beginning of two wings, vertical to one another and parallel to the external wings. They form the core of the unit, including the common areas and the services of the ward, as well as providing the space for the rest of the services available in Albany Lodge, i.e., the ECT unit, the consultation offices and the activity area.

5.2.7. Forest Lodge

Regarding its location, Forest Lodge stands in a residential area, close to the centre of Southampton. It is close to local amenities: shops, leisure areas, parks and the post office, and the local bus service is quite frequent. Additionally, service users may get a lift from staff. The unit is located between a commercial garage and the police station. Across the street is a residential area.

The unit follows the long and narrow geometry of the plot of land and comprises three two-storey houses, attached to one another, and a small one-storey detached build-

Figure 103. Houses' main entrance

Figure 104. Houses' individual backyards at the rear

Figure 105. Garden view with a pond, a gazebo and a gardener's shed

ing at the rear. The exterior of the main building resembles a normal housing project (figure 103). The south side of the houses is divided, to provide three more private gardens, giving each house its own outdoor space (figure 104). Gates enable movement between the gardens. A garden house and a gazebo occupy the south-east end of the garden (figure 105).

The main buildings have two main functions: administration and accommodation. The accommodation is further divided into three houses. These areas, the administration and the three houses, have their own entrances, and on the ground floor level are separated from one another. However, a spinal corridor on the upper floor level runs through all four areas and its interconnecting doors allow controlled internal communication (figure 106).

Figure 106. First floor corridor (Bedroom area of one of two houses)

Figure 107. The seclusion room

Figure 108. Smoking room

Figure 109. Service users' dining room and kitchen

Figure 110. Lounge

5.2.8. Lakeside

Lakeside Acute Mental Health Unit is located in the premises of West Middlesex University Hospital site, a major acute hospital at Isleworth, but not part of the hospital organisation, despite the lack of any separate fenced outdoor space. It comprises two wards each of 20 individual beds, and one of 12 in-patient and four intensive care beds with a seclusion room (Finch Ward) and an out-patient function, which comprises a day hospital of 34 places and its activities, acute day treatment, ECT, therapies and a gym.

Figure 111. Shared bathroom   **Figure 112.** Service users' bed- **Figure 113.** Service users' bed-
facility   room   room

Once service users leave the main entrance they are in the heart of the campus. The building is U-shaped, on two floors. The ground floor has four wings, forming an almost square shape with two protected patios, the only outdoors area where sectioned service users may go, their condition permitting. Initially, these used to have fountains, but they proved difficult to maintain. Service users who can go out of the ward use the hospital campus grounds, which have green space to walk, by the river. The ground floor comprises doctors', psychologists' and consultation offices, one of the three wards, and the day hospital. Upstairs, three wings create a U-shaped layout overlooking the two patios and a semi-enclosed area. The west wing is Finch Ward, the north the ECT unit and the east wing the third ward. Apart from single bedroom accommodation, each ward has the following spaces: quiet room, staff room, treatment room, games room, kitchen, dining, tea station and TV room. Of the three wards, only Finch Ward (figure 114) is participating in the study, since the research will be more concise if all participants come from one ward. Finch Ward has been selected since it includes provision for intensive care and a seclusion room. At the time of the study, the intensive care beds are functioning as normal beds.

Figure 114. OT room

To get to Finch Ward, service users or visitors enter through the main entrance, pass by the reception and take the stairs up. The ward develops on both sides of a double loaded corridor divided into three zones. The northern part, near the entrance, contains the clinical and day activity. The central part is the in-patient accommodation. The southern part, near the emergency exit, shelters the former intensive care accommodation and the seclusion room.

Figure 115. The dining room, where reheated food is passed through the hatch

Figure 116. The games room with the table tennis

Figure 117. The kitchenette has no cooker or microwave

Figure 118. In the corridor opening is a payphone with an armchair. However, the height of the phone is suitable for standing use

Figure 119. Ward corridor alcoves form projecting closets or mild turns

Figure 120. The mattress on the floor of the seclusion room: typical and with white cell reference

Figure 121. Service user bedroom

Figure 122. Part of the bedroom

Figure 123. The assisted bathroom hasno hoist, yet it is spacious for staff to move around

5.2.9. New Bridges

New Bridges, in East Hull, is a facility that combines an Acute Admissions Mental Health Unit and a Community Mental Health Centre under one roof. However, the shared projects have no interaction between them, so the focus will be on the acute unit only. It is located in a residential area, right in front of the railway lines (figure 124). The building is placed centrally in the plot. The front part, as in Albany Lodge, serves as a parking lot (figure 125). The rest, i.e., the two sides and the rear, remain green free space. Only

Figure 124. The railway lines are unprotected and just outside the service users' garden

Figure 125. Part of New Bridges' main facade. This elevation is symmetrical on the entrance axis.

Figure 126. Ground floor bedroom

Figure 127. The quiet room

Figure 128. The Clinic, with a one way mirror on the wall of the former bedroom

Figure 129. The dining room

Figure 130. The lounge

Figure 131. The conservatory

a small part at the rear, about 60sqm, outside the ward, is fenced for service users to use for smoking and some fresh air.

New Bridges is a two-storey, U-shaped building. The front elevation has a strong symmetry, with the entrance placed in the middle. The two halves on each side of the entrance do not correspond to the same function. The west half is the CMHC and the east half belongs to the ward.

The ward (figure 161) is organised on two floors. The ground floor houses the "public" activities and the first floor is the private "sleeping" area. A double-loaded, L-shaped corridor serves each floor.

5.2.10. Small Heath

Small Heath is in a dense inner-city area with a large Asian community. The unit is located near the main street (figure 132), and is very close to the Mosque. The Post Office is two minutes' walk from the unit and there is a park close by. The relationship with the immediate neighbourhood is practically non-existent, as there are no houses in the immediate vicinity.

The building has two storeys. Inside, apart from the mental health services, it contains GPs and a family care clinic. The mental health services comprise a Small Heath In-patient Unit, an Acute Day Unit of 30 places, and a Joint Health/Social Services Team Base and the Northern Birmingham Community Trust Base. It is L-shaped, located in the corner of the plot, occupying the entire west side and part of the north side. The garden is in front of the mental health facilities, providing an outdoor area for games and recreation. Small Heath Community Centre has two wings. The northern wing is single-storey and the west wing has two storeys. A spinal, double loaded corridor runs through each floor (figure 133). A staircase at the end of the corridor connects the ward to the Day Centre and the garden.

Figure 132. Main street view of the centre   **Figure 133.** View of the centre from the car park

The Day Centre and the in-patient unit are not under the same management yet, due to lack of space in the ward, the dining area and the laundry facilities are common. However, the relationship between the day centre and the ward has arisen out of necessity and not because of a shared therapeutic regime.

The lack of spaces necessary for the autonomy of the ward differentiates Small Heath from other acute wards, where there is a day centre in the same building but which does not relate to the life of the unit. Nevertheless, what is shown by all cases, including Small Heath, is that the presence of the day centre in the building does not necessarily guarantee any therapeutic activity for the service users. Even in the case of Small Heath, where service users have to go downstairs, the majority of the service users cannot not attend the activities there. A brief description of the day unit is necessary under these circumstances, because of it being a space where in-patients have to come every day. Still, this description will be very brief for two reasons. First, the research focuses on the ward and second, the two facilities are organisationally different and fundamentally serve two different service user groups.

The day unit runs around a double loaded corridor. The east rooms of the centre have access to the garden. It comprises art therapy, activity, group therapy, clinic, two rooms, one of which is used as quiet room, dining room, rehabilitation kitchen, laundry and a pantry. The dining room is very close to the staircase that leads to the ward (figure 134). Apart from bedrooms, the ward comprises only one lounge, a kitchenette, an interview room and a quiet room doubling as a non-smoking lounge (figure 135). The central feature is the corridor (figure 136).

Figure 134. The dining room   **Figure 135.** The dining room in the day centre   **Figure 136.** Ward corridor   **Figure 137.** Bedrooms

5.3. Qualitative Evaluation of Case Studies

5.3.1. Safety and security

Regarding safety issues, French foyers tended to be more relaxed than the UK acute mental health wards. As far as their location was concerned, in general facilities were in areas where there were no major problems regarding service users' safety, especially in the foyers, which were open units. In the UK, occasionally location raised safety concerns: New Bridges was directly in front of the railway lines and Small Heath in an area with social problems with no houses in the immediate vicinity. On the contrary, the presence of a police station next to Forest Lodged increased the degree of safety.

The safety of gardens and courtyards could be an issue for some of the foyers as well as the wards. Geraniums lacked a fence around the perimeter of its premises. Small Heath lacked a fence in the car park area and there was a nook for the garbage bins where somebody could hide. For those reasons, Small Heath CHC was employing security at the main entrance but that extra cost was not sustainable according to the manager. In New Bridges only a small part of its grounds was fenced and accessible to service users. Lakeside, on the contrary was in a hospital campus and was protected by the hospital security. At Albany Lodge, despite the fact that its semi-enclosed courtyards were fenced, staff allowed service users to access only the central, fully enclosed one, where they could have no interaction with people outside the ward nor abscond. In general, the lack of secure external areas might exclude service users from having access to fresh air. However, what a 'secure' external area might mean differed among the wards, as for Small Heath it meant 'fully enclosed' whereas in New Bridges and Forest Lodge it was just 'fenced'.

Another factor that could prevent sectioned service users from having access to the outside was the siting of the ward on first floor, as was the case of Finch Ward and Small Heath. Wards sited on the first floor limited the accessibility of sectioned service users as

Figure 138. The stairwells in the main staircase   **Figure 139.** Looking down the main staircase

they spent much time away from the ground floor. For staff, steps increased the difficulty of escorting people or running down the stairs behind somebody who was absconding. The rest of the UK case studies were placed on the ground floor. On the contrary, in France, service users had access even to balconies and terraces, wherever those were available, i.e., in Elan, Geraniums and Bois St Jospeph.

Single-level wards were featured in Albany Lodge, Finch Ward and Small Heath. However, in one case service users had to use the stairs to go to the dining room on the ground floor, twice a day. The rest of the UK wards developed on two floors, whilst of the foyers only Francois Tosquelles developed on more than two floors. Staircases in all cases but Geraniums and Rene Capitant were in enclosed compartments for fire regulations. Stairwells and parts where service users could fall had been closed after the opening of Elan, with the use of jardinieres (figure 138) and, after New Bridges began operation, with toughened glass. On the contrary, Geraniums had a wide stairwell of four storeys (figure 139). Moreover, the main staircase was very steep and with badly designed steps that increased the chance of an accident or self-harm incident.

Observability inside the foyers and the wards raised several issues. In Elan, there was a window from the reception to the staircase, a window to the main corridor and a CCTV to control the entrance. In Francois Tosquelles and Rene Capitant, there was control of the entrance through the office, if its door remained open. In Geraniums, despite the fact that the office was situated next to the entrance, the placement of the door did not permit any visibility to the entrance and the main staircase. In the case of Bois St Joseph, the reception desk could control only one of the entry points of the building. In the UK on the contrary, in the wards the office or the nursing station tended to have a better control of the entrance, as was the case at Albany Lodge, Finch Ward, New Bridges and Small Heath. However, in the latter two, there was no window to the corridor from the office, and staff had to leave the door open, unless confidential issues had to be discussed. Still, in the case of Finch Ward, somebody could enter or leave unnoticed if they crawled. For supervision purposes, the common room had a large window on the corridor wall, for supervision.

Access to dangerous areas is not really an issue of building design but a policy issue. Yet, cookers tended to be avoided in service user kitchenettes in most wards but Forest Lodge. Foyers, apart from Elan, lacked a service user kitchenette where service users could go unsupervised.

Corridor layout could cause problems in some of the wards. In Albany Lodge corridors at some points were around 1.2 m wide, which promoted a domestic atmosphere,

and the low and wide windowsills invited people to sit and rest. Yet, space was insufficient when escorting a violent service user. The semi-circular benches proved obstacles
in cases of violent service users, allowing service users to catch hold of them. In Forest
Lodge corridors had many dark hiding spots and corners that service users could cling
onto when staff needed to escort them. In Finch Ward, corridors lacked clear visibility.
Similarly in New Bridges, corridor width was not enough to escort service users in crises,
with doors opening against the flow of traffic and with a few blind spots, especially at
turning points. Blind spots were also a concern in Small Heath. In foyers, these issues
were not really a concern. A similar concern applied to ward bedrooms, where they might
be too small for staff to handle a service user having an episode. This was the case at
Small Heath and Lakeside.

Figure 140. The dining room of Bois St Joseph

The fittings of foyers could bear weight and there were normal towel hangers at
normal height, apart from Elan where there were no weight-bearing towel hangers and
curtains. In general, in terms of safety, foyers' detailing resembled that of student accommodation. On the contrary in Albany Lodge and Small Heath, towel hangers were
at the washbasin level and curtains could not bear weight. In New Bridges, staff placed
toughened glass above the curtain rails in the shower. In the rest of the case studies, curtains and other fitting from which service users could hang themselves also could not
bear weight.

Windows could open and there were no bars apart from some of the windows of
Geraniums for decorative purposes and the windows of Rene Capitant, which had a restrictive metal panel on the exterior. Additionally, all windows in French facilities had
normal glazing. In Bois St Joseph there was even glass over the dining room tablecloths (figure 140). Moreover, glazing and mirrors were unbreakable and windows had
restricted openings. In the cases of Lakeside and Small Heath the plastic mirrors dis-
torted the reflected image and could interfere with service users' pathology or affect their
self-esteem.

Regarding bedroom doors, foyers tended to lock from the outside as well, whilst in
the wards, doors could only lock from inside and staff could still come in, and there were
vision panels on doors as in the cases of Albany Lodge, Finch Ward, New Bridges and
Small Heath. Occasionally, as in Albany Lodge and Finch Ward, these panels had flaps
with a key to allow controlled visibility from staff, for privacy, and in the case of New
Bridges they had semi- transparent glass. The bedroom doors of Albany Lodge were
reinforced with metal on the lower part.

In some of the wards, rooms had alarm buttons connected to a board in the reception as in the case of Albany Lodge, or one heard in all wards, and staff could attend from everywhere as in the case of Finch Ward. In Forest Lodge, alarm buttons had been replaced by personal alarms as a more secure option.

Last but not least, in two wards there were seclusion rooms, and one of the two had an intensive care area, which was, however, used as normal space. In Forest Lodge the seclusion room was on the first floor and located far from the service user area, which proved difficult when violent service users needed to be transported. Yet, it was at a distance from the wards, so as not to distress other service users. At Lakeside, safety received attention. The intensive care suite and the seclusion room testified to this. The seclusion room toilet had to be removed after incidents of staff getting trapped. Instead, a new door had been provided where the toilet used to be.

Maintenance is interconnected to safety in a two-way relationship, as neglected buildings might facilitate incidents of harm and self-harm and as the service users' violent behaviour can result in damages to the buildings' infrastructure. Regarding damage as a result of violent behaviour, this was mostly anticipated at the wards. Even at Forest Lodge, at the time of the visits, half the service users were under section and could act violently. According to the Forest Lodge Manager, a lot of equipment needed replacement and there was a lot of wear and tear on the building. However, the maintenance level was very good, as management tended to see to repairs swiftly. A similar approach was the norm in the UK cases, as in all of them there were instances of violence, however continuous repair works gave an impression of respect for the environment of the wards. In some of the wards, changes had to be made to facilitate maintenance, such as changing the carpets to carpet tiles for easier repairs, in Finch Ward. A few pieces of furniture had been broken and not repaired in Albany Lodge and Finch Ward but the overall condition of the furniture in those facilities was good. In Finch Ward, emphasis was given to matching curtains and bedspreads, though many of the original bedspreads had been lost.

An inadequate quantity of sanitary facilities in Small Heath resulted in their not being as clean as in the rest of the UK cases. More serious problems were reported in Albany Lodge. Surfaces had scratches, occasional holes from kicks and the smoking room carpet and furniture had cigarette burns. Some instances of damage, however, could have been prevented if the designers had employed a different design solution in the first place. For instance, the carpet in the smoking room, no matter how homelike it seemed at the beginning, would be impossible to maintain in an acute unit. Also, walls should have been of more solid and strong materials to avoid holes, since disturbed service users can be expected to throw objects at or kick them.

In foyers, there was less violence but the variations among the foyers were more notable. Thus, there were cases of foyers in excellent condition, i.e., Bois St Joseph, Elan and Francois Tosquelles, though the rest of the foyers were found in rather poor condition. In Bois St Joseph and Francois Tosquelles, the materials that had been used helped in that, as they were wear and tear resistant, walls were kept clean and tiles made maintenance easy. Elan was clean, with freshly painted walls. Furniture and fittings were immaculate. The quality of the materials and the attention of the staff certainly contributed to this fact. Additionally, there was initial anticipation of potential problems. For instance, all plumbing pipes in the bathrooms were accessible through the corridor. Also, the cork on common area and corridor floors was a costly choice, but was justified as a material of high endurance that was resistant to dirt and cigarette burns.

By contrast, in Geraniums and Rene Capitant, furniture was old and broken. Bathrooms were in very poor condition with missing tiles, mould on the walls, furnishings were old and stained and pipes exposed and decayed. Some doors did not close properly or doorknobs were missing. In Geraniums, there was even a door to a terrace blocked with a chair in order to keep it closed. Service users had to cope with unacceptable conditions such as pest infestations. Walls were dirty and in places the plaster had peeled off. Furnishings were old, broken, scratched and of poor quality.

5.3.2. Competence

Flexibility levels in the buildings differed among the case studies. There were cases with extended degrees of multiuse and flexibility of resources, and on the other hand also case studies with specialised areas for each separate function. The facility where each function had its own room was Bois St Joseph, with an activity room for each different type of activity, even if theoretically there could for example be multiuse of rooms for similar tasks such as the Language and Maths classes. Thus, there were offices for clerical or administrative work only, therapists had their own offices, the dining room served only for meals, and common areas for their exact purpose, such as socialising in the bar, reading or watching films in the resource room etc. Users in each area were distinct, and certain areas such as offices or workshops would be closed, out of their official hours. For that reason the building was vast in size with a complicated layout, yet with clear separations of groups of areas. This separation was in accordance with the separation of user groups: staff in their offices mainly, service users in bedrooms or common areas. The only area where all user groups merged i.e., service users, nursing staff, administration staff etc, was the dining room, where they all had meals together. However, that was about to change as there was a plan for separating part of the dining area for staff only.

Similarly, Elan had distinct zones for different functions, such as the administration area, sleeping area, the common areas and the utility areas, with distinct user access, i.e., service users, staff, visitors or even the students that had apartments in the broader body of the foyer to be on call at nights, but did not access the foyer normally. The activity existing in the facility had a casual character, like that of roommates doing something after working or studying hours, and for that purpose took place in common areas, similar to what would happen in a house with several flatmates.

On the other hand facilities were seen that had a great deal of multiuse, such as the Foyer Francois Tosquelles, where the dining room-lounge was the only common room for service users. It catered for different and occasionally contradictory needs: medication arrangements, social interaction, TV area, indoor activity area, dining and sitting-relaxation area. The use of furniture indicated the function each time: chairs would be on the tables when not in use, movable partitions would separate areas for activity or when the meals were taking place and the activity space was not used, or tables would be separate for a certain activity and then be united again to form a long dining table where service users and staff would have a meal (figures 141-142).

Another interesting example of flexibility was that of separate facilities sharing one building at different times of the day, as in the example of Rene Capitant. Since space was arranged to serve both facilities, there was an imbalance between activity areas and

Figure 141. Part of the common room, the TV corner **Figure 142.** Part of the common room, activity area 'corner'

offices in the foyer, and at the same time bedrooms could be crowded and without privacy. Most offices were empty when service users returned from their day, leaving patches of unused space in the heart of the foyer. This applied to activity areas too. Since service users had a busy day, rest and normal activities were more likely to be the evening option. Moreover, the dining room was too small for all service users to use simultaneously and the lack of a staff room increased the load of the secretariat, as nurses used it for that purpose as well.

In Rene Capitant, there was multi-use of areas even for incompatible functions: thus, the TV room had folding chairs instead of comfortable sofas, in order for it to be transformed easily to an exercise room for day service users. Or service users suffered many thefts due to unauthorised persons having access to the bedrooms, either because domestic staff might forget to lock them or because day service users might break the locks. In general, this combination of functions was adverse to the quality of life in the foyer. As it was based on the concept that both facilities used the premises at different hours, it appeared to achieve an economy of building resources, particularly in such a very expensive area as Central Paris. Yet, it failed to address the social and therapeutic parameters of both facilities.

The idea of separation of functions by areas, separating accommodation functions and placing them axially in shared communal or therapy functions creates the core and cluster model that was discussed in the literature review. This model, enabling smaller, more private accommodation with options for more interaction according to service users' ability to be involved in communal life, was met in some of the case studies. Critics of Albany Lodge and MAAP architects themselves related the unit to the 'core and cluster' model with "houses" of four to six "residents", developing around the core of common areas and services [216], [163]. "Houses" differed from one another, each having a different room that could be used by all the ward's service users, such as a laundry or an assisted bathroom or a quiet room. That way, MAAP architects intended to create small interacting communities and attempted a domestic approach to ward design. However, this solution was more complicated than a straightforward core and cluster model and some aspects of "domestic like" criteria were not met. "Houses" were connected to one another and only the T-shaped houses were immediately connected with the core. Additionally, their linear placement one next to the other enabled the creation of long corridors, which is an institutional feature, although this also allowed space for walking. The fact that there was no visual differentiation between the houses, by colour or material for example, did not promote their local character. Neither did the use of rooms with a unique function help to create a local focus. Instead, they encouraged service users to use the long corridors and to mix. If instead of a "global" function these rooms had a local function, like a small lounge or a local kitchenette, the core and cluster model would have been clearer.

A variation of the core and cluster could be seen in the case of Forest Lodge, where three houses acted as separate clusters, with administration and activity placed in the periphery, away from the normal living activities. Yet, even in that case, the unifying element appeared to be the bedroom corridor that was not in the communal areas but in the most private, contradicting the actual purpose of the model. The rest of the case studies did not present any references to the core and cluster model, as they either spread functions around the building as in the case of Geraniums or grouped accommodation together, as the examples of Elan or Finch Ward indicate.

Regarding physical accessibility, Elan and all the UK case studies had provision for service users with mobility problems. However, in New Bridges the design of the bathrooms raised questions. The wheelchair-accessible bedroom was on the ground floor, yet the hoist for assisted bathing was placed in one of the upper floor bathrooms (figure 143). Moreover, none of the bathrooms upstairs was designed for people with physical disabilities, yet all were larger than the assisted bathroom downstairs. Despite their size, the placing of the bathtub in the corner did not facilitate staff to wash somebody. As there was about one bathroom or shower-room for every two service users, which was very convenient, there was some waste of space there.

Apart from Elan, in France the rest of the case studies did not consider accessibility. Bois St Jospeh had a comfortable elevator and proper width of corridors but no other provision for physical accessibility. Geraniums, despite its ground-floor bedroom option, was not accessible to people with mobility problems. There was no lift, handrails or accessible toilet. As accidents were frequent, service users who suffered from mobility problems stayed in bed all day. Even less accessible were Francois Tosquelles and Rene Capitant that lacked an accessible lift, WC or showers and all bedrooms were on the upper floors.

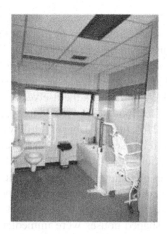

Figure 143. The assisted bathroom on the first floor of New Bridges

Regarding orientation, double loaded blind corridors and a deep core, combined with the lack of focal or reference points, hindered orientation in most parts of Bois St Joseph;

in bedroom areas in Elan; the ground floor bedroom area and the first floor in Geraniums and Rene Capitant; the first floor interconnecting corridor of Forest Lodge and the core of New Bridges. Furthermore, the existence of turning points with no areas of focus, as in the cases of Geraniums or Forest Lodge, or the twisting form of the aforementioned spinal corridor in Forest Lodge accentuated the problem. The latter effect was created despite the linear organisation of the building volume, to break down the long hospital corridor reference, yet instead of solving the problem this created areas of poor visibility that could increase anxiety.

The disorientating layout was more obvious in the case of Bois St Joseph due to the frequent turning points as a result of a large and complex organisation of the floors. In New Bridges, fire doors interrupted the opportunity to walk naturally in the corridor and broke its continuity. Since the enclosed courtyard was small, a more pleasant corridor with visual stimulation and external views could be a focal point. On the contrary, the open organisation of the common areas in Elan that allowed external views to the square or the patio, the small sitting areas with views to the campus developing occasionally on both sides of New Bridges corridor or the large windows in other parts of the corridors in Geraniums with views to the trees and good quality daylight, enabled a good sense of orientation. Another interesting attempt of a linear corridor with no references to external views was the case of Small Heath ward. Despite its location deep in the building, its linear development, its small size and the limited number of day spaces eased orientation. This could be attributed to the design of the corridor as a gallery. Nonetheless, it lacked external views to make the location and cardinal orientation of the building intelligible from the inside.

In an attempt to avoid the disorientating effect of double loaded corridors and the maximisation of natural daylight, Small Heath had single loaded corridors with large glass surfaces, and views to the atria, which increased the quality of life for residents and staff. An additional benefit was the creation of internal courtyards, which was discussed earlier in this chapter. However, the strong symmetry of the design and the repetition of the details did not facilitate orientation in the ward, as had been expected. Maybe a colour scheme on doors and corridors or artwork could give a cognitive map of the space.

The real answer to the problem came from smaller, compact layouts with external references. In Francois Tosquelles this was obtained through the great extent of multi-use and the fact that there was partial room sharing, and wayfinding was easy. Additionally, the upper floor corridor, which was the longest, had external views to the courtyard, enabling orientation (figure 144). Alternatively, in Forest Lodge the division of the ward into three smaller houses partially facilitated orientation and allowed external views. On the ground floor, the layout allowed the minimum amount of corridors, and the visual perception of the entire house from a central point.

Finally, a major issue for service users' competence is activity. Activity is a core matter of policy that determines the role of the mental health system in the facility. In short, the placement of activity, i.e., internal or external, the variety and the structure of its provision, i.e., casual or organised, reflected the care philosophy of each case study, determining the individuality of each project, especially in France, where major differences regarding activity were detected.

As far as unstructured, everyday life activity was concerned, such as preparing a meal or playing games, a domestic kitchen and a common room would suffice. The domestic kitchen option was available only in Elan and Forest Lodge, where service users

Figure 144. Large window panel at the end of the corridor

had access to a domestic kitchen with a cooker, as they could do later in their home or in a protected apartment. Alternatively, service users either prepared food in a professional kitchen once in a while, as in Bois St Joseph and Finch Ward or on an everyday basis and in large quantities as in the instance of Francois Tosquelles. Both those practices differed from a casual domestic activity, because of the spatial configuration and equipment of the kitchen and of the quantities that were involved. Service users in Francois Tosquelles used the kitchen as part of their rehabilitation because they had to cook for twenty people, but a more domestic approach would have been more helpful for their rehabilitation and less stressful too. The rest of the case studies lacked cookers accessible to service users.

For structured activities involving tasks and skills not necessary in everyday life, such as professional laundering and artwork, there was either the option of an organised activity area and equipment, or mobile equipment with the activity taking place in a common room. The former was the case of Bois St Joseph and Rene Capitant, even if in that case the OT areas were underused by the foyer service users; Francois Tosquelles only as far as the wood workshop was concerned; Geraniums theoretically, as in practice the OT room was rather underused and insufficient in size and Forest Lodge, the only UK case study with an organised OT room accessible to all its service users. The remaining UK case studies had to resort to using adjacent solutions, limiting the opportunity to voluntary service users only. So, in four of the UK case studies any form of OT where available would take place in common areas. In chapter 7 the thesis will refer to the sufficiency of available activity from a service user and staff perspective. Their views will help address the key questions on the actual need for activities, their suggested types and the necessary resources from an insider perspective.

Regarding outdoor activity such as games or gardening, that was again determined initially by the availability of such an area, excluding the two Parisian case studies, and the opportunities of access to sectioned service users to use those areas security-wise. In France, where the latter was not a problem, outdoor activity would take place in Francois Tosquelles and Bois St Joseph. Regarding the UK, we will discuss the issue further when we examine the users' feedback on the subject.

5.3.3. Personalisation and choice

Privacy in bedrooms differed between the two countries. Regarding room sharing, in the UK in all case studies single room accommodation was available except for one bedroom in New Bridges, after the transformation of a bedroom to a staff room. In France, only

Elan provided single accommodation only, Bois St Joseph shared with two service users per bedroom and the rest offered a choice between single and shared accommodation that in the case of Geraniums and Rene Capitant included triple bedrooms as well. The choice between single and shared accommodation was something common among the French case studies, since sometimes service users might choose the cheaper option of sharing.

Regarding sanitary facility provision in bedrooms, only Elan and Bois St Joseph provided en suite accommodation throughout, whilst Geraniums, Small Heath and Albany Lodge had some en suite showers. Francois Tosquelles, Geraniums, Rene Capitant, Forest Lodge, Finch Ward and Small Heath had one washbasin per room, where there was no en suite accommodation provided. Here it should be mentioned that the provision of those facilities did not per se determine quality in private space. More precisely, in some triple rooms of Geraniums, the WC fittings were in the middle of the room, in no separate compartment, with curtains partially hiding the toilet. By contrast, privacy inside the bedrooms was taken more seriously in Small Heath, as special consideration had been given to how staff might observe service users, and using the sanitary facilities to protect the privacy of the bed area. Regarding the first, staff could check service users' beds in a very discreet way, through a tiny square window on the door, placed in such a way as to reflect the top part of the bed from a mirror but without direct visibility to the bed (figure 146). The washbasin and the wardrobe formed the initial part of the service user's 'compartment' leaving the actual bedroom closer to the exterior wall and direct light.

Figure 145. A small, enclosed, shady sitting area for service users to relax. The garden was the work of the gardening group

Figure 146. Washbasin inside ward bedroom

Figure 147. Information leaflets were discreetly tucked in a corridor bay

On the question of privacy, we will further discuss the communications infrastructure available to service users and more precisely the access to telephones for service users. Service users had personal land-lines only in Elan as each one had a card-operated telephone inside the bedroom. In the rest of the facilities there were public payphones tucked somewhere in the corridor system of the foyers or the wards with limited privacy. To receive incoming calls service users would have to go to the staff office or the reception. In the case of Finch Ward and Bois St Joseph, the payphones were located in the openings of corridors that created local sitting rooms, where service users could speak seated. Similarly, in Albany Lodge, the payphone, although in one of the corridors, was in a wall recess that left space for a bench (figure 147). Access to public computers was provided only in facilities that had IT workshops, specifically Bois St Joseph and Forest Lodge.

Finally, on service users' privacy we will briefly discuss the opportunity to protect their personal belongings in lockers. Thefts are a frequent problem in mental health facilities and service users could lose personal belongings because of other service users' misbehaviour but also as a result of staff malpractice. In that sense, even in single room accommodation there could be incidents of theft especially since service users, especially in acute care, could not lock their bedrooms from the outside. However, in none of the case studies was there any provision for service user lockers inside the rooms. The only case where service users could lock private things was in Elan, in the kitchen, where each service user had a lockable compartment in the refrigerator. On the contrary, there were occasionally lockers for staff, as the cases of Finch Ward and Small Heath indicate.

The gender policies have been discussed during the presentation of the institutional operational and care policies section earlier in the chapter, where it became clear that at the time of the fieldwork, three foyers and all the acute wards operated under mixed gender policies. In this section there will be a presentation of the privacy levels regarding gender in mixed gender wards. First, bedrooms were single gender in all the wards. However, only in Bois St Joseph women's only bedrooms were clustered together, forming a part of the facility (with female only bedrooms) that was not however a female only part as male service users could use the corridors. In that area there was an open sitting arrangement by the corridor amid the female bedrooms, yet with no clear restrictions to forbid male access, especially since in the same corridor there were common areas such as the dining room, and therapy areas such as the infirmary. The same applied to the male service users' bedroom area that occupied an entire floor. In none of the wards there was no female only or male only lounge.

Similarly, there was a mixed gender house at Forest Lodge and the other two houses were single gender, as men tended to be the vast majority of service users. Yet, during the day Forest Lodge service users had access to all three houses, no matter what their gender. The only spatial restriction regarding gender in mixed gender foyers/wards was the existence of separate sanitary facilities, where there were no en suite bedrooms for all service users. However, in the case of Small Heath, because of the inadequate number of sanitary facilities, showers and bathrooms were common for both genders.

Common areas	
Cs	sq m per patient
FrT	9.77
New	8.39
Forl	7.8
Fin	6.17
Elan	5.93
Bois	5.65
Rene	4.72
SmH	4.26
Alb	3.85
Ger	3.71

Table 9.: Common area square footage per service user

Regarding opportunities for socialisation, Francois Tosquelles and New Bridges had the highest metric area of social space per service user and Albany Lodge and Geraniums the lowest, as table 9 indicates. Francois Tosquelles for example, had a spacious common room but with very few seats for all service users to sit and no other alternative for the rest at the same time. So, despite the fact that it had the largest amount of common space, it remained inadequately equipped and insufficient for service users' needs. Similarly, in New Bridges common areas were fairly spacious and service users had a choice of day spaces. However, the quiet room, which was adequate for its original purpose, should not have served as the smoking area, as it was too small for that purpose and it had only one sofa for sitting. Similarly, the conservatory was too crowded after the addition of the table tennis. Regarding the quality of its day areas, the main lounge had a domestic feel with comfortable sofas with colourful spreads, lamps, pictures and plants but lacked natural daylight, encouraging service users to use the conservatory, which was rather small, during most of the day. In the case of New Bridges, design features such as windows, or policies, such as the smoking policy, influenced the use of space by service users rather than the actual size or the furniture arrangement.

Alternatively, in Finch Ward, the third facility in terms of square metres of common areas per service user, the corridor, that was rather narrow, constituted an important part in the social life of the ward. Service users formed a line outside the nursing station, something that happens in psychiatric institutions like Geraniums, occupying almost half of its width. The rest of the areas were functionally large but institutional in decoration (figure 148). Armchairs and sofas were not comfortable and looked like those in NHS waiting rooms. In one of the lounges there was even a seclusion room chair, which consisted of foam covered with plastic. The dining room furniture was rather institutional and there were photocopied reminders and pamphlets on the walls and doors. These rooms lacked decorative objects, plants and tablecloths and chairs were vinyl covered.

In Bois St Joseph however, despite the fact that the seating arrangement was not in proportion to service users, common areas did not feel crowded. The dining area was the only noisy and congested area. The only area with the more domestic option of timber was the sitting area in a niche of the main lounge. It was spacious, with direct access and views to the garden and contained a bar. It looked like a normal pub-bar, unusual for a psychiatric environment, where alcohol is normally forbidden and coffee or tea consumption is sometimes discouraged. It did not serve any alcoholic drinks but contained coffee and tea making facilities. Also, in the lounge recess, a more socio-friendly furniture arrangement and a slight change of level, of one step, created a calmer environment. Sofas and armchairs upholstered with man-made bright coloured leather, in cheerful colours yet easy to keep clean compared to fabric, and the bar lounge decorated with trophies, translated to a youth-friendly environment, much closer to a college refectory than a home and quite popular among the relatively young population of the foyer.

Two interesting examples of sociofriendly common areas were Elan and Forest Lodge. To prevent overcrowding, the foyer was spacious, with a variety of day areas of different styles that provided opportunities for social interaction so that there was a choice, and service users could move around the building. The only area that might have proved insufficient was the patio, the only outdoor place of the foyer. However, the fact that it was overlooked by residential flats and lacked privacy discouraged service users from using it. As for Forest Lodge, the service user population inside the ward was evenly distributed. The three houses model broke common areas into three smaller areas instead of one and created local focal points. The only crowding occurred in the three smoking rooms. Each was furnished with only five chairs and the ventilation was insufficient. In the dining room there were three smaller tables instead of a bigger one, which was not like a home but on the other hand catered for people who might not get on well with one another.

On the contrary, two facilities with poor organisation of common areas were Rene Capitant and Geraniums. The former did not present pleasant living spaces. Light was scarce even in vital spaces. The first floor internal offices and the corridor borrowed light via the light well above the Rotonde. The same applied to views. Materials were cheap and institutional; plastic floors, metal beds, plastic shutters and practically no curtains. There was a total lack of pictures on the walls but pamphlets were stuck on the walls near the entrance or on the ground floor corridors. The TV room had folding chairs because of the shared functions, instead of comfortable seating. The basement, however, retained its original character, since the structural elements were dominant. The thick stone walls and the vaulted roofs referred to the age of the building and the area was artificially lit and without windows: it looked like an old cellar. The only area that had some natural light was the bar, through glass bricks in the ceiling. In the dining room, plants compensated for the lack of views.

Figure 148. The Finch Ward smoking lounge looked rather like a waiting room

Figure 149. Small Heath Kitchenette

Figure 150. Small Heath smoking lounge, with low maintenance issues, and one of the most used rooms in the ward

In Geraniums, similarly to Finch Ward, service users gathered outside, seeking attention and interfering with the workload. That is institutional behaviour that is frequently observed in asylums, sometimes because service users seek attention from staff and there are no other more attractive alternatives for them. A similar accumulation of service users was present in corridors outside the doctor's office, nurses' office and the bridge leading to the dining room, before meals. The only pleasant area was the dining room, which was very spacious and with windows that covered almost the whole west wall and a large part of the northern wall and permitted views to the garden. The furniture had a domestic feel, wooden chairs and tables painted all in white and was in better condition than those in the rest of the unit. The foyer had potential for improvement in many aspects of quality of life as there were positive elements too. Nature was integrated into the foyer with a strong aroma of the forest and pleasant views. There was light but the foyer was on the whole very institutional. Geraniums was the facility that had the least number of square metres per service user for common areas among the case studies, yet the common areas were practically empty for the aforementioned reasons. In the rest of the acute wards, Albany Lodge and Small Heath common areas appeared insufficient as well (figures 149-150).

Albany Lodge was quite crowded. There were only two lounges, the smoking and the non-smoking each slightly under 16 sq m, for 24 people. The smoking room was the most crowded and noisy, since most of the service users smoked. It appears that in the UK facilities, as the case of New Bridges and Forest Lodge indicate, there was insufficient provision for smokers, who tended to be a majority then. In Small Heath, apart from the lounge, the other common areas were small with room for only a couple of people at a time. The only physical activity available to ward-bound service users was to walk up and down the corridor. The kitchenette lacked space for a small group of service users to sit there and have snacks or tea together. The lounge had plenty of light in the afternoon, yet it would have been even better if there had been a cooling system for the summer months, especially since the windows had restricted openings.

From the above it is clear that square metres are only indicative, as matters such as the quality of space, including comfort and the actual room arrangements are very important to service users' decisions not only to use the space but to participate in social life and engage in interpersonal relationships with other service users. The service user and staff perspective on where service users prefer to go in order to meet other people inside the facilities will be discussed in the interviews chapter. As for a more systematic exploration of the social areas, such as for example if they have sofas or coffee tables, this will be discussed with the analysis of the questionnaires.

The last part relevant to the personalisation and choice criteria is the atmosphere of the foyers or the wards, in terms of being related to the psychosocial aspects of care and the reduction of discriminating aspects that stem from the institutional appearance of the buildings as well as the domestic references and references to the fact that they are treated in environments that receive attention from staff and society, including the State in the case of NHS.

Forest Lodge more closely resembled a residential building as it retained the size, the volume shape, the materials and the window types of the neighbouring houses without any sign of labelling. The only difference between Forest Lodge and a neighbouring house was the fact that the entrance was at the side and not in front of the building.

Rene Capitant had kept the interior of a listed building that retained all the characteristics of the architecture of its neighbourhood and could be the most integrated building that could go completely unnoticed were it not for the view from the street to the photocopy room and the label that declared the public use of the facility, as opposed to residential, clearly marked above the entrance with capital letters: "CENTRER CAPITANT". Additionally, protective panels outside the windows indicated the need for security. Similarly, Geraniums could be well integrated, if a sign on the street did not inform passers-by both about the name and the function of the institution, (figure 136). The building was rendered, with ceramic roof tiles. Windows had wooden frames with wooden shutters and resembled a plot of land with a local housing estate, were it not for its size and the siting of the entrance at the rear that gave it the appearance of a care home for older people.

Albany Lodge blended well with the surrounding domestic environment. The scale, the use of materials and the size of the windows constituted part of the architectural vocabulary of the locality. Small courtyards underlined its use as accommodation. The absence of entrances that would break the relatively large volume from the two main roads was indicative of a more public use. However, one could think that it was the building such as a students' hall of residence.

Bois St Joseph was the largest institution participating in the study, not only in service user numbers but also in square footage. It covered approximately 4,000 sq m, taking the discussion about domesticity to its upper limits. Despite its size, an effort was made to merge the unit with its surroundings. Using large stripes of colour, the architect gave the illusion of terraced houses and broke the monotony of the large volumes. The pitched roofs, clad with ceramic roof tiles, and the size and shape of the openings suggested the residential character of the building: it could be anything from student accommodation to an old people's home or even flats. There was no label or any indication of use nor bars in front of the windows. There were instead large terraces and open doors. The garden was under development from the gardening group and was rather inviting.

Francois Tosquelles' atmosphere was welcoming, as the interior was small, with an interesting elevation that made references to domestic architecture. Materials had a variety of colours and textures, familiar and warm. For the ground floor, the architect used two types of brick to mark the entrance. The upper floor was timber clad, with patterns in bricks creating lines framing the volumes and the openings. The roof was slated. Most openings were the size of single doors, bringing plenty of light inside, but for safety and security reasons, they had restricted openings. The garden that surrounded the facility was well maintained with paved areas to walk in and flowers.

Elan extended to part of the first three floors of a block of flats. The housing association, however, did not want the architect of the whole building to be the architect of the foyer. They trusted another architect who was familiar with their ideas and therapeutic work for the interior. The co-operation was not ideal and, according to the manager, the openings defined the size of some rooms, because of the inflexibility of the site architect. Although the idea of the foyer being part of a residential block of flats would be considered the optimum integration criterion, the discrimination of the part that the foyer occupied, with an entirely different architectural vocabulary regarding the design of its volume, which was more compact than the rest of the building and had a different type of windows, and different materials from the rest of the building, made it obvious that this part of the building did not house normal residences.

New Bridges and Small Heath wards were parts of larger community services, so that the scale of both differed from the adjacent houses. In both cases the existence of a clearly marked main entrance, the lack of a front garden and the existence of a large car park very close to the entrance, were enough of a reference to announce the public function of the facility. New Bridges, however tended to look more domestic than Small Heath, which had stronger architectural gestures, including different materials to mark the different functions.

Finch Ward was a ward in a CMHC that was located in a hospital campus, following the hospital campus architecture very closely. It had no external landscape area of its own to distinguish it from the surrounding volumes, and had an entrance reminiscent of a hospital entrance. The long development of the layout around a double loaded corridor accentuated the hospital ward type architecture that was reflected in the building volume as well.

The focus will now move from the exterior to the interior of each facility. The facilities could be separated in four groups regarding the quality of the interior decoration: those that presented innovation with high quality options, in materials, fittings, and amenities provided; those that presented and emphasis on creating a warm, welcoming environment with domestic references in materials and fittings; those that aimed at creating a decent, functional environment, with emphasis on enduring materials and fittings that did not aim at a domestic look - closer to a student hall of residence than a home; and finally, neglected environments with references to asylums.

Elan was in the first category. The entrance was elegant and integrated in its environment, with timber clad walls, decorative objects and furniture, without any "health care" pamphlets or posters. The same approach continued also inside the unit. All equipment was normal and of good quality and design. The quality of materials and furnishings inside the foyer was impressive. The cork floorings were soft, noise absorbent and warm to the touch. Bathrooms were tiled floor to ceiling and the washbasins and toilets were domestic looking in a variety of colours and styles. The furniture in bedrooms and common areas was in a domestic style, elegant and expensive, and in excellent condition. Dark wood and bamboo were widely used. Decorative objects, such as metal and granite side tables, flowers and pictures gave the impression that the decoration was carefully chosen. The same applied to lighting, where a variety of fixtures and light sources was employed to create atmosphere. The only area with poor lighting, and no natural light at all, was the visitors' room, which was not in the core of the life of the foyer, encouraging service users to meet people on the outside. Bedrooms were comfortable and distinctive. Each bedroom had a large fitted wardrobe, a bed, a desk with a chair, some shelves and a bedside table, with individual colour schemes. Curtains came in sets of lighter and heavier ones, so service users adjusted the amount of incoming daylight. Furniture was domestic in style and of good quality and floors were carpeted. Each bedroom followed its own colour scheme and furniture style. Bathrooms comprised small but high quality prefabricated units with an ergonomic design. They had varying colours and details. Most were spacious, apart from a couple that had to be smaller because of the window arrangement.

In the second group, Forest Lodge presented an environment with strong domestic elements of good quality materials and attention to detail. Decoration enhanced the domestic character of the houses. Different colour schemes, furniture and accessories in each house prevented the institutional "buying in bulk" approach. Furnishings were soft, floors were carpeted and the wallpaper was in homelike patterns and in good condition. Plants, framed pictures on the walls and decorative objects accentuated the warm character. The decoration was a result of staff and service user collaboration and both brought in objects and plants. However, ceilings had fitted lights, nothing hanging, and had alarms and sprinklers. Internal doors were heavy fire doors, but locked with keys and had no observation panels, looking like student accommodation doors. Bathrooms and showers had linoleum floors, handrails that could double as towel hangers and soap dispensers above and by the washbasin. Still, apart from the assisted bathroom, they more resembled those of student accommodation. Light was satisfactory. Apart from the hallways, all other spaces were naturally lit. Ventilation was inadequate in the smoking rooms.

Francois Tosquelles was not as domestic looking as Forest Lodge, yet it still had domestic references. Regarding the quality of space, the foyer was airy and with plenty of light. The interior was also of good quality but with not much visual stimulation and a uniformity, even in bedrooms that followed the same colour and pattern scheme, emphasised homogeneity rather than an individualistic approach. Each service user had a bed, a double wardrobe, and a shared desk with a chair in double rooms. Apart from wall colour, all rooms had exactly the same furniture and fittings, yet they were domestic in appearance. Art and plants enhanced common areas and corridors, and uniform door decorations adorned bedroom doors, without intending to differentiate (figure 151-152). Colour was introduced in walls, doors and furniture, but floors were uniformly tiled.

In the third category, the remaining UK wards may be placed, as well as Bois St Joseph. In Albany Lodge the materials of the ward showed that a high quality of environment was among the design intentions. The design was not homelike - in the all-carpeted and wallpapered sense - but it was not clinical either. Wood was widely used, including for some structural details, and the dining room floor was of timber. Large surfaces of unbreakable glass brought light into the building. Windows had two types of curtains to control the amount of daylight. There was carpeting in almost all common rooms and bedrooms and tiles in circulation spaces. Bathroom walls were tiled from floor to ceiling, but they were closer to a hotel style than to home aesthetics. Radiators were placed elegantly below benches and desks instead of standing alone. Ceilings were plastered, instead of the usual tiles, and lighting was soft and adjustable.

Figure 151. Service user's bedroom door ornament   **Figure 152.** First floor corridor artwork

Albany Lodge was not homelike, but it was not like a hospital ward either. Service users did not have much say as to their bedrooms, which looked more like hostel accommodation. Desks were nice but fixed to the wall, limiting room rearrangement. A framed wall area in each bedroom indicated the place for pictures. The doors were hospital doors allowing staff to enter and watch service users. The dining room was not homelike either, as there were no tablecloths nor decoration. There was instead a billiard table and a vending machine. The nursing station was like a fishbowl. Yet, the wooden floor looked luxurious and there was natural light and a view to the courtyard. More institutional details included soap and paper dispensers in toilets, numbers on doors and photocopies stuck on the walls to remind service users of rules. Last but not least, fire regulations imposed certain fittings such as sprinklers, fire doors and fire extinguishers, in all units.

In New Bridges, apart from a set of vinyl sofas, the rest of the furniture and wallpaper had a domestic feel and it was kept in a decent state. All areas, except bathrooms and toilets, were carpeted. Walls were painted in various colours and had decorations. Furniture and doors were timber. Beds and bedroom furniture were domestic-like. The dining tables had flowers and there was a tea trolley. Quality standards varied in the ward. Lighting was ample in the conservatory or the staircase, yet corridors were dark and the main lounge was deprived of a window. On the other hand, bathrooms were over-equipped with handrails, hospital bins, soap and paper dispensers and photocopied reminders. Tags on doors labelled the use of the corresponding room. Yet, the most institutional trait was the lack of a kitchenette. Service users could not prepare anything for themselves, having to depend on ward meals, and for drinking water they had to use the toilet tap.

Small Heath was designed with the hospital rather than the domestic concept in mind. Yet, the environment had interesting touches. The corridor followed a plastic geometry; with recesses to play with the width and two rows of columns broke the monotony and enhanced linearity. Colours, daylight, the carpet and a few details such as plants and some wooden furniture, gave a user-friendly impression. Privacy was taken care of in the clinic as well, with a changing area behind a curtain, something that sounds obvious, but is rarely encountered in other case studies. All ward areas, apart from toilets, had natural daylight.

In terms of its finishes and fittings, Lakeside was reminiscent of a hospital ward, with standard NHS furniture in common areas, hospital bathrooms and doors, as well as pamphlets and photocopied sheets on the walls. Yet, there was extensive carpet use in day areas and bedrooms and co-ordinated curtains and bedspreads. Similarly, in Bois St Joseph, decoration was of good quality, yet it was not domestic. Materials, fittings and colours did not vary; walls and floor tiles were white, with colour only in furniture and doors. Homogeneity characterised the bedroom furniture too. The unit displayed service users' work in the art workshop, an empowering gesture for service users. Additionally, there were some plants, tablecloths on dining room tables, despite the fact that they were protected by a sheet of glass for easier maintenance.

Finally, Geraniums and Rene Capitant belong in the last category (figure156), both of them in France. Those facilities presented strong elements of neglect, with broken furniture and fittings, very limited use of decorative objects and plants and only in specific areas such as the dining room in Geraniums and the basement in Rene Capitant. Both facilities were in serious need of extended renovation. Geraniums had good quality daylight and views, whilst in Rene Capitant day areas lacked views and natural day-light as common areas were mostly in the basement.

5.3.4. Does size matter?

The ten cases provided a great degree of diversity regarding functions, services available, policies, service user numbers and degrees of domesticity. As appears in Table 4, facilities tended to differ considerably in the amount of space per service user, with acute facilities having a higher percentage of total facility area per service user. This was however not so straightforward in regard to actual space, nor did it bear a direct relation to the quality of the facility, as Rene Capitant, with a poor quality of environment, did not score as low as expected, despite the high amount of multiuse of space in that facility. Additionally, Albany Lodge was the second lowest from the last as to actual metric area per service user, despite the single room accommodation. Forest Lodge, that did not have a sense of crowding and had single room accommodation, scored much lower in actual numbers than Newbridges.

The findings in Table 10a and Table 10b show that space per se or its proportionality to service users is not the fundamental issue, nor is it a reliable indicator of the quality of space or services, nor does it guarantee that the facility will be fit for its purpose. This is important if one considers that buildings are a costly investment in the health care sector, in terms of both the capital cost, as infrastructure, and in terms of maintenance throughout the working life of the building. In that sense, investing in good design and thought could economise a considerable amount of resources over the working life of the building.

(a)

Facility	square footage per service user (%)
Newbridges	60.31 sqm
Elan	53.75 sqm
Small Heath	27.67 sqm
Bois St Joseph	44.48 sqm
Francsois Tosquelles	43.52 sqm
Forest Lodge	39.07 sqm
Rene Capitant	32.66 sqm
Finch Ward (Lakeside)	32.00 sqm
Albany Lodge	27.30 sqm
Les Geraniums	24.04 sqm

(b)

Facility	percentage of the building per service user (%)
Newbridges	8.33
Francssois Tosquelles	7.69
Small Heath	7.14
Finch Ward (Lakeside)	6.25
Forest Lodge	5.56
Rene Capitant	4.17
Albany Lodge	4.17
Elan	4
Les Geraniums	2.13
Bois St Joseph	1.23

Table 10.: a) Rank ordered of total facility area per service user b) Rank ordered percentage of facility space per service

Functions	Sq m/ function	Sq m/ function %	Sq m per patient	% total area/patient
Bois St Joseph	**3603 sq m**	**81 patients**	**44.48 sq m per patient**	**1.23 % total area/patient**
	Sq m	**%**	**Sq m per patient**	**% per patient**
bedrooms	802.6	22.28	9.91	0.28
hygiene space	341.86	9.49	4.22	0.12
utility space	542.79	15.06	6.7	0.19
circulation space	586.29	16.27	7.24	0.2
common area	458.04	12.71	5.65	0.16
administration-nursing area	351.18	9.75	4.34	0.12
clinical area	52.38	1.45	0.65	0.02
staff area	0	0	0	0
therapy area	475.06	13.19	5.86	0.16

Table 11.: Distribution of areas in facilities according to function

Elan	1343.76 sq m	25 patients	53.75 sq m per patient	4 % total area/ patient
	Sq m	%	Sq m per patient	% per patient
bedrooms	479.2	35.66	19.17	1.43
hygiene space	109.76	8.17	4.39	0.33
utility space	164.23	12.22	6.57	0.49
circulation space	324.65	24.16	12.99	0.97
common area	148.34	11.04	5.93	0.44
administration-nursing area	108.86	8.1	4.35	0.32
clinical area	5.7	0.42	0.23	0.02
staff area	15.58	1.16	0.62	0.05
therapy area	0	0	0	0

Fransois Tosquelles	577.9	13 patients	44.45 sq m per patient	7.69 % total area/patient
	Sq m	%	Sq m per patient	% per patient
bedrooms	153.99	26.65	11.85	2.05
hygiene space	38.45	6.8	2.96	0.52
utility space	73.05	12.97	5.65	1
circulation space	119.98	21.2	9.23	1.63
common area	127.05	21.98	9.77	1.69
administration-nursing area	27.71	4.9	2.13	0.38
clinical area	0	0	0	0
staff area	12.31	2.13	0.95	0.16
therapy area	25.36	4.39	1.95	0.34

Les Geraniums	1129.88 sq m	47 patients	24.04 sq m per patient	2.13 % total area/patient
	Sq m	%	Sq m per patient	% per patient
bedrooms	523.96	46.37	11.15	0.99
hygiene space	58.76	5.2	1.25	0.11
utility space	146.46	12.96	3.12	0.28
circulation space	202.32	17.91	4.3	0.38
common area	165.66	15.42	3.71	0.33
administration-nursing area	19.92	1	0.24	0.02
clinical area	21.99	1.95	0.47	0.04
staff area	25.79	2.28	0.55	0.05
therapy area	0	0	0	0

Rene Capitant	783.85 sq m	24 patients	32.66 sq m per patient	4.17 % total area/patient
	Sq m	%	Sq m per patient	% per patient
bedrooms	165.92	21.17	6.91	0.88
hygiene space	30.27	3.86	1.26	0.16
utility space	140.82	17.96	5.87	0.75
circulation space	190.8	24.34	7.95	1.01
common area	113.39	15.56	4.72	0.65
administration-nursing area	62.07	14.47	2.59	0.6
clinical area	0	0	0	0
staff area	11.67	1.49	0.48	0.06
therapy area	88.39	11.28	3.68	0.47

Albany Lodge	655.30 sq m	24 patients	27.30 sq m per patient	4.17 % total area/patient
	Sq m	%	Sq m per patient	% per patient
bedrooms	226.48	34.56	9.44	1.44
hygiene space	65.46	9.99	2.73	0.42
utility space	34.7	5.25	1.45	0.22
circulation space	225.62	34.43	9.4	1.43
common area	92.46	14.11	3.85	0.59
administration-nursing area	10.58	1.61	0.44	0.07
clinical area	0	0	0	0
staff area	0	0	0	0
therapy area	0	0	0	0
				5.56 % total area/

Table 11.: (Continued.)

Forest Lodge	703.18 sq m	18 patients	39.07 sq m per patient	Patient
	Sq m	%	Sq m per patient	% per patient
bedrooms	209.62	29.81	11.65	1.66
hygiene space	42.19	6	2.34	0.33
utility space	86.75	12.34	4.82	0.69
circulation space	169.83	24.15	9.44	1.34
common area	140.41	19.97	7.8	1.11
administration-nursing area	15.32	2.18	0.85	0.12
clinical area	11.08	1.58	0.62	0.09
staff area	11.29	1.61	0.63	0.09
therapy area	19.69	2.8	1.1	0.16
Finch Ward (Lakeside)	512.02 sq m	16 patients	32	6,25
	Sq m	%	Sq m per patient	% per patient
bedrooms	156.93	30.65	9.81	1.92
hygiene space	33.4	6.52	2.09	0.41
utility space	41.07	8.02	2.57	0.5
circulation space	115.04	22.47	7.19	1.4
common area	98.76	19.29	6.17	1.21
administration-nursing area	21.32	4.16	1.33	0.26
clinical area	24.15	4.72	1.51	0.3
staff area	3.12	0.61	0.2	0.04
therapy area	18.23	3.56	1.14	0.22
				8.33 % total area/
Hull Newbridges	723.68 sq m	12 patients	60.31 sq m per patient	Patient
	Sq m	%	Sq m per patient	% per patient
bedrooms	168.19	23.24	14.02	1.94
hygiene space	59.4	8.2	4.95	0.68
utility space	81.09	11.2	6.76	0.93
circulation space	217.93	30.11	18.16	2.51
common area	100.37	13.87	8.36	1.16
administration-nursing area	64.04	8.85	5.34	0.74
clinical area	14.25	1.97	1.19	0.16
staff area	18.43	2.55	1.54	0.21
therapy area	0	0	0	0
Small Heath	387.44 sq m	14 patients	27.67 sq m per patient	7.14 % total area/patient
	Sq m	%	Sq m per patient	% per patient
bedrooms	165.3	42.66	11.78	3.05
hygiene space	27.52	7.1	1.97	0.42
utility space	23.12	5.97	1.65	0.51
circulation space	89.15	23.01	6.37	1.64
common area	59.69	15.41	4.26	1.1
administration-nursing area	11.05	2.85	0.79	0.2
clinical area	10.81	2.79	0.77	0.2
staff area	0	0	0	0
therapy area	0	0	0	0

Table 11.: (Continued.)

Bois St. Joseph

2nd floor

bedroom

hygiene space

utility space

circulation space

common areas

administration - nursing area

clinical area

staff area

therapy area

areas not included in the ward

Bois St. Joseph

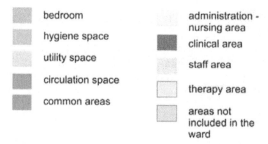

1st floor

	bedroom		administration - nursing area
	hygiene space		clinical area
	utility space		staff area
	circulation space		therapy area
	common areas		areas not included in the ward

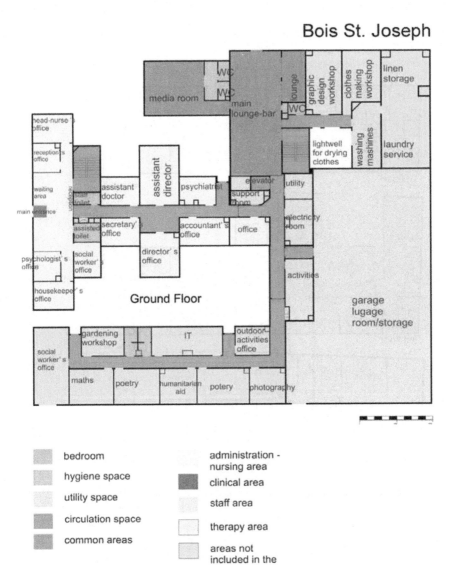

Figure 153. Bois St Joseph, ground, 1st and 2nd floor plan

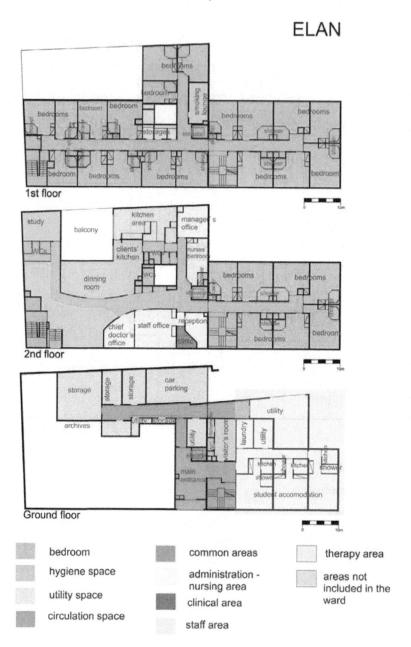

Francoise Tosquelles

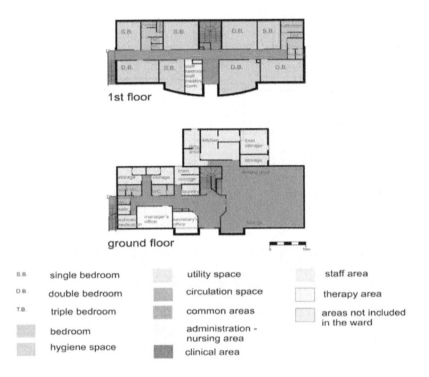

1st floor

ground floor

S.B.	single bedroom		utility space		staff area
D.B.	double bedroom		circulation space		therapy area
T.B.	triple bedroom		common areas		areas not included in the ward
	bedroom		administration - nursing area		
	hygiene space		clinical area		

Figure 155. Francois Tosquelles, ground and 1st floor plans

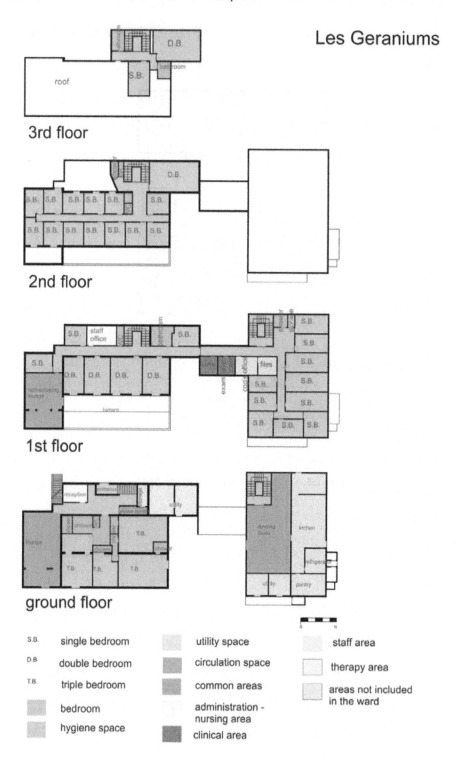

Figure 156. Geraniums, ground, 1st, 2nd and 3rd floor plan

Rene Capitant

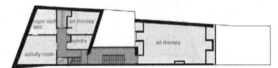

4th floor

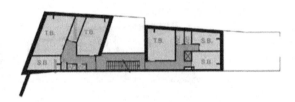

3rd floor

2nd floor

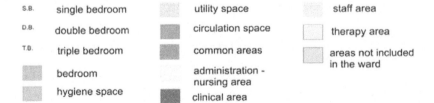

S.B.	single bedroom		utility space		staff area
D.B.	double bedroom		circulation space		therapy area
T.B.	triple bedroom		common areas		areas not included in the ward
	bedroom		administration - nursing area		
	hygiene space		clinical area		

Figure 157. Rene Capitant, floor plans

Albany Lodge

ground floor plan

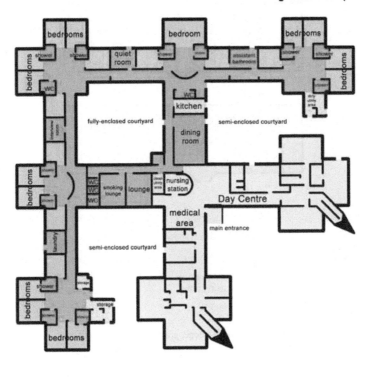

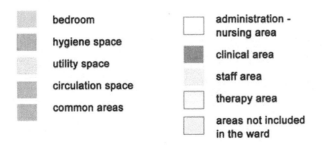

bedroom

hygiene space

utility space

circulation space

common areas

administration - nursing area

clinical area

staff area

therapy area

areas not included in the ward

Figure 158. Albany Lodge, floor plans

Forest Lodge

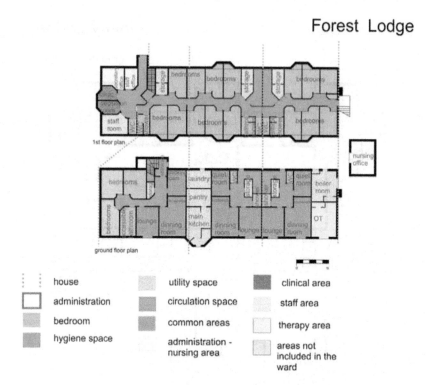

Figure 159. Forest Lodge, ground and 1st floor plans

Finch Ward, Lakeside

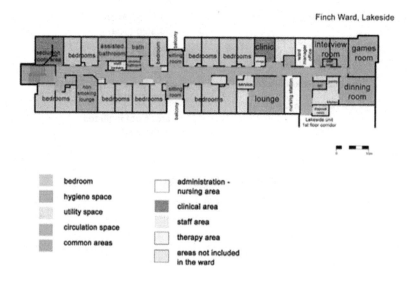

Figure 160. Lakeside, floor plan of Finch Ward

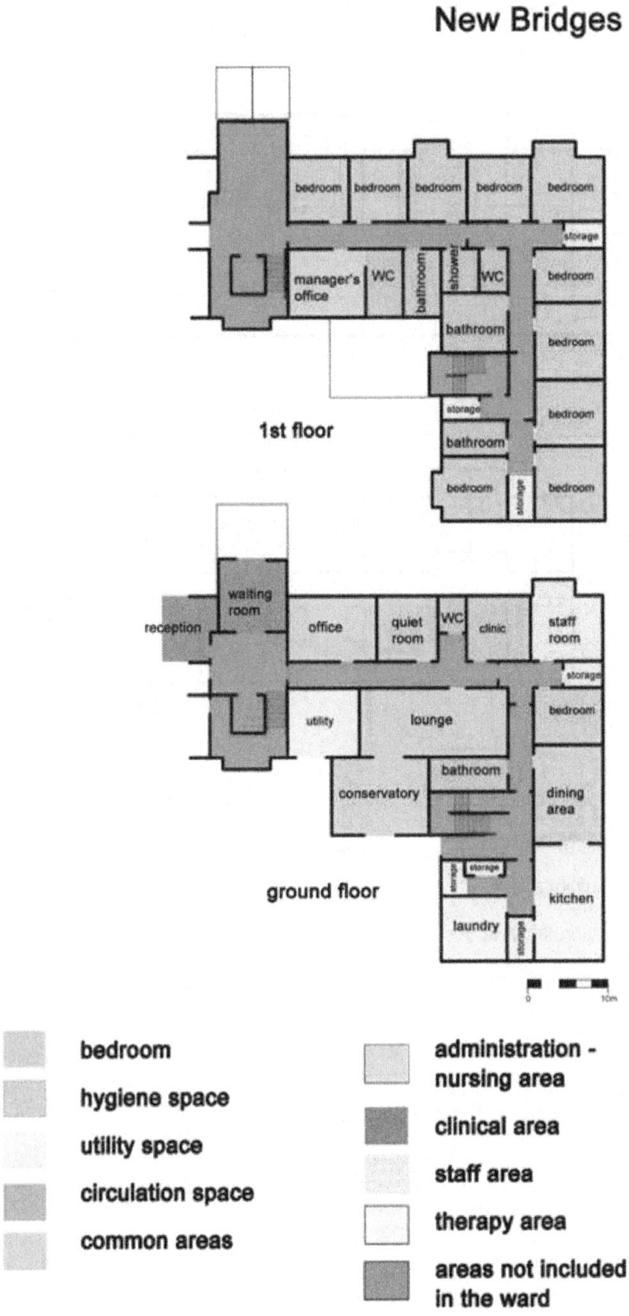
New Bridges
bedroom
storage
manager's office
WC
bathroom
shower
1st floor
waiting room
reception
office
quiet room
clinic
staff room
utility
lounge
conservatory
dining area
kitchen
laundry
ground floor
0
10m
bedroom
hygiene space
utility space
circulation space
common areas
administration - nursing area
clinical area
staff area
therapy area
areas not included in the ward

Figure 161. New Bridges, ground and 1st floor plan

Small Health

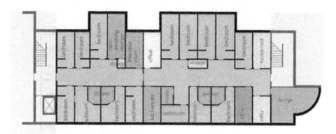

1st floor

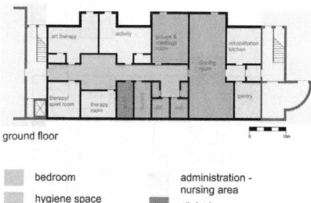

ground floor

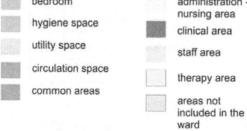

bedroom

hygiene space

utility space

circulation space

common areas

administration - nursing area

clinical area

staff area

therapy area

areas not included in the ward

Figure 162. Small Heath, ground and 1st floor

Chapter 6

Architectural Checklist analysis

6.1. Overall performance according to the checklist

6.1.1. The foyers'/wards' performance according to the checklist

Regarding the mean percentile scores for the premises including all of the features from the Checklist (table 12), revealed that Forest Lodge and Elan Retrouve performed significantly better in respect of not containing institutional features than the rest of the units. Finch Ward displayed the strongest institutional profile. Overall, there was no marked difference between the French and the UK case studies. Also, there was no immediate relationship between the type of the unit, i.e., acute or aftercare, and the domestic profile of the facility. Forest Lodge, the least institutional building according to the checklist, served acute care purposes, even if it was closer to rehabilitation than the rest of the UK cases. Contributing to this was the small scale of individual dwellings and the separation of administration and therapeutic areas from the service users' houses.

It was also noticeable that the units did not have the same rank order in the three subgroups, with the example of Rene Capitant, scoring very low regarding its surroundings yet displaying a high degree of institutional features related to the building layout. However, the two least institutional and the two most institutional case studies were both relatively high or low respectively in all subgroups.

Facility	Mean	C&S	B	S&R
FORL	26	31.82	30.00	24.00
ELAN	30	22.73	47.50	26.00
FRT	41	59.09	45.00	37.41
ALB	44	40.91	48.57	43.33
BOIS	44	40.91	62.50	39.73
NEW	47	45.45	62.50	43.15
REC	47	13.64	62.50	47.62
GER	48	59.09	47.50	46.38
SMH	48	63.64	68.62	59.55
FINW	56	72.73	64.10	51.70

Table 12.: Percentages of Institutional features per building

6.1.2. The Context and Site features

The Context and Site features are the group of features that relate to the placement of the facility and the relationship of the facades of the case studies to the local residential buildings. Regarding the location of the building and its integration into the surroundings that this subgroup has explored, the French cases appeared much less institutional, and the reason for this was that four out of the five UK cases were part of health care schemes, whilst all the French were either stand alone or integrated into general housing schemes.

The most integrated into its surroundings unit was Rene Capitant followed closely by Elan. Both of those units were French and they were the only two sited in inner city areas, surrounded by many local amenities. Rene Capitant was exceptionally well integrated externally, as it was housed in a converted listed building and the function followed the existing facade and did not intervene in it. On the contrary, in the case of Elan, which was part of a general housing scheme, the decision to separate the mental health part of the building visually, affected the result to some extent. Nevertheless, its location and local service network placed Elan high on the list. The only UK unit that displayed a strong domestic profile according to Context and Site features was Forest Lodge, the only UK facility that was stand alone and not part of a hospital campus or a community health care or mental health care building.

The units with the strongest institutional features were Small Heath and Finch Ward. Those two were integrated in larger, general health care schemes, with Finch Ward located in a large mental health facility, built in the heart of an extensive hospital campus. However, it was the architecture of the facade, which had few domestic elements that placed them so low in the ranking.

In short, facilities that were located centrally in urban areas, with lots of amenities and a facade most resembling local residential architecture presented the least institutional feature in this group, whilst facilities situated in the periphery of rural areas, and with facade architecture that differed from the local style of residences appeared to be the most institutional of the checklist. However, the policies of the facilities, for example if they were open or closed, and if in fact the facilities were actually using their local networks, did not affect the results of the Checklist in this category, as the checklist dealt only with architectural features. Thus, if Rene Capitant were housing a project with sectioned service users that did not have opportunity to go out, the network on offer might not make much difference to their quality of life and the degree of integration in the community. On the other hand, this category was of added importance for the facilities where service users were expected to go out as part of their social re-integration. Moreover, facilities that faced issues of NIMBYSm, as did Geraniums, and more precisely vandalism, as in the case of Small Heath (before they employed security staff) and New Bridges, tended to score higher regarding institutional features than the rest. It is worth mentioning that the case of Finch Ward, which appeared the most institutional but did not face any vandalism problems, was different as it was located in the protected environment of the centre of the general hospital campus.

6.1.3. The "Building" group of features

The features relevant to the Building regarded the entrance area, the layout and the circulation in the facilities, as well as the decoration of those areas and their relationship to the administration and day areas. The units were rank ordered according to their performance on this part of the checklist from least to most institutional, in Table 13.

(a)

Facility	Mean
REC	13.64
ELAN	22.73
FORL	31.82
ALB/BOIS	40.91
NEW	45,45
FRT/GER	59.09
SMH	63.64
FINW	72.73

(b)

Facility	Mean
FORL	30
FRT	45
ELAN/GER	47,5
ALB	48,57
NEW/BOIS/REC	62,5
FINW	64,1
SMH	68.42

Table 13.: a) Institutional features of Context and Site per building, b) Institutional features related to the Building per building

There was no significant difference between the two countries. The French Foyers, which referred to service user groups closer to their rehabilitation stage displayed similar levels of domesticity to the rest of the UK case studies.

Small Heath was the most institutional among the ten case studies regarding building features. The case studies presented considerable diversity regarding internal organisation, overall size and facility provision. None of those factors, however, seemed to differentiate the domesticity factor according to this group of features, as independent projects could be at similar levels of institutionalisation to integrated schemes, foyers tended to be at similar levels to wards and small units could be more institutional than the larger ones. However, there was a differentiation according to the overall layout, between facilities that were closer to the 'family home' organisation and those that more resembled hospital wards. In more detail, only one unit, Forest Lodge, displayed a domestic character among the ten case studies, following the pattern of terraced houses, with optional connection on the upper floor and administration, service and therapy functions kept separate from the houses where service users lived. On the contrary, the two most institutional case studies in this ranking, Finch Ward and Small Heath, showed buildings with the greatest resemblance to hospital wards, as in both of them the layout had a long, straight, double loaded corridor with all areas developed on either side.

6.1.4. The Space and Room Group of features

Space and Room was the broadest category of the three. That group constituted the features relevant to specific rooms within the unit, regarding their function, their fixtures and fittings, their furniture and decoration. The country or the type of the facility did not differ in terms of domesticity, and environments for acute cases were as domestic as those for the service user group that was a bit more stable, according to this checklist.

In Table 14 we can see the means of the ten units that were relevant to the Space and Room, rank ordered. The French Elan and the English Forest Lodge were the least institutional units in Space and Room terms and those were the facilities that invested more in design and where there had been stronger involvement of the users at the planning stage. In the case of Elan, staff used their past experience from the old facility and teamed up with the architect, giving their input from the very beginning. Similarly, staff from Forest

Facility	Mean
FORL	24
ELAN	26
FRT	37.41
SMH	39.55
BOIS	39.73
NEW	43.15
ALB	43.33
GER	46.28
REC	47.62
FINW	51.7

Table 14.: Institutional features of Space and Room per building

Lodge formed a team that included service users as well, and after visiting other facilities around the country and discussing their views arising from their experience they contributed their input at all planning stages.

The two neglected facilities, Rene Capitant and Geraniums, however, were among the lowest in that group of features, yet not the lowest.

6.2. Overall Frequencies of Institutional features

It will next be reported which among those features constituted common factors for all units, which appeared in some and which features were the odd cases or did not appear at all. This procedure emphasised the features themselves, and helped to point out any stereotypes for the units, especially those features that were included in the checklist because they were mentioned in the literature, or appeared in some other buildings or formed part of the psychiatric buildings of the past. Alternatively, rare cases could be ideas that had been piloted in those units, and since the Checklist was formulated after the visits, those features were included and could be highlighted and compared. Additionally, features that were common in most cases will be highlighted.

The following five tables give in rank order the common traits from the most to the least met common traits, starting from what all the facilities shared. Those traits have been classified according to their relation to the model parameters, indicating how the model parameters affected the decision making and if those design decisions were justified from the three parameters angle or happened to be so for other reasons, such as prevailing institutional practices with no clear benefit or even financial gain.

Institutional features that were related to the prevention of harm and self harm have been classified under the safety and security parameter. These features were relevant to the medical purpose of the facilities, such as the features regarding the clinics or the psychiatric offices attached, or the jurisdictional aim of the facilities, such as anti-ligature features, or for example the restrictions of access to external doors. The features relevant to competence were features related to the nursing purpose of the facilities and the restoration rehabilitation of the disabilities caused to the service users as a result of their illness. Such features were relevant to physical accessibility means, such as the existence of a hoist or related to their rehabilitation such as the existence of activity rooms. Finally, the Personalisation and Choice category included the features that were relevant to stigma, such as those that differentiated the appearance of the facility from nearby housing, or the existence of labels, or even other aspects connected to the psychosocial models such as the existence of decorative objects or plants in common areas.

The classification of the 215 features was not straightforward and sometimes a feature could relate to more than one parameter for different reasons. For example, an elaborate facade with bays and balconies protected service users' privacy as it helped the building to merge with the surroundings, compared to a plain facade, but it might relate to safety as well if its architecture enabled people to abscond more easily, or if external features permitted drugs to be hidden and passed in to the units. Similarly individual mailboxes increased privacy but staff might want to check mail first for safety reasons or even clinical purposes, if mail came from a source that might cause distress to a service user.

A decision had therefore to be reached on many features as to the gravity of each parameter for the specific feature. Moreover, there were parameters that when presented from their domesticity aspect were relevant to one parameter, such as the placement of the facilities next to housing that was related to personalisation and choice as a stigma reducing feature, yet if it were observed that the placement of the rest was only in health care settings or next to police stations, it could be argued that this was related to clinical or safety reasons and in that case it was best suited to the parameter of safety and security.

What 10/10 units shared			
parameter	Feature	institutional	domestic
Safety and Security	Locked storage areas and closets	▓	
	Clinic inside the ward	▓	
	Psychiatric offices, attached or included in the ward	▓	
	Front doors that opened out automatically	▓	
	Exit sign indications in circulation areas	▓	
	Mobile bedroom furniture		▓
Competence	Notices on walls and doors of circulation areas	▓	
Personalisation and choice	No mailboxes for individual service users accessible to the postman		▓
	Fluorescent lighting on circulation areas		▓
	Lack of separate staff dining area		▓
	No use of concrete, concrete blocks or metal panels on facades		▓
	No use of resilient flooring in lounges		▓
	No urinals		▓
	Natural light in kitchenettes		▓
	No sliding or revolving doors		▓
	Service users' stereos, radios or TVs in bedrooms		▓

Table 15.: Common features of all case studies

As Table 15 makes clear, there were few features common to all facilities and for each context. Regarding safety, all facilities had clinical and managerial functions within the premises as well as locked areas that were inaccessible to the service users. Points made in the literature regarding fixed furniture for safety had been largely abandoned in acute environments. Among visits to mental health facilities in both countries during the time of the case study selection, this practice was met only in Broadmoor that at the time belonged in the Jurisdiction system. Lately though, in the name of so called safety and without any serious justification these institutional practices of heavy and immobile furniture have an institutional come back. It is also sad that these practices appear as innovative in several undocumented attempts of so called "better bedrooms" ignoring all the effort of medical architecture after the 50s and the input of enlightened psychiatrists, such as Prof Sivadon, in several parts of the world to alter these institutional references of a custodial system. The other key feature referred to fire safety regulations. Regarding competence, the existence of photocopied messages or notices on walls or doors, was definitely an institutional practice on behalf of staff, denoting an attempt to substitute the written word for staff input through personal interaction and verbal communication that could perhaps increase the effectiveness of the message written on those photocopies.

Regarding Personalisation and Choice features, the prevalence of fluorescent lighting installations arose from decisions to contain costs, which reduced the quality of the environment. This decision could be reconsidered, especially since research indicates that there are potential health hazards related to fluorescent lighting [42]. The lack of service user mailboxes accessible to the postman that compromised service users' privacy was probably related to safety and security reasons, especially since the facilities faced drug trafficking problems, but that speculation was not tested in the staff interviews. As far as staff privacy was concerned, there was no provision for a staff dining room area, the lack of which could increase staff burnout as staff would still have to attend to the service users during their meals.

Design elements that enhanced the domesticity of all case studies constituted the absence of materials that were connected to public building architecture on the facades, the avoidance of resilient flooring in lounges, and the absence of urinals and revolving or sliding doors. The provision of light in kitchenettes, where kitchenettes were provided, was relevant to the quality of life in the buildings. Service users had the choice of bringing in electronic equipment such as stereos and TVs in all case studies, yet restrictions regarding TVs in service users' bedrooms existed in Elan. The limited number of domestic elements in the Personalisation and choice category, indicated a tradeoff between quality of environment and institutional design elements that became apparent to a greater or lesser extent in the rest of the tables as well.

What 9/10 units shared			
parameter	Feature	institutional	domestic
Safety & security	No office for a resident (full-time) GP		■
	No mirrors to allow visibility to a corridor turning point or a room		■
Competence	Administration offices inside the wards	■	
	No rooms especially designed to accommodate activities	■	
	No hoist in a bathroom	■	
	Location close to shops		
Personalisation and choice	More than six residents per ward		
	No coat-hanging area near the entrance		
	Automatic door closers		
	Identical bedroom furniture		
	Common WC with automatically self cleaning toilet seat		
	Freestanding toilet in bedrooms		
	No continuous table arrangements in dinning room		
	No individual food lockers in the kitchenette		■
	No stands for leaflets		
	No areas accessible to external service users only		
	No access to internal areas for external service users		
	Lounge and dining room with external views		
	Kitchenette, if existing, with eating area and direct connection to dining room		
	No walk-in cooler for food		
	Elevator close to front door and visible from it, if there was one		
	Stairs, if existing, at the centre of the ward		
	Variety of decorative objects, vases or plants in common areas		
	Outdoor areas visible from interior social areas		
	Bathrooms not opening directly into social areas or main corridors		
	No more than one sink and more than one toilet cubicle in bathrooms		
	Variation of windows followed size and shape		
	No access to living areas for external service users without internal service users' presence		
	Couch or comfortable seating in the TV area		
	Room shape, window location and window size varying in bedrooms		■

Table 16.: Common features of 9/10 case studies

Regarding safety, almost all units had common practices that questioned the one-off practices in the remaining case studies. In this sense, there was an office for a resident GP only in Geraniums, which might however be related to the inclusion of older people in the service user group. Observability in circulation areas tended to be addressed by other means than the use of mirrors, and there was use of a round mirror only in the seclusion room of New Bridges.

As far as competence was concerned, almost all facilities were located close to shops. Furthermore as to competence, only in Lakeside was the core and cluster model implemented, moving all administration areas outside the service users' areas. Having earlier discussed the case of Forest Lodge, which will be further discussed in terms of the users' responses later, it was the only case of a facility that functioned successfully with no managerial and therapeutic areas within the service users' accommodation (table 16).

Regarding the aspect of competence that related to activity, activity rooms, where provided inside the wards, lacked the designated provisions for what would be necessary for that activity, such as a sink for washing brushes and paint in the case of Art Therapy in Bois St Joseph. Another interesting single case related to physical disability and therefore to competence, was the hoist that existed in one facility only. The hoist will be discussed again in the following chapter, where staff express their opinions.

Personalisation and Choice aspects that appeared as unique cases related to privacy, included the freestanding toilet in Geraniums, which was an extreme case that indicated the degree to which some institutional remnants could still find their way into today's world. Moreover, only in Small Heath did bathrooms open directly onto the main corridor, whilst only in Francois Tosquelles was there more than one sink or one toilet cubicle in the bathrooms. On the other hand the self cleaning toilet in Elan was considered a luxury for the rest of the projects. Also, apart from Rene Capitant, there were no internal areas, including living spaces, accessible to external service users. Finally on privacy related issues, the only form of locker that enabled some privacy in service users regarding personal belongings appeared at Elan and concerned individual food lockers.

Regarding socialization opportunities and the welcoming factor of common areas to promote interaction, social areas, in all but the lounge of New Bridges, had natural daylight, as well as views to the outdoor areas, and they tended to have decorative objects, vases or plants, that were absent in Geraniums. The kitchenette, where available, provided the option of sitting or was directly connected to the dining room for service users even to prepare some tea and share some company while eating. Dining rooms had free-standing tables enabling service users to form groups of their own, despite the fact that this might appear non-domestic, as in homes people gather around one table.

The rest of the major tendencies that were related to Personalisation and Choice were mostly around the reduction of stigma, with choices that appeared domestic from the outside, i.e., the variation of windows as to size and shape, and design choices that reflected domestic architecture in the interior. Those concerned the siting of the elevators close to the front door, or stairs located centrally in the facilities, there were no stands for leaflets and bedrooms presented variety in shapes, sizes and window location. On the contrary, only in Forest Lodge were there coat racks close to the entrance, and only Elan lacked automatic door closers and presented variety in bedroom furniture.

What 8/10 units shared			
parameter	Feature	institutional	domestic
Safety and security	Plain facade (vs brok	■	
	No fireplace	■	
	Bars on bedroom windows	■	
	Bathroom window restrictions	■	
	No pieces of fixed furniture in bedrooms		■
	No seclusion room attached to or inside the ward		■
Competence	Laundry service for service users		■
	Parks or recreational areas within walking distance		■
	Tea or coffee equipment for service users		■
Personalisation and choice	Different sizes of lot compared to neighbourhood	■	
	Different distance between buildings	■	
	Different parking arrangements to adjacent buildings	■	
	Different front doors to adjacent buildings	■	
	Staff areas inside the ward for staff's short retreat	■	
	Tables seating more than eight people	■	
	Bedroom doors with labels or decorative elements	■	
	No armchair in each bedroom	■	
	No curtains on bedroom windows	■	
	No en suite WCs for all rooms	■	
	Bathrooms close to bedroom areas	■	
	Paper towel dispensers	■	
	No natural light on staircases	■	
	Non institutional materials for the surfaces of circulation areas		■
	Natural light and operable windows in the kitchen		■
	Food prepared in the units		■
	External doors in kitchens		■
	No dedicated room for staff to sleep inside the ward		■
	Varying furniture in social areas		■
	No fluorescent and overhead lighting only in common areas		■
	TV was in social areas instead of TV room		■
	Stereos in common areas		■
	Coffee tables in front of sofas or armchairs		■
	No dedicated staff area for rest inside the wards		■
	Decorative items in dinning room		■
	No triple bedrooms		■
	No resilient flooring in bedrooms		■
	Plastered ceilings in bedrooms		■
	Service users' posters, decorations or pictures in bedrooms		■
	Service user bathrooms with a bath or bath and shower		■

Table 17.: Common features of 8/10 case studies

The majority of case studies had elements that characterized the facility as non-residential from the exterior to prevent self-harm, such as the avoidance of balconies, yet only two French case studies had bars on bedroom windows, as acute wards had restricted openings on windows. Yet, the exterior differed from the neighbouring residential buildings for reasons other than safety, and these included a different size of lot and differences in distances from neighbouring buildings, in parking lots and front doors, marking its use as a non-residential building and thus affecting service users' privacy. Internally, related to safety was the absence of fire places, although they were a feature in Forest Lodge that catered for acute service users as well. On the contrary, only in two facilities were there seclusion rooms inside the wards and only in two facilities were there fixed pieces of furniture. Regarding competence, service users in most cases had access to a laundry, parks and recreational areas within walking distance and access to tea or coffee equipment.

Regarding aspects of greater privacy than those mentioned above, most facilities lacked curtains on bedroom windows, or extended use of en suite accommodation, whilst bathrooms tended to be located far from bedroom areas. Triple rooms were avoided in most facilities. Features that differentiated the unit from nearby housing, and therefore could increase the stigma, concerned the size of the lot, the distances between buildings, parking arrangements and front doors. Similarly, there were features that increased the public building atmosphere in the interior, such as tables seating more than eight people and bedroom doors with labelling or decorations, a feature associated with institutions such as older people's homes. However, there was a tendency to avoid institutional materials in circulation areas and bedrooms.

Features that diminished the quality of life and the wellbeing of service users and staff, and therefore related to psychosocial factors, included the lack of daylight in staircases and kitchens, and the absence of staff areas for a retreat or to sleep in the buildings, and armchairs in bedrooms. Moreover there were paper towel dispensers. However, most facilities had freshly prepared meals in the units, variety in the furniture of common areas, which tended to be equipped with TVs and stereos, and decorative items that adorned the dining rooms. Bathrooms had a bath or a bath and a shower, instead of a shower only. In most foyers and wards, service users had the choice to put decorative objects and posters in their bedrooms.

It may be seen from the above that some domestic elements such as curtains were missing for no other apparent reason than neglect, or perhaps easier maintenance, as in the case of paper towels, but here we have to report that the remaining two facilities did not provide any sort of towel at all. Spatial constraints could be blamed for some of the institutional features, such as the lack of daylight in some areas and the lack of armchairs. Lack of staff areas could be associated with older prejudice that staff should at all times be with the service users, and therefore should not have 'hiding' places, an idea however that ignored the problem of staff burnout in mental health environments. Interestingly, there were two facilities with fireplaces, extending the limits of domesticity over safety, and especially since this was not commented on negatively by staff later on.

The following three tables show the lack of a clear definition of what was deemed necessary for safety among the facilities, as those were spread between the two countries and not universal among all the case studies. These tables indicated that either the inclusion of domestic elements in the design of mental health facilities was not justified by the actual necessity for them, as otherwise how would the rest of case studies in the case of wards cope without them, or that there were inadequacies in the provision, compromising user safety. In consequence, apart from the features that appeared in Table 21, connecting the features with partial application among the entire sample to a specific country, there was a large number of features that needed attention at the planning stage: they were either overrated or neglected.

Similarly, regarding Competence as well as Space and Room, it became clearer that there was an ambivalence about which institutional features were necessary for the best function of the wards or the foyers. It is worth noting here that the volume of the features increased compared to previous tables indicating that many of the institutional features, either including the location and the external environment, or architectural details and decoration, were a result of poor investment in thinking or in a lack of resources rather than a functional or therapeutic imperative, such as in the case of the absence of pavements or even tablecloths.

What 7/10 units shared			
parameter	Feature	institutional	domestic
Safety and Security	Differentiation of fencing and landscaping to the neighbouring buildings	■	
	No direct access from social areas to out-of-doors areas	■	
	Non operable windows or external doors in the dining rooms	■	
	Smoke detectors and sprinklers on the dining room ceiling	■	
	Sprinklers, smoke detectors and alarms on bedroom ceilings	■	
	Bedroom windows with restricted opening	■	
	No watch-panels on bedroom doors		■
	Operable bathroom windows		■
Competence	No paved pedestrian paths around	■	
	Dedicated laundry area with professional equipment I more than one washing machine	■	
	Service users could prepare tea or coffee		■
	No elevator within the residence		■
Personalisation and choice	Different front width	■	
	Non-residential locations	■	
	More than one office in the ward	■	
	Different height than nearby buildings that were used for housing	■	
	More than one door at the entrance	■	
	No furniture by the entrance	■	
	No natural light in circulation areas	■	
	Entrance far from public spaces and close to bedrooms and bathrooms	■	
	Bedroom interiors opened directly on public corridors or public areas	■	
	Bins in lounges	■	
	No curtains on dining room windows	■	
	Dining room far from the lounge	■	
	Food served through a door instead of designated hatch	■	
	Vending machines or water coolers	■	
	Washbasins in bedrooms	■	
	No chests of drawers and bookshelves in bedrooms	■	
	Watch panels with mechanism to control visibility from the corridor	■	
	One couch instead of more than one or none in the lounge		■
	Seating in socio-friendly arrangements		■
	Curtains or shades in common areas		■
	Side tables in lounges		■
	Framed pictures instead of blue-tacked posters		■
	Kitchens with external views		■
	Service users could lock bedroom door from the outside		■
	No framed areas on walls for service users' pictures		■
	Normal instead of hospital beds		■
	Mirrors in bedrooms		■
	Only one shower in the shower rooms		■
	Ordinary instead of hospital bins in bathrooms or WCs		■

Table 18.: Common features of 7/10 case studies

parameter	Feature	institutional	domestic
	What 6/10 units shared		
	Security desk or reception at entry point	▓	
Safety and security	Sprinklers and smoke detectors on lounge ceilings	▓	
	Double corridor widths	▓	
	Only fixed lighting fixtures	▓	
	Interview room or room dedicated to psychiatric consultation	▓	
	Ward entry as differentiated part of circulation area	▓	
	Unlocked access-points to out-of-doors areas		▓
Competence	Ward entries not immediately connected to a lobby or to a waiting area	▓	
	Specialised activity rooms	▓	
	Attached rooms equipped to accommodate activities accessible to external service users too	▓	
	Professional cooker, dishwasher and fridge	▓	
	Larders for food storage	▓	
	Lack of both a kitchen for professional use and a kitchenette for service user use	▓	
	Option of domestic cookers and refrigerators		▓
	No wheelchair accessible bathrooms		▓
Personalisation and choice	Different distance from street compared to adjacent buildings	▓	
	Different access point to nearby housing	▓	
	Labels or inscriptions before or by the entrance	▓	
	Similar facade colours to nearby buildings	▓	
	Similar size front entrance doors to public buildings	▓	
	No wallpaper, wall decorations or pictures in wall circulation areas	▓	
	More than two social areas	▓	
	More than one sink or double sink	▓	
	Separate food preparation and washing up areas	▓	
	Staff-only WC within the wards	▓	
	Gender segregation for each bathroom	▓	
	No windows in all or in most of their bathrooms	▓	
	No shelves in the bathrooms	▓	
	Fixed soap dispensers in common WCs	▓	
	Paper towel dispenser or a hand drier in bathrooms	▓	
	Similar facade materials to nearby buildings		▓
	Living rooms by the ward entry		▓
	Social spaces grouped together		▓
	Direct access into kitchens from social areas		▓
	One kitchen only		▓
	Direct access dining room from the kitchenette		▓
	Decorative lighting fixtures in circulation areas and the entrance		▓
	Variety of decoration or colours in social areas		▓
	Blind enlarged corridors with no sitting areas		▓
	No kick-plates or crash bars on doors		▓
	At least a double wardrobe for each service user in the room		▓
	Presence of side table for each bed		▓
	A desk for each person in the bedroom		▓
	Rugs or carpets on bedroom floors		▓
	No fixed soap dispensers in bathrooms		▓

Table 19.: Common features of 6/10 case studies

From all features, only 16 tended to be related to the type of facility, i.e., acute ward or foyer, and therefore, country oriented. More specifically, immediate neighbours in all French Units included housing, but this was not the case in the UK units. Moreover, almost all French units were integrated to a general housing scheme or stand alone, apart from Rene Capitant that shared the premises with a day centre.

By contrast all UK units, apart from Forest Lodge, were integrated to a health care scheme. That did not necessarily result in what it implied for interaction between the services, as interviews showed that wards tended to be self-contained and dealt with their own resources during crises, apart from Lakeside where the alarms were connected to the rest of the wards as well. Therapeutic interaction was also minimal, as low staff numbers did not permit staff to escort sectioned service users to the neighbouring facilities. This practice therefore mainly prevented absconds, as the location of Forest Lodge, the only free-standing UK case study, next to a police station emphasised. Most of the rest of the

parameter	What 5/10 units shared Feature	institutional	domestic
Safety and security	Front doors open to public	■	
	Open stairs within residences (vs enclosed or between fire doors)		■
	Lounges with windows or doors to the outside operable by service users		■
	Doors opening inwards		■
	Glass mirrors in bathrooms and WCs and weight bearing fittings		■
Competence	No handles by toilets		■
	Microwaves in kitchens		■
Personalisation and choice	Signs or notices on lounge walls	■	
	Table cloths		■
	Stainless steel kitchen counters	■	
	Provision for some en suite accommodation		■
	Neighbouring to houses		■
	Either integrated to general housing schemes or stand alone	■	
	Window size similar to adjacent housing		■
	Designated waiting area such as a recess/portico outside the entrance	■	
	Stair surfaces built from materials such as wood, carpet, marble or mosaic		■
	Laundry area located near kitchens or bedrooms		■
	Single room accommodation		■
	Variety in lighting (vs fluorescent only)		■
	Variety in style and colour of curtains and bedspreads		■
	Curtains around the shower		■
	Decorative elements in bathrooms		■

Table 20.: Common features of 5/10 case studies

common features in the UK that were not met in France also focused on safety: bedroom doors opened outwards to avoid barricading, mirrors were of plastic and fittings like curtains could not bear weight. Additionally on Safety and Security, all UK wards apart from Forest Lodge that was an open unit, had controlled access to the outdoors. On the contrary, in France service users could access the outdoors areas freely.

Regarding differences in Competence related features, the situating of all UK units but Forest Lodge in health care premises promoted the existence of specialised rooms for activity under the concept that internal and external service users would use them, economising the resources necessary for providing separate provisions for OT or other therapy. Yet, as it appeared in chapter 5 and as staff interviews in chapter 7 will confirm, the idea did not work as planned due to limited staff to escort internal service users there.

The rest of the parameters that were met in one of the two countries only, but did not have a full implementation there, were Personalisation and Choice related, with a few of them being as a result of increased safety and security needs. More precisely, the existence of kick plates in UK wards could be justified by the violence occurring in the units, and the fact that rooms opened directly onto corridors, as that way visibility could be increased. Watch panels furthermore increased the sense of observability, even in cases where staff still had to enter inside bedrooms. Watch panels were not used in Forest Lodge, where service users tended to be more stable than on the rest of the UK wards. Yet, the emphasis here was that all the watch panels had devices for controlled vision or employed intermediate devices to aid vision through the use of strategically placed mirrors, to protect service users' privacy. So, even if privacy in the UK was hindered compared to France as the result of increased needs for observation, the design of those panel aimed at lessening this intrusion on privacy.

The rest of the features that presented differences between the countries referred to the territoriality and psychosocial features and more precisely the atmosphere of the facilities. Under the concept of territoriality, and the personalised appearance of rooms in almost all French case studies (the exception being Geraniums) service users had placed rugs and carpets in their bedrooms, even in triple bedrooms in Rene Capitan. Yet, in three French cases, common area windows lacked curtains and shades, increasing the institutional appearance of the area and preventing users from adjusting the natural day-light to desired levels. Similarly, three French Cases lacked mirrors in service users' bed-rooms, encouraging service users to use common washing facilities for personal grooming. Under the same prism of reduced privacy, three French cases had bathrooms with more than two showers.

More on the psychosocial aspects of the facilities, in the UK, only Finch Ward presented uniformity in bedroom wall colours, bedspreads and curtains, and Elan was the only French case where each room had its own personality. The former two features as well as the rest of the traits that appear in table 21 were institutional features that restricted privacy or service users' territoriality and sense of a domestic looking environment, without really contributing to the therapeutic role of the facility or its function. Similarly, for no apparent therapeutic reason, UK wards tended to have hospital bins in the bathrooms, despite the fact that mental health wards do not have the hygiene needs of pathology or other clinical NHS wards.

Feature	Institutional	Fr	UK	Characterisation according to model
Immediate neighbours include housing	No	–	5	s
Bedroom doors open inwards	No	–	5	s
Mirrors are plastic	Yes	–	5	s
Weight bearing fittings	Yes	–	5	s
Ward entry	Undifferentiated part of circulation	–	4	PC
Access to the outdoors	Locked or partially	–	4	s
Attached rooms have been especially designed or equipped to accommodate certain activities, like gym (size), crafts (sink) or music (accoustics), and can be used by external service users too	Yes	–	4	C
Doors have crash bars/ kick plates.	Yes	–	4	PC
Rugs or carpet in bedrooms	No	4	–	PC
Bedroom interiors opening to corridor or public area	Yes	–	4	PC
Living room and dining room windows	No curtains or shades	3	–	PC
Food is served through an designated pass- through	Yes	–	3	PC
mirror in each bedroom	No	3	–	PC
There is a watch panel on bedroom door, with no curtain but with controlled vision	Yes	–	3	PC
Bathroom with more than one shower inside	Yes, or in some cases	3	–	PC
Bathroom hospital bins	Yes	–	3	PC

Table 21.: Country related features

Chapter 7

The users' perspectives

7.1. Safety and security

The safety and the security section of the questionnaire explored those measures employed by the units to enhance the safety and security of the service users and was intended to identify the reactions of the user groups to them. It focused on staff considerations about the necessity of policies, if more secure approaches were needed or if with input from them the units could become "closer to home". Alternatively, it explored their perception of safety and security measures. In short, were these measures restrictive or reassuring?

7.1.1. Staff

Staff characterising the performance of the building during normal days raised a number of issues. Safety and security constituted the majority of staff concerns even when it was not a case of an emergency situation in the foyers/wards. The various qualitative data deriving from the individual comments were initially grouped together as positive (satisfied), negative (dissatisfied), mixed or irrelevant. Negative responses prevailed, yet French staff tended to be satisfied.

Apart from the trends of the two countries, it should be mentioned that there was a relation between the architecture of the building and the responses. Elan, which received a total satisfaction rate, was the second least institutional building according to the checklist and was the building with the highest standards. The rest of the French case studies gave more uniform responses. In the UK no building gathered more than one satisfaction point, irrespective of the condition of the ward. In accordance to that, the vast majority of further comments came from UK staff. From the above, it appears that the service user population may have affected the staff's perception of the building. Facilities with a less challenging population, i.e., foyers, received more positive comments on the performance of the building under normal circumstances.

Individual comments regarding the performance of the buildings on normal days were then classified according to their relevance to one of the three parameters. The majority of comments concerned safety and security, with the vast majority of concerns arising from UK staff. As for individual comments, topics varied considerably. Only a few comments were mentioned more than four times and among those only one comment was from the Personalisation and Choice perspective and regarded staff spaces. Regarding the rest, all were related to safety and security.

Regarding emergency situations, on the other hand, staff appeared more satisfied with the buildings' performance. The opinions of those who were satisfied with their buildings compared to those who were not, was almost even. Yet, looking more closely, the French units seemed more satisfactory as these figures were very close to those of non-emergency days, disproportionately to the UK units where there was less satisfaction, but more staff were satisfied with the performance of buildings during emergencies than during normal days. That could be related to differences in the service user populations and the fact that the UK buildings were designed with safety and security as a stronger priority than competence or personalisation and choice, which could be expected in acute care.

Concentrating on specific facilities in the UK, only in Small Heath was the staff satisfied in emergencies, despite the fact that Birmingham facilities generally, amongst which was Small Heath, tended to care for more acute cases, as Birmingham health authorities had an extensive network of community teams, which tended to keep service users at home more than other health authorities, and provided in-patient treatment only when home care was inadequate. The rest of the UK wards scored average in staff dissatisfaction, despite the fact that part of them or all could be on the ground floor. Yet, all those wards had more complex layouts.

The difference between the countries in satisfaction regarding the safety measures provided in the buildings and the numbers of dissatisfied staff, were to a great extent retained, even when staff were asked to identify danger-points in the foyers/wards. Yet, few staff appeared satisfied with the overall safety measures, which still left a few dangerous spots. However, this could be a result of the question itself, as it was directing staff to focus more on the safety of the buildings. 21 staff in both countries did not identify any dangerous parts in the building. Most were French, but there were 9 British among those that were satisfied therewith. Regarding alterations to improve safety one tenth considered the building inappropriate, with its replacement necessary. They also suggested that the units be rebuilt.

Regarding the sense of safety, staff felt safe in both countries with French staff feeling safer, despite the fact that staff in both countries had felt threatened in the past, especially the UK staff. The UK staff that reported insecurity came only from Newbridges that had currently issues with a service user that they could not control.

7.1.2. General organisation of the building and building features mentioned by staff

The layout was reported to cause problems on normal days when there was no emergency situation in the ward, by seven UK staff, in that it was reported to create obstacles to easy access and observation. When staff were asked to name specific dangerous parts the size and the general layout of the building was mentioned only three times, yet specific aspects of the layout such as the existence of more than one floor increased the importance that layout-related issues had for safety, according to staff. However, when staff were asked to propose specific alterations to improve safety, 10 staff members, mostly in the UK, proposed changes in layout, such as level buildings and more compact buildings, i.e. with less distance between the main functional areas.

Stairs and the existence of more than one storey were raised as a problem even if there was no emergency situation in the facility, by 5 members of staff, 4 of them in the UK. In case of an emergency situation the overall comments regarding these two features increased. Thus, the number of floors that the building spread over raised four comments, half of them in French units, and five mentioned the need for a level building, of which three were in France. The facilities in France, where the staff were dissatisfied, were Geraniums and Rene Capitant, where there were no elevators and, also, those were the only facilities with more than three stories. When staff were asked to name dangerous parts, stairs and steps were mentioned 7 times, mostly in France. Interestingly, in the UK steps were mentioned in Small Heath, a ward on the first floor that was dependant on a ground floor unit and staff had to escort all service users there twice a day for meals.

Regarding observability, historically there was much discussion about the value of being able to observe service users from a central point. The modern equivalent could be either the nursing station or the staff office. Staff offices were the points where staff could do clerical work and exercise control over the ward. Arrangements varied from a glazed nursing station close to the entrance, to a reception point with glazing to watch the entrance, to an open reception or an office close to the entrance, where an open door allowed some control. In Forest Lodge, however, the office was in a separate house and staff only did clerical work there. Staff opinions regarding the nursing station or the staff office were divided too, yet these did not follow a pattern linked to the spatial options.

Control of entry/exit points concerned staff, mostly in the U, even if there was no emergency situation. Moreover, 7 French and UK staff addressed the need for improvements regarding the control of intrusions and abscondings. Interesting comments, spread among the case studies with emphasis on emergency situations, included the inability of staff to cover all floors, the lack of visibility and the inadequate size. To the lack of visibility could be added the comments referring to the difficulty staff encountered in emergency situations due to the presence of narrow and twisting corridors that were mentioned 6 times, and in almost all the UK case studies. Moreover, 9 UK staff proposed improvement to visibility and entrapment areas in and outside of the ward as a necessary means to improve safety. Monitoring and security equipment such as alarms was proposed by 10 staff members in both countries as a means to improve safety. Other issues that aroused staff concerns regarded windows, mostly by French, and balconies.

A very important aspect of the safety of the service users was staff observation at night, especially in acute facilities where the risk of self-harm was present. Yet, even in post cure, some of the staff declared support for night time observation as well. Apart from staff at the two facilities where service users were permitted to leave during day, all staff agreed with the practice of entering rooms at night. It should be noted here that in Rene Capitant staff made night rounds, and maybe that is why staff agreed with that policy. However, in none of the French case studies was the issue of having watch panels on bedroom doors raised. In the UK staff checked inside the rooms, despite the presence of observation panels. Overall, 14 staff stressed the need for observation at night and 11 confirmed that observation windows were necessary. In Small Heath, all staff mentioned that they felt that they needed to open doors despite the careful design of the observation window combined with an indirect mirror reflecting the bed. However, staff mentioned that they faced problems due to the weight and noise of the door or service users blocking the view.

Features that could enable self-harm or accidents, received only four mentions as necessary alterations, all in the UK. Yet, if the answers that were given for dangerous parts mentioned features such as balconies or terraces, details that could block access, showers or baths and slippery floors, this number increased. Still, none of these features, if examined of their own, provided a substantial number. Finally, there were a few mentions from staff regarding environmental factors that related to health and hygiene, such as temperature, inadequacy of hot water or ventilation, especially in the UK, and in France in the two old and neglected cases of Rene Capitant and Geraniums, which caused problems for the everyday life of the facilities.

7.1.3. Service users' concerns on safety related issues

The service user questionnaire on safety aimed to identify sources of worry and possible elements in the environment that could trigger hallucinations for service users. This was based on concerns that were raised in the literature review, for example surfaces that reflected light and caused visual hallucinations, as factors that could aggravate service users' conditions or that would indicate such pathological traits that this would require caution in specific elements of design.

Regarding sources of worry in the facilities, quite a large proportion of service users, reaching almost half for the UK, could not detect anything worrying in the unit or anything that made them uncomfortable. Additionally, three service users in the UK characterised their illness as the origin of their problems and not the premises. The rest of the service users' issues spread over policy, environmental and service user or staff interaction issues. The most common concern was about violence. This concerned more French than UK service users, with a significant number of service users in Bois St Joseph. The fact that violence was most reported in France might be related to the fact that service users in acute care accepted violence as part of their life. Problems with staff were reported only in Geraniums. "Environment" was spread in four units in both countries, yet not the poorest environmentally. On the contrary in less privileged environments, social or policy issues were reported. Bathrooms, in terms of shared provision or challenging design, concerned three acute service users, two in Albany Lodge. Those answers however, did not focus on the question about worry, as their concerns related mostly to discomfort. This applied as well to other replies, for example "boredom". In that sense the percentage of service users that did not worry in their environment was higher, whilst there was no substantial indication that there was a direct connection to features of the environment and service users' worries.

Service users were also asked a question about their preferences in respect of night time observation. Yet, for service users the emphasis was not on the watch panel but on the observation levels they desired to have. As with most topics that were addressed to service users, the point was to identify their perception of the entire experience of their stay and their perception of needs, and how this was in accordance with the three parameters, rather that asking service users directly on spatial issues. More than half of the service users questioned preferred their door locked or closed at night instead of being supervised, with theft concerns being the most common reason for that, equally proportioned between the two countries. A bit more than one tenth preferred being supervised by staff at night, with a slight difference between the two countries (slightly higher for France). An additional relatively small number wished the door to remain open at all times, or wanted the door open but as a habit, all of them French. Finally, even less preferred their door locked or closed at night but with staff being able to enter. In France that number was almost a triple of the UK. There were also very few that did not mind.

7.1.4. Issues related to safety and security that could be connected to design implications

Hallucinations could affect all the senses. Thus, potentially service users could experience hearing, visual, tactile and olfactory hallucinations and the aim was to investigate if and how those issues might be taken seriously in the design of community mental health care facilities. As service users could not be asked directly if they experienced these problems, more generic questions regarding noise for example, in the case of hearing hallucinations, were brought into the interviews. Additionally, as there were references in the literature review about service users' sensitivity to environmental factors, in this way the existing units could be evaluated. The point of this section was to identify any potentially grave sources of hallucinations in the buildings or potential environmental stressors, as this could then be an area that evidence based design could help.

Regarding noise, over half the respondents in both countries, equally proportioned between France and the UK, commented on noisy spaces in the wards. Noise seemed to bother service users regardless of their condition. Reported annoyance levels did not differ among acute and post-cure service users. Most sources of noise were related to the life of the facilities. According to service users, TVs and stereos were the most frequent sources of noise, followed by people and crowded spaces and external noise. All those responses were related to the conditions that existed in the facilities and did not indicate any pathological origin. As for echoes, apart from a single case in the UK, no other similar source of noise was detected, and another acute service user admitted that the noise was in his head. The vast majority of service users did not detect any glary surfaces in the units or any areas where light was reflected in a peculiar way. Out of 65 service users only five in the UK and four in France reported problems from glare, mainly because of large windows or too much light coming in. There were no reported cases of hallucinations stimulated by light on surfaces. No particular problems were reported due to artificial light. Specifically on light levels, which was an issue that derived from this discussion as there was an issue of sensitivity of service users to light because of medication, the majority of service users were satisfied. In France, a third of service users were in need of more light, though. On the contrary, a tenth of the UK service users needed lower light levels. Additionally, in the UK, two service users needed some night light. Almost all Enan service users needed higher light levels. Service users' needs differed regarding artificial and daylight. There were no associations to service users' pathology.

Most service users did not report problems with surfaces in the facility. The vast majority were satisfied with the surfaces. In France, that percentage rose to almost 8/10. There was a tendency that acute service users seemed more concerned about surfaces, patterns and materials than the residents of foyers, even if the majority did not pay attention to these. Women in foyers seemed to pay more attention to their environment compared to their male counterparts, even if men were staying in similarly poor conditions. In acute care there was not such a clear sample to check if the case applied there too, as the female sample was too small and scattered around the case studies.

Service users were mainly concerned about poor condition and maintenance. In more acute environments, where the buildings were not so old, hygiene was the commonest concerns, as it appeared in Finch Ward, New Bridges and Albany Lodge, followed by isolated remarks about specific materials in three among the case studies. Thus, black gravel in Albany Lodge, or a particular wall in a facility in New Bridges which had patterns that seemed to move, and remarks about laminate and cement that were mentioned by two service users in Small Heath, could all be relevant to specific service user's pathology. A similar case, where a service user associated red sofas as generating distress, was met in the pilot study. In foyers, mention about specific materials by one service user occurred only in Bois St Joseph. It regarded tiles as an annoying texture. Yet, Bois St Joseph was a building where tiles were a strong element, as they covered all areas and without change in pattern or colour. They were very reflective too and overall gave a clean but institutional atmosphere. Generalisation from these data about the specific materials would therefore be premature, but a larger sample of acute service users might identify if there are lessons there about surface treatments. However, there was indication from the above that responses to specific materials that could not be predicted or generalised, could be related to service users' pathology.

More than half of service users' sample reported problems from smells. Service users reported problems in almost all units apart from Francois Tosquelles, and even in new and well-constructed environments, in both acute care and post-cure establishments. There were no marked differences among the countries, with the number being slightly higher in France. The main sources of bad smells were toilets, followed by cigarette smells and bedrooms. The rest were isolated cases that did not present indications of olfactory hallucinations.

7.1.5. Staff and service user perspective on the safety and the security of the facilities

In more acute settings, where staff had a tougher job, staff's opinion about the performance of the building on regular days appeared unrelated to the architecture of those buildings, as increased job challenges influenced their opinion about space. From staff's comments, it appeared that there were a variety of criteria that they used to evaluate the buildings. Those were mainly control and observation factors, such as layout, connections, control of the entrance and ease of movement, all related to safety and security. The adequacy of staff areas, environmental factors and the date of construction were also among the parameters.

To outline staff opinions on unit safety, the service user population, in terms of dependency, determined the number and the type of issue that staff pointed out as dangerous in a building. The foyer de poste-cure as opposed to the UK acute mental health wards raised fewer concerns about safety. French staff tended to be more satisfied than the UK staff, both on normal days and in emergencies, and that could be a result of the fact that French facilities accommodated more stabilised service users. Yet, that did not much affect the sense of safety in the facilities, as both acute and post cure staff tended to feel safe, even if they had been threatened in the past. The condition of the building or the number of storeys did not seem to affect this parameter.

Buildings for more unstable service users needed more alterations to improve safety, even though they were already designed to include a greater number of secure and institutional features. The French units, despite the fact that they had more "ordinary" materials and fittings, such as glass and weight-bearing details and fully opening windows, appeared adequately safe. Monitoring equipment was a common demand among staff, in both closed and open facilities. Looking more closely at the facilities, in open units the control of the entrance gained in importance as service users interacted more with the community. In more acute settings, just controlling the entrance did not suffice nor did the proximity of the control point to the entrance, and the resemblance to more clinical patterns of control were more effective, according to staff, as they had to be present everywhere instead of attempting to control the entire ward from a single point. Visibility was inadequate even in "fish bowl" patterns.

Staff made rounds at night in acute wards checking inside rooms, irrespective of the watch panel of the bedroom door. However, even in the most independent units staff might make rounds at night. Observation panels were deemed necessary in acute settings.

Service users did not report sources of worry related to the unit, with acute service users tending to be more satisfied, perhaps due to their increased passivity. Interestingly, violence, which was more frequent in acute wards, was most commonly raised as issue in France, and was the most common concern among service users. Policy factors as well as social factors, were most frequently reported, and environmental concerns were not necessarily mentioned more often in the poorer buildings, but those were not necessarily related to worries. Regarding night time observation, from service users' responses, the majority of service users in acute and post-cure preferred having their door closed or locked at night instead of being supervised. There were no differences between acute and post-cure service users on that. However, the acute wanted that for supervision, which might increase their sense of safety, while post-cure service users had that preference as a personal habit. In general, however the night supervision preference did not differ much between the two countries.

As for potential environmental stressors or possible triggers of hallucinations, the research did not detect any problems with noise due to service users' condition and in isolated cases of hearing hallucinations service users could relate them to their pathology. Service users were generally satisfied with the light levels in their environment, with acute service users preferring less light and foyer service users more. Only isolated cases, mainly in acute wards, reported issues that would indicate visual hallucinations or materials causing discomfort that could relate to pathological reasons. Maybe a much larger sample might be able to detect a more precise number and pinpoint potential environmental factors that could trigger such instances.

7.2. Competence

7.2.1. Staff views on service users' competence

A few staff members in both countries mentioned that the buildings had been designed in accordance with service users' competences. The vast majority of staff though, made specific comments about their existing building that could be gathered under the following major topics, presented here according to the times each was mentioned:

- Lack of activity space or activity equipment (i.e., gym, workshops)
- Lack of normal living space or equipment (bicycle store, garage)
- Lack of external/ open space (i.e., garden)
- Lack of therapeutic space (i.e., quiet room, relaxation areas)

Regarding the need for more activity space and equipment as well as of normal living space, there was no significant difference between the countries. Lack of external space was mentioned mostly in the UK, where service users tended to be ward-bound and where many facilities did not have access to a garden. Even in the two French inner city facilities, the lack of a garden was expected in Paris. Finally, lack of therapeutic space was equally divided between the countries but with a very small number.

Staff opinions varied on the difficulties that service users encountered in their environment, and most responses were isolated cases where no more than two answers were given on a country basis. According to 14 staff members, non-building related problems, such as social, family or medical issues, were equally divided between the two countries. The next most frequent was the communal life in the facilities. Lack of space was also higher among the UK staff. By contrast, the location of the unit was less of a problem in the UK. Since service users were wardbound, the location did not seem to make much difference. Few mentioned the smoking policy, mostly in France.

Finally, there arose from the above the importance of the role of the facilities' structure and policy. Staff in both countries tended to agree with the structure policy of the unit in which they worked. Overall, the vast majority agreed, and only a small percentage disagreed, and a slightly higher percentage did not reply. In France those who agreed were even more. Yet, as staff might present an "improved" view of service users' regime on a daily basis, they were also asked directly about the details of the service users' programme.

7.2.2. Spatial organisation issues related to service users competence according to staff

As far as accessibility was concerned, mobility issues were not mentioned by staff as compromising service users' competence. Stairs and accessibility were mentioned only 3 times and surprisingly it was mentioned in a UK single storey, ground floor facility, despite the fact that foyers in France could spread across several floors. The only point that was discussed regarding physical accessibility concerned assistance that service users might need when bathing, a topic that was though raised by the author, and thus a topic that did not initially cross staff's mind when asked about service users' competence. Nevertheless, the vast majority staff members had encountered service users who needed assistance when bathing. According to staff, this need for help could be due to pathology, and could result in them refusing to wash part of their body and thus staff needed to intervene, or low motivation as service users under normal circumstances were fully mobile. Activities, on the other hand, either as structured activity or as outdoors activities or as unstructured everyday skills activity such as cooking and room maintenance, were more extensively discussed. The levels of required activity - in terms of structure, numbers, kinds of activity, especially the structured ones but also unstructured such as cooking, have strong implications to the spatial organisation of the facilities, as these activities claim their space in the wards/foyers, in their internal or outdoors areas. Depending on their kind, they might require the relevant infrastructure and would affect the whole organisation of the ward/foyer. For example, activity provided externally only, might enable more homelike organisations, as activity areas would not be required. For example, decisions on service users being involved in food preparation might imply the existence of a kitchen accessible to them that would not be too challenging to use: in short would raise the issue of a domestic kitchen for service users.

In France, of the staff that expressed a clear opinion on the placement of activities, most suggested that these should be provided externally or both, and very few suggested only within the unit. There was no clear connection between staff suggestions and the existing organisation of the facility. However, in Elan and Bois St Joseph, staff supported the existing practices of external or external and internal activity respectively.

In the UK only a very limited number of staff took the view that activity should take place outside the ward while the majority suggested that it should be both, mostly outside but with on site activity provided too . These that found the dedicated activity area inadequate came from Small Heath. In Newbridges most staff suggested that activity should take place outside only, despite the fact that service users rarely participated in the adjacent day centre activities due to a lack of staff to escort them. The remaining units were divided among various degrees of activity taking place both inside and outside.

Concentrating on the everyday activity of food preparation, architecturally there were five possible scenarios, graduating from options that were less demanding spatially (i.e, from a preparation room, where food could be reheated) to having both a professionally equipped kitchen and a homelike one. Policy-wise this translated into eight different options. Looking more closely at the combinations, one can see that the stability of service users and their proximity to independence was not necessarily relevant to the policy regarding the use or availability of a kitchen. The result was not determined by central planning, both spatially and policy-wise, but it was determined by a combination of the intentions of the people who designed the place and the people who ran it.

A wide range of opinions emerged from answers to the question asking staff if they believed that service users should use the kitchen. Staff opinions varied considerably, and occasionally "misunderstanding" of the relevant legislation was brought up to justify current practices. In general, staff adopted the ward policy, with a few exceptions, mainly in Francois Tosquelles and Rene Capitant. In the former, staff questioned the practice of service users providing the ward meals, which did not replicate normal domestic cooking from a quantity and equipment perspective. The answers also indicated that, depending on the facility where they were placed, staff supported all options from the most dependent to the most "normal".

The majority of staff supported that staff could use a kitchen, preferably with supervision, yet the majority amongst them believed that this should be a domestic kitchen and only few staff members supported that this could be the main kitchen. In the UK the answers were grouped into the following categories regarding service user use of the kitchen: use of a domestic kitchen under supervision, no cooking and no use of professional/main kitchen. UK staff were less influenced by the existing policy. Apart from Forest Lodge and Albany Lodge where staff agreed with the co-presence of a professional and service user kitchen, and the no-cooker policy respectively, in the rest of the case studies, where there were no cooking facilities available for service users, staff welcomed the idea of staff-supervised cooking options. These staff had embraced a position that was closer to the 'normal' concept, despite the fact that the UK service user population was in more vulnerable state.

Half the staff found the kitchen size big enough, with some amongst them even considering it too large or too professional for service users to use. The number of positive answers was divided between the countries. The rest considered the size of the space inadequate. Most were from the UK. Staff tended to be satisfied in Elan, Francois Tosquelles, Bois St Joseph, Geraniums, Newbridges and Small Heath.

Regarding the everyday activity of service users' bedroom maintenance, only a fourth of staff members answered that most service users were able to keep their rooms tidy. Here it should be mentioned that bedroom maintenance did not have immediate design implications. However for reasons of relevance to the rest of activity topics it has been discussed in this section. Positive answers were divided among the countries and regarding the rest of the answers there was no significant difference as well, despite the fact that French service users were more stable. Even in facilities closer to independence like Elan, answers were not different. The only ward where most staff answered positively was Geraniums, a female only ward.

Finally, regarding staff suggestions for the use of the garden, overall passive activities and relaxation were suggested by more than a third of staff, closely followed by sports/ physical activity and gardening. Less suggested were meals, socialising and therapies. The countries differed significantly, with passive activities being proposed by most UK staff members, and, while in France only few staff proposed passive activity and outdoor meals. That could be due to differences in the motivation of the two service user populations. There were no other significant differences.

7.2.3. Service users' concerns regarding competence

Service users' replies on the difficulties they encountered in the facility regarding things they could do but were not given the option to do, covered a wide spectrum, encompassing policy, activities, structure and, indirectly, a few issues that had spatial implications. In general UK service users seemed to express fewer such difficulties, which could be related to the degree of their illness as that could encourage passive behaviour. In France almost a third of service users replied that they had experienced no limitations on what they actually wanted to do in the facility, while in the UK the number rose considerably. The issues that were felt as restrictive by service users were, according to frequency: lack of activity and sports, difficulty in complying with policy issues such as going out of the facility or accepting visitors and lack of several facilities.

On the other hand, regarding things/situations that service users would find hard to cope with, almost half of the service users did not find any particular difficulty in their environment. This percentage was higher in France than the UK. The most common source of trouble was other service users, followed by boredom, and social problems and noise. Next, service users reported difficulties, with staff behaviour, treatment, hygiene, lack of space, quality of environment. Issues such as structure, lack of privacy, and lack of specific practical amenities raised even less concern.

Boredom was considerably higher in the UK, (almost a quarter of the local population, compared to a very small number in France), followed closely by issues arising from co-habitation (other service users), staff behaviour and treatment issues. Among the French service users the most common issue was cohabitation, "other service users", followed by the closely related "social problems" such as thefts, violence and racism. Noise received few mentions and there were also isolated comments that are not presented here. Social problems, institutional regime related issues, and smoke bothered only French service users.

7.2.4. Spatial organisation issues related to service users competence according to service users

The only feature regarding physical accessibility from service users' perspective concerned bathrooms. Regarding the size of the bathroom, a third of UK service users preferred a family like bathroom, as opposed to an assisted bathroom, as opposed to two thirds in France. There was also a considerable number of service users in the UK who prefered a larger assisted one as compared to a smaller number in France.

There was, by contrast, a major input from the service users regarding the activity in the wards/ foyers, either as structured or everyday activities, internal or external. Service users' daily activity programme was very much determined by the ward policy, and the availability of options in the area. In France, all facilities but Geraniums, either provided options in the facility or had a local network, or were in a locality where there were many options. In the UK, Albany Lodge service users might use the day hospital. In all other cases, passive behaviour was reported, forming the commonest choice of behaviour among the service users, followed by ward activity and then going out for leisure. Going out for work or study was not among the UK options.

From the total service users' sample, the vast majority liked some of the available activity The number was higher in the UK than in France, which still was higher than the two thirds of the French sample. The boredom that acute service users faced was maybe the reason for the wide appreciation of activity in the facilities. Service users in France who did not like the activity provided or would not bother with any activity came mainly from Elan, Geraniums and Rene Capitant. The strong external activity orientation of Elan and Rene Capitant might explain their service users' lack of interest in on-site activity. Regarding Geraniums, the strong institutional character of this facility might have resulted in service users' passivity, yet when Geraniums' service users were asked about difficulties they encountered in their environment they complained about the sort of activities on offer and the lack of sports facilities. In the UK, mainly the service users who were unwilling to get involved in activity came from Finch Ward and Small Heath, the two wards that did not have any activity schedule or where this activity was very limited.

Regarding specific activities, service users mostly preferred OT, mostly comprising art, pottery and arts and crafts, which were most frequently available. Next were games, followed by organised outings and trips and finally, music. The other activities, which were numerous, were considered non-indicative. Games were more favoured by the UK service users. The majority of service users did not want any other activity than the ones on offer. Yet, in that case, sports was the activity mostly missing from what was on offer.

As far as unstructured everyday activities were concerned, service users commented on food preparation and room maintenance. Regarding food preparation, almost half of service users preferred food to be prepared by a chef. In France that percentage rose more than half while in the UK the percentage dropped to less than one third. In total a third of all of service users preferred to cook for themselves, mostly the British. In between those two extremes, there was a relatively small number who wanted to be able to cook and have a chef as well; mostly in the UK. From some service users' comments it could be inferred that their preferences were mainly personal habits unrelated to issues of trust in respect of food preparation. Additionally, there was no unit where service users were in complete agreement on the subject. Even in open units or units where service users went out for the day, food preparation responsibility generated various responses. Nor was gender indicative of a direction.

Regarding room maintenance, well more than half of the service user population replied that they tidied up their rooms, which reached a bit less than two thirds of the UK sample. A quarter, evenly divided, replied that the domestic staff did the cleaning anyway since they needed help. The rest mainly said that they needed some help, mostly the French. In the only female-only unit, service users tended to say that they tidied up by themselves as opposed to the sole male only unit, where respondents reported that the ward was tidied for them. Both were in France.

Finally, service users commented on the opportunity they had regarding the use of the garden and what they were doing there. As some wards lacked gardens or secure external areas, service users there tended to reply negatively. Overall, a bit less than half of the service users replied that they did not or could not go to a garden or an external area like a terrace. Apart from all the service users from Rene Capitant, and 3 from among the Elan, more than half of the French respondents came from facilities with large gardens. By contrast, in the UK only less than a third of service users, mostly in Finch Ward, did not use a garden, but although the rest were in places where there were easily accessible gardens for the service users.

French service users mostly preferred gardening activities, next enjoyed passive activities and relaxation as well as the contact with nature. In the UK almost a third enjoyed passive activities and relaxation, followed mainly by sports, next enjoying nature, and even fewer gardening and socialising. Those who enjoyed sports were from Small Heath, where they played football.

7.2.5. Main findings related to competence for staff and service users

Regarding competence according to staff, facilities needed more activity space and equipment, both in the UK and France. Staff also recommended that service users could benefit from more normal living spaces, especially in acute wards. Therapy spaces both in wards and foyers were mostly adequate for staff. According to them the most common problems that service users faced in acute wards or foyers were not directly related to the building. In closed units the lack of space and the obligatory communal life were the most reported space- related issues, while location was the most reported problem in foyers. Focusing on the type of activity the majority of staff deemed both internal and external occupations as necessary. There were variations among staff about the proportion of an interior activity as opposed to external, with staff of acute wards tending to prefer more ward-based options. Research also suggested that internal activity in British wards was not sufficient and there were concerns from staff about the adequacy of allocated spaces.

Regarding unstructured everyday activities, food preparation and bedroom maintenance were discussed. The attitude of staff towards meal preparation depended largely on the existing ward policy, especially in France. In terms of the cooking options for service users, staff were divided in both countries. Staff disagreed with the option of a professional kitchen to be accessible to service users and meal preparation was not related to service users' progress. A substantial proportion of staff in both settings proposed a domestic type of kitchen available for service users to use individually under supervision. About maintenance, domestic staff were needed to clean service user bedrooms in both acute wards and foyers. That applied even in facilities where service users worked or followed day-care programmes outside. Staff opinion agreed with the current state regarding maintenance.

Closing the subject of activity from the staff perspective, the garden was important in places where service users tended to be ward bound, and it dropped in the needs scale where they had access to open space. In more acute settings, it functioned as an opportunity for relaxation and passive activity and for, more stabilised service users as an opportunity for gardening, sports or social activity such as meals.

According to service users, now, the sources of difficulty, either from things they would like to do, i.e, limitations to their competence, or things that were too difficult for them to cope with, differed among acute and foyer service users, as acute service users tended to report difficulty less often. Acute service users mostly complained about the fact that they could not go out and suffered from boredom, where some activity could perhaps help, whereas foyer service users mostly complained about the lack of activity, sports and the rules imposed. Yet, a large number of service users were satisfied with the activities on offer, especially OT. However, they would like sports to be included as an option.

If food needed to be cooked in the unit or reheated there, there was no clear agreement between service users. From the service users' perspective, there was an important part of the acute ward and foyer population that wanted their meals to be prepared by staff. However, in the UK the service user population that preferred to prepare their own food was larger than those preferring to have meals made by somebody else. Similarly, there was no relationship between service user state and increased motivation to tidy their rooms. Service users from France tended to say less often that they could do their own rooms, but this could be a result of cultural differences between the French and the British service users in admitting independence. Service users used a garden when they had access to it, especially the wardbound ones. The activity in the garden varied according to service users' state, with more stable service users being less passive or even not using it at all if they went out during the day.

Finally, the section on competence did not bring up issues of physical competence, other than bathing. The vast majority of staff had encountered service users who needed assistance during bathing. Service users, especially in France, preferred homelike bathrooms.

7.3. Issues related to personalisation and choice

7.3.1. Staff on issues regarding psychosocial aspects of care

As there is a prejudice in mental health that too good surroundings might prevent service users from being willing to move on, staff opinions on the issue were important, this being a very sensitive topic since unsupported similar statements could serve as excuses for poor conditions. Most were divided between that it depended on the service user or the staff input to that direction and that service users had motives for discharge. A minority supported that there was this possibility based on spatial, comfort and dependence reasons.

Here it should be mentioned that there was an inverse relationship to those replies about the opinions of staff comparing the wards/foyers' condition to service users' homes. Most recurring opinions are presented listed from high to low, from those that regarded the ward as positive compared to service users' homes, those who perceived that it depended, those that rendered it as negative. In the UK, amongst the three groups, the strongest was the one supporting that the wards were better than service users' homes. In France, the most potent opinion was the "it depends".

Staff positively viewing the wards commented that sometimes service users' homes were the origin of their problems, or that service users were lonely and isolated there, or in better living conditions in the facilities or in some cases that they had spent long periods in the psychiatric system so service users might not have homes at all. On the other hand, some staff maintained that service users faced difficulties with communal life, the lack of privacy and independence, the structure and the fact that they had to follow some activity programme. There were instances where staff rated the ward building in poor condition as compared to service users' homes. Overall, the concept that the environment might be too good to provide motivation to move on did not appear in the interviews but as an isolated case, as staff perceived their role to encourage service users to progress.

It seems that from acute care, service users could go more easily to the next step, but from foyers more work was needed, although eventually service users would want to leave. There was no detectable relation between the design of the building and the responses, as service users could be willing to go from Elan, which was the better constructed and more spacious facility, and less willing in facilities like Geraniums where living conditions were rather poor. In foyers, where service users during the daytime did not use the bedrooms or could not access the foyer, there were no negative replies to the question regarding whether service users left the foyer willingly. Answers in all those cases varied from 'it depends' to 'yes'.

Yet, despite the fact that the majority of staff did not consider the environment as an obstacle to service users' willingness to move on, they did not support the view that it should be a substitute for home during service users' stay, either. So far as the staff were concerned, in order to identify the place of the wards/foyers, in an axis from more hospital-like to more home-like orientation because of service users' condition, this raised a variety of individual answers, with hospital and home the extremes and the hotel option appearing in between. Obviously, not all answers belonged to a particular type or referred to particular traits that could be then attributed to one of the previous types. In both countries the vast majority of replies, or parts of them, were classified as hospital-type traits, even more those that came from the UK. Interestingly, comparing between countries, the French prioritised a hospital- type model and traits as the most appropriate, then the hotel and last the home model. Yet in the UK the home traits were more than the hotel traits, with the hospital-related ones being the vast majority.

Safety and security issues overpowered the personalisation and choice options that related to more homelike choices, whilst competence issues were practically not brought up. In this way, they set an initial threshold to personalisation and choice dilemmas to favour those options that would not contradict safety. More analytically, some staff raised concerns about suicide risk, even in France, where foyers did not have many of the self-harm considerations incorporated into the design of the buildings. Fire risk raised some comments, most in France, while policy to encourage discharge was mentioned as well, mostly in the UK. Low buildings (mainly a French concern), anti-violence and anti-vandalism considerations (UK concerns), and hygiene concerns (all in the UK), and the comment that it would be like a hospital (mainly a UK concern), occurred as well. There were also few staff members, took the view that the building should feel like a home, and the 'core and cluster' model was mentioned as well.

Staff's persistence on safety as it was expressed by the hospital concept, however, did not rule out the importance of stimulation for service users, even in the acute cases. In response to the question about what service users needed most regarding stimulation levels, well more than a third of staff members answered stimulation, few answered calmness and a significant number answered both, while almost a third suggested that this depended on the case. For the UK only, most valued both as what was most appropriate, followed by those who answered that that it depended on the case or calmness. This was relevant to the state of the UK service users as they were during or close to the acute episode. By contrast, in France the vast majority suggested stimulation. This was expected as post cure service users had to start to act independently. However, there was a chance that these findings were affected by the country of origin, as culturally the British seemed to value calmness over stimulation, while the French had the opposite attitude.

The UK gathered a larger sample of responses that allowed a pattern to be detected. On calmness, half of valid responses were space-related comments. On stimulation, quite a few related to space, unlike France. The most common comment regarding calmness was related to the individual's care programme. The space-related comments were about the need for individual rooms and the decoration of the environment and then isolated comments regarded space to come back to from external activities and a low stimulus room. Regarding stimulation, spatially, the most common comment was ward activity and activity rooms, followed by common areas and isolated comments on environment and stimulation rooms.

Before looking in greater detail at service users' opinions on spatial consideration issues in the facilities, two policy issues will be discussed, gender segregation -a policy that raises a dilemma between privacy and normality, as gender segregation in general is associated with institutions-and the smoking policy, relevant to smoker service users' comfort and personalisation of space and at the same time non-smoker service users' choice of a smoke free environment. The vast majority of staff supported mixed sex units, with a small number only disapproving of mixed sex. Numbers did not differ significantly between the countries, with the French raising a few more negative answers. Those were concentrated in Rene Capitant and Geraniums, which were the French single gender facilities. In the other French case studies that were mixed, even with occasionally limited female presence, all staff wanted mixed units. In the UK there was no such relation as all units were mixed sex, and staff in one ward only proposed that it should be single gender. No staff member raised the issue of a single gender area within a mixed gender facility. The most commonly reported problems resulting from mixed sex wards were the formation of relationships, which interfered with service users' care programmes and the vulnerability of female service users, while the most common reason for mixed gender was that it was normal. Other comments were mentioned no more than twice.

The vast majority of staff in both countries, even more in the UK, suggested that smoking should be allowed in allocated areas only. In the only case study where service users could not smoke inside, all staff agreed that there should be a smoking room. Comments on difficulties to implement the smoking policy were more common in France, most from Les Geraniums. Concerns about ventilation were limited.

7.3.2. Staff on personalisation and choice design features

The location of facilities so far were attributed to the Safety and Security section, partially justified by the fact that in the UK case studies, actual planning indicated a major interest therein as they were either in health care premises or, in the case of Forest Lodge, next to the police station. However, staff interviews shifted the focus regarding the location of the facilities to service users' opportunities and choices in the surrounding area. In more detail, regarding the location of the facilities,

Mostly, staff positively rated the proximity of the facility to the city or town centre, as offering more opportunities to their service users. Next in importance was the location in the catchment area, followed by the public transport network available. By contrast, open grounds and nature, proximity to other healthcare facilities, integration to the local community and acceptance by it as well as activity opportunities comprised lower priorities. The rest were isolated cases.

The UK priorities were the location in the catchment area, followed by proximity to the town/city centre and open grounds, space and nature. Public transport was mentioned three times. By contrast, in France the catchment area was not mentioned at all, whereas proximity to city or town centre and public transport appeared the most important location parameters. In that sense, French staff rated the importance of the location as offering stimuli to the service users to integrate and move independently, which was feasible in a more central placement that was served by public transport. In the UK, because service users were more dependent and arrived directly from their homes, the location within the catchment area was far more important and the choice between calm environments and stimuli was not obvious.

Normalisation theory references suggested that a building integrated to the surroundings would help eliminate problems of NIMBYism and would lessen social exclusion. Trying to identify the wards/ foyers relationship with the local area would indicate the status of the actual relationship of the case studies to their neighbourhood and possibly be able to identify major trends behind those relationships. Most staff rated positive (good to OK) the relationship of the existing unit to its surroundings. Few considered that the neighbours were not aware of the presence of the facility and one did not know. The rest made points on a bad relationship. Those included:

- Drug trafficking from the community towards the unit
- Complaints regarding service user behaviour outside the unit
- Need to control the entrance and the territory around the unit
- NIMBYism
- Bad reputation of the unit
- Vandalism from the community

The positive responses were almost evenly divided between the countries, indicating no culturally determined relationship or distinction of service users' state (sectioned or voluntary) between the service user group and the public's acceptance. The responses concerning indifference were divided too. As far as specific issues were concerned, drug trafficking was mentioned most in the UK, together with vandalism, complaints regarding service users' behaviour and that staff had to control the entrance and the territory of the unit. The bad reputation of the ward was mentioned concerned Geraniums.

Looking closer at the case studies to identify patterns, regarding drug trafficking Bois St Joseph had unmonitored entry points, and Albany Lodge staff had to prevent service users from using the external courtyards and needed extra care to prevent drug dealers from passing drugs through windows left ajar or the external garden shrubs. In the remaining UK buildings that were located in residential areas, staff mostly rated the relationship to the community negatively. On the contrary, positive comments were received from Finch Ward and Small Heath, both situated in larger health care schemes and Forest Lodge that was located in a residential area but with no immediate proximity to housing. In France where none of the units were located in a broader campus or healthcare scheme, the only two units that received mostly positive comments were the two inner city Parisian ones, Elan and Rene Capitant, where the anonymity of such a dense area was relevant. However, Elan, being embedded in a large block of flats, originally had troubles with the community in the form of complaints and prejudice. Yet, the immediate response of staff to the complaints restored the relationship.

Here one could detect two contradictory patterns; facilities that appeared less institutional regarding their exterior and placement according to the architectural checklist, such as Elan, Rene Capitant and Forest Lodge, as well as facilities that were well integrated in health care schemes, as the case of Small Heath that was in the core of a general healthcare scheme or Finch Ward that was located deep in a general hospital campus, - in short the better integrated or the most isolated - appeared to have the least problems with the interaction with the local community.

The question regarding a therapeutic environment received a great deal of individual and isolated answers. Some French staff member supported the view that the environment should be bright, airy and naturally lit and emphasised the balance between private spaces and those that favoured interaction. Homelikeness as such was barely mentioned, yet some staff commented design qualities such as pleasing environments, or furniture. A calm environment, spaciousness and closeness to nature as well as closeness to human scale received limited mention but could be added up to reinforce the spatial quality group.

Safety was not mentioned at all in France, but there were isolated comments on the balance between security and freedom and the need for a level building. Personalisation and choice was mentioned in the balance of private and public spaces, individual rooms, and in respect of the provision of recreation spaces. There were also some more isolated comments.

In the UK a quiet and calm environment was highest rated by staff, followed by a homely environment, a choice of activities and comfort and spaciousness. Parameters that related to safety, including durability, received limited comments despite the fact that the service user group was more dependent and aggressive. Competence was mentioned only in relation to choice as a choice of activities, as again service users were more dependent than in France. Personalisation and choice received more extensive mention, if we include isolated comments on the balance between private spaces and those that favoured interaction as well as individual en suite rooms.

Additionally, as in France, the majority of spatial elements regarded design qualities: quietness, agreeable welcoming environments, homelikeness, comfort, cleanliness, spaciousness, bright, airy and naturally lit space and close to nature. To sum up, regarding both countries, quietness was the most frequently mentioned element for a therapeutic environment, followed by homelikeness, and then a nice, welcoming environment and choice of activity.

Moving on into the interior, the sufficiency of day areas, regarding opportunities to meet people or to withdraw, were discussed. As far as the day areas are concerned and their adequacy for promoting/enabling service user interaction, i.e., the socio-friendliness of day areas more than half participants replied positively, one third negatively and few considered some places as well designed. There was no major difference between the foyers and the acute wards on that subject, yet the sample of valid answers was limited in order to draw conclusions for specific facilities.

As for places where service users would go to relax, bedrooms were mentioned by the vast majority of staff members, followed by those who mentioned common areas other than a quiet room, and the quiet room or study received also some mentions. The garden/terrace was mentioned less. One explanation of these results was that quiet rooms or studies were not available in all facilities. The same could be argued about the gardens, as in fact not all of them had sheltered areas where service users could sit or in France where they were not available in two cases and they practically lacked an adequate number of sitting arrangements.

In each country about half of the participants, found the quiet spaces adequate. Also, half of the total sample, did not find spaces adequate, while the French were less clear on the subject. The units where staff tended to find quiet spaces adequate were Elan, Bois St Joseph, Forest Lodge, Small Heath and Albany Lodge. There was no immediate connection between these responses and the actual day spaces available. It could be said that staff in units with shared bedroom accommodation tended to be less satisfied. There was no detectable relation to population size, pathology stage or country, nor if service users could leave the ward, either. Even the existence presence of a quiet room did not guarantee that the staff would consider the unit as satisfactory in terms of private areas. Regarding more private areas, and more precisely bedrooms, besides their aforementioned role as withdrawal areas, staff discussed issues of privacy, and more precisely the en suite provision of a shower, the opportunity for service users to intervene in their personal space and the adequacy of storage for their personal belongings. In greater detail, most staff preferred en suite facilities for service users, some shared, few proposed a mixture and even less suite showers but retaining a common bath as well.

There was no clear pattern between staff replies and accommodation type, or quality of environment. For example, both Elan and Geraniums staff answered "en suite". This could be accounted for by the stage of the service users' illness. As the possibility of self-harm was higher among acute service users, staff might be more prepared to compromise as to the issue of privacy. However, safety was not mentioned as a justification but rather practicality, hygiene, maintenance and the need for supervision because of the difficulty service users had in washing themselves.

Almost half of staff in both countries supported that service users should be able to decorate their rooms, with two thirds from France. One fifth of staff regarded that service users should bring only personal belongings and small things, most coming from the UK. Almost a similar percentage, about equally distributed among the two countries, considered that service users could bring equipment and that interventions should occur within limits, but they did not define the limits. Few staff members in France, considered that service users should put pictures and posters only on framed, dedicated parts of the wall, to prevent damage. Also, a limited number in the UK, objected to service user interventions. Staff that did not approve of changes came mostly from New Bridges and the UK staff that were more open to suggestions on changes were from Forest Lodge, which was closest to the foyer concept and where service users tended to stay longer. There, in practice service users even brought furniture such as armchairs and a considerable number of personal belonging like books. Focusing on electronic equipment specifically, all staff agreed that service users should bring stereos into their rooms. Very few added that

TVs should be allowed but there were also those that raised concerns, most in the UK. There were also few concerns on the noise levels.

In France more staff members reported that the storage space available to service users was inadequate than those that found it sufficient. By contrast, in the UK more agreed that it was adequate. This could be relevant to the service user population, as service users closer to independence may have gathered more personal belongings or had not retained their homes, as they were supposed to be on longer stay than acute service users. Characteristically, Forest Lodge, where service users were closer to independence and had started going out as a first rehabilitation stage, was the only UK facility where most staff members considered storage to be inadequate, and one in particular commented that service users tended to have all their belongings there. Additional staff comments included that storage should be able to bear tough use and that service users lacked secure storage that could prevent thefts. Elan was the only case study where all the staff agreed that there was enough storage. Here the staff had contributed the experience from their former old building to the design of the new facility at the planning stage. Storage was carefully planned. Cupboards were unusually large and spacious, with a variety of shelves and drawers and substantial depth for service users to store suitcases. There were also chests of drawers and shelves plus shelves in the en suite bathrooms. Moreover, there were individual food lockers in service users' kitchenette.

7.3.3. Service users on personalisation and choice regime related issues

Regarding the psychosocial aspects of care and more precisely the elements that could contribute to increase service users' morale, there was considerable variation, allowing further grouping in broader categories. Non-spatial or environmentally related responses mainly comprised "people" (more if the response "children" was added), "going out", or "nature and views to the exterior", "organised activities" and "music". Spatial qualities that were reported as morale boosters for service users were a sense of friendliness and comfort, spaciousness in the ward, private bedrooms and plants and flowers in the ward. Other responses, like a drink at the bar downstairs or a glass of chilled water, or even the views from the ward could be translated into environmental qualities although also ward equipment.

Comparing between countries, non-direct environmental factors or factors that were not relevant to the ward/foyer environments, such as activity and nature or outings or therapeutic regime, were mentioned mainly by the French service users. UK service users gave more gravity to the ward environment and issues related to that, which was justifiable, as they tended to be ward-bound. Surprisingly though, nature that includes "views to nature" was mainly brought up by the French, strengthening the idea of the ward-oriented/introvert attitude of the acute service users.

Regarding the importance of environmental factors for service users, almost half found as most important non-building related issues such as interpersonal relationships, their independence or a pet. Second in the service users' hierarchy of importance regarding their environment was quality, including the atmosphere of their surroundings and relevant details. There was a difference in priorities between the two countries, with most of the French sample valuing as most important non-unit related issues, and fewer concentrating on quality of environment, with the UK having reversed priorities. Apparently, French service users had started building their bridges with the community, while many of the British service users were still wardbound.

Next was hygiene and tidiness issues, with eight service users in the total sample, yet this was the third shared priority with calmness, nature and opens spaces in France, and the fourth in the UK, sharing the position with comfort. Activity was the third priority in the UK, yet this was a very low priority for the French service users as it was mentioned by one case only. In the UK, calmness was lower on the list, followed by personal space. Nature and space could be added to the broader group of issues concerned with quality of environment.

A final issue relevant to personalisation and choice related policies that arose through the interviews, and more precisely relevant to privacy, was the gender policy of the foyers/wards. Similarly to staff, the vast majority of service users from both countries preferred mixed gender environments. Service users who answered single in France were mainly from Geraniums (a female only facility). In the UK, only one service user would prefer a male only ward. Reasons regarding normality, in the sense that in the broader social context genders mix.

7.3.4. Service users on personalisation and choice issues that were relevant to the space of the foyers/wards

Regarding the placement of the facility in order to fit service users' needs, the research explored the activities, unstructured or structured that service users were engaged in. The most popular activity in both countries was walking. It constituted almost a third of service users' responses in both countries, mostly for the French. The next most popular outing was shopping and visiting markets, which appealed to one fifth of the total population, mostly the British service users. Leisure places like cinemas, theatres clubs and museums appealed equaly to service users, mostly to the French. Cafes and restaurants, as well as family and friends came next. Nearby towns as well as sports appealed to some and next followed visits home. Education and health facilities scored rather low as well as work, trips and religious places. Finally, almost a fifth of the UK sample never went out.

The choices of service users were to some extent influenced by local geography and the availabilitof options. In facilities, especially in France where service users were voluntary, where more options were encountered in the locality, such as the case of Elan and Rene Capitant, as opposed to facilities that offered very limited options, such as Francois Tosquelles and Geraniums, service users were engaged in a broader network of activities including visits to museums and following educational courses at the university.

Regarding the appearance of the facility externally, the majority of service users preferred the unit to be fully integrated into the community or like home. About a fifth said they liked the building to be the way it was, somewhere between hospital and home, few more like hospital and even fewer would like the building to stand out. Those that preferred the hospital model all came from the UK. The French supported more strongly the homelike model, while some of the Elan service users preferred the unit to stand out.

Proceeding to the interior and the organisation of the facility, the vast majority of service users initially responded positively as to their satisfaction regarding the size of the ward. Satisfaction was almost evenly distributed between the countries. One fifth was divided between those that wanted more people around and those that wanted less. The actual size of the foyer was not related to the reply, neither was the fact of being in single or shared accommodation. For example, Bois St Joseph, which was by far the largest facility in term of service user numbers, had only positive answers and a service user there wanted more people around. Francois Tosquelles had very small choice of day areas and, since rooms were locked during the daytime, that could be a reason for the high percentage of negative answers. Geraniums had an extensive room-share, in triple rooms with limited privacy, but then again Albany Lodge was single room accommodation. Yet, the latter two had a relatively small percentage of negative replies. Isolated cases who wanted more people around came from various wards, including those of Geraniums.

When service users in the unit replied "as it is" they were asked more specifically if they wanted more or fewer people around and the result did not differ much, with only nine out of fifty service users wanting more or fewer people around. Those were almost equally divided again, but with service users in France giving more "fewer" answers, one of them in Francois Tosquelles, raising the number of negative answers in that facility to a ratio of 4/6.

The vast majority of service users had friends in the unit. The very few negative answers were equally divided between the two countries, yet not equally spread among the case studies, where for the UK Finch Ward accounted for all the negative replies. Lounges and bedrooms were the spaces where service users met their "unit-mates". The smoking room followed, mentions, which in some wards could be the same area as the lounge, as well as the TV room. The dining area was also a meeting point. In Geraniums, where two service users reported that they did not have friends in the facility, corridors were a rather institutional option. The music room and games room where available, could also gather people, as in the case of Finch Ward. In general, depending on the options available, service users tended to use several diverse places for their social life. The meeting places tended to be the places where service users would go if they felt lonely. In that case service users would try the social interaction areas, such as the lounges, the TV and smoking rooms as well as bedrooms, as both a place of retreat and not meeting people or as a place where they could host people as visitors to their room. Additionally, other service users' bedrooms were mentioned. There were also few service users that would try to find company in the staff room. The rest of the spaces, the music room, games room, kitchen or visitors' room, received fewer mentions as a place where service users would go to confront their loneliness issue. There were also few UK service users that did not specify a place, and one could not find any such a place in the facility. Also, some would go outside, most of those being in France. As with the previous responses to similar questions, the alternatives available were highly relevant to the geography of the ward and the ward policy regarding bedrooms.

Regarding the design of common areas related to various topics, from the size and shape of a room and the size of population it catered for, to furniture arrangement and decoration details, looking at each country separately did not shed a great deal more light on the responses.

In common areas, service users did not appear to mark specific areas as their own territory, a practice that is connected with institutions. More analytically, almost half of service users did not have a particular place where they sat, and about a third mentioned specific rooms but no particular seat in them and few would go anywhere but had a preferred chair or table mostly in the dining room. Yet, some service users preferred a seat mainly in the lounge. From those, one was in the UK, in Finch Ward, and the rest in France, spread among all the case studies with more replies in Geraniums and in Rene Capitant, the two most institutional facilities in France according to previous analysis.

Moving from the need for socialization to the need for retreat, and more precisely the spaces that service users preferred when they wanted to be on their own, the vast majority of service users stayed in their bedroom when lonely. Additionally, few went to bathrooms that were private areas too, even more than bedrooms and few replied "nowhere" which could either mean the bedroom or nowhere in particular. Some of the French might go out. The garden was the next preference, mainly in France. Almost all UK service users that replied that they went to their bedroom to be on their own and the vast majority gave bedroom as their only reply. UK service users were also the ones where the "nowhere" replies came from. There was no discernable pattern in the replies between single room accommodation or shared, yet the two wards where service users tended not to stay in the bedrooms had shared accommodation. In particular at Francois Tosquelles, only one service user went to the bedroom in lonely times, obviously not during bedroom closure times, because service users did not have access to bedrooms during the day with the garden as the main option.

In France the majority of service users stayed in their rooms at night and for a couple of hours during the day, with few service users going there only to sleep, while seven spent more time there, some for physical or mental illness reasons. In the UK service users were more evenly divided among those who did not withdraw much and those who spent many hours there, while the group who would go for few hours apart from at night was slightly smaller. In France it was necessary to take into account that quite a substantial proportion of the sample could not access their bedrooms during the daytime. Yet, there was no hint that service users spent most of their time in bed. Service users in facilities with single rooms did not spend much time in their rooms either.

Service users' most preferred activity in their rooms was listening to music. This had no connection with either single or shared room accommodation. Listening to music was mentioned by almost half the service users, followed by those who would read and those who preferred to have quiet or a siesta, and some that would watch TV or DVD. Few replied "nothing". The other activities received even fewer mentions in total, including writing, playing music, receiving people, sleeping, playing games, studying or tidying up. Dancing, playing with a pet, talking to a room-mate and staying alone were mentioned once.

Looking closely at the two sample groups, the French majority mentioned music, while the British equivalent was about a third, and the French had a higher percentage too regarding TV and DVD. Overall, apart from reading that was equally spread, the British tended to have more passive behaviour, like sleep, or doing nothing, as opposed to music and TV. Small scale variations, with limited mentions in total and those divided among the sample, were treated as non-indicative trends, yet these results suggested that individuals might have their own preferences regardless of country or stage of the illness. Regarding TVs and their percentage in acute wards, it could be that staff in the wards did not encourage them, and hence some service users did not have the option.

The vast majority of service users in both countries were happy with their bedrooms. This was even higher for French service users, with almost all replying positively. The negative responses were, in general terms, spread among the case studies for France, while in the UK the greatest service user dissatisfaction came from Albany Lodge and Small Heath, two wards with single bedroom accommodation. Small Heath had quite small bedrooms but the same could not be claimed for Albany Lodge. One of the Small

Heath service users complained about storage, which was small and there were no different alternatives, such as surfaces or shelves.

Yet, regarding single room accommodation, the vast majority preferred single room accommodation with the percentage rising among UK service users. The percentage of service users who preferred shared accommodation was for the UK only very small, while for France that rose to more than one fifth of the sample questioned. Looking at particular units, the one with more service users wanting shared accommodation was Rene Capitan, followed by Francois Tosquelles, and Geraniums. The significant majority of service users preferred en suite accommodation to but a quarter did not mind sharing. The French were more positive regarding en suite.

About two thirds of service users in France and the UK were satisfied with the size of their rooms, about one third and one fifth respectively found the rooms too small. Looking more closely at specific wards, the results did not follow a specific pattern. In France, half the service users in Francois Tosquelles, which had large double rooms, were dissatisfied. In Bois St Joseph, a few service users were dissatisfied, due to the fact that they were in smaller rooms, shared as well. By contrast, in Geraniums, where most service users were in triple bedrooms with not even private WC facilities, service users were satisfied with the size of the bedroom, while in Rene Capitan, which also had a large amount of triple accommodation, all service users found the rooms too small, even the single bed ones. In the UK, Albany Lodge which had quite spacious accommodation received answers equally spread among satisfied, average and dissatisfied service users. And apart from Albany Lodge and Small Heath, there was no pattern connecting responses about room satisfaction and size to any of the other characteristics of the wards.

Regarding furniture, the vast majority of the total service user population was satisfied with their bedroom furniture. French were even more satisfied than the British. Looking at specific units, once more the relative dissatisfaction of service users with their bedroom were again in Albany Lodge and Small Heath, where approximately half the service users were not satisfied. In France, the two wards where half the service users were not satisfied were Rene Capitan and Geraniums, which were very old buildings with old and torn furniture, so that the responses reflected the actual state of the environment.

About half the service users had not made any changes in their rooms. In the UK, the ratio constituted the majority of the service users, while in France the ratio was lower. On the other hand, there was a minority who effected several changes, the majority being in France. There was no significant difference between France and the UK for those who put pictures and posters on the walls and two in each country brought objects carpets or pieces of furniture. Only few re-arranged furniture, mostly in France. Most of "several changes" were reported in Elan and in Forest Lodge. Yet, even those sharing triple bedrooms in France brought objects.

A final issue when dealing with personalisation and choice issues concentrated on the opening of the facility towards the community as this was expressed by the reception of visitors. About visitors, almost a third in France and couple in the UK replied that they never received visitors. Some service users in France and couple in the UK, replied that they meet their visitors outside the unit. A fifth of the French service users and a third of the UK service users, received visitors in the common areas. Inside bedrooms, could happen in some instances in France and close to a third of cases in the UK, while at the entrance or in the garden was rare for France (3%) but a quarter of the UK service users. Visitors' room was the answer given only from Elan service users, where there was such an option and where the service users that replied to that question found that solution private enough. However, in that case the visitors' room was one of the most deprived areas of the foyer, and not welcoming from the architectural perspective. Interview rooms were mentioned by British and one British service user answered that s/he received visitors in the office. There were few service users in France who replied that visitors could not come inside.

Regarding whether the privacy that service users had during visits sufficed, the French sample was not adequate to obtain valid results. However, it should be mentioned here, that because the foyers were open, French service users could see visitors outside the facility if they wished, the foyer policy did not allow visitors on the premises, in which case that question was not applicable to them.

For UK service users this option was not always available as many among them were sectioned and could only leave the unit when escorted by staff or even not at all. Hence, in the UK that question was of more importance for the quality of life of the service users. Only very few service users did not have enough privacy during visits and 20 were satisfied with the privacy they got. It should be mentioned here that not all service users under section were allowed full privacy for safety or therapy reasons, or that their privacy was limited to specific individuals when staff decided so. Also, children were not allowed in mental health wards, so service users would see children either outside or at the entrance. There were also units that allowed service users to receive guests in their rooms, but that depended on the ward policy. Yet in cases where service users received visitors in common areas, that did not always reduce their sense of privacy, as was indicated by service users' responses from New Bridges.

7.3.5. Main findings on personalisation and choice

Regarding privacy issues, staff, especially in the UK, suggested that service user bedrooms should have en suite facilities. Additionally, staff in both contexts supported the idea of mixed gender facilities over single gender ones. As for infrastructure available to service users, all staff agreed on electronic equipment brought into the facility by service users but did not make a particular mention for internet connection – that was not as widespread at the time of the interviews. Staff considered personal storage for service users tended to be inadequate in foyers, yet one foyer case study was considered as an exemplar case among its staff, and sufficient for ward service users according to staff, unless those wards tended to cater for service users staying longer. Units that catered for longer stay had a greater need for storage space of a variety of types and sizes, where standard mobile wardrobes might not have the necessary space or depth.

Service user's territoriality issues that arose in the staff interviews concentrated on the areas available for service users to withdraw to. There were divided opinions on the adequacy of quiet areas/areas for service users to withdraw, with some tendency for staff of shared accommodation facilities to find quiet areas less satisfactory. Single bedroom accommodation was connected with adequacy of quiet spaces. Service users would mostly relax in bedrooms, but day areas could prove relaxing for service users according to staff.

There was some difference in the opinions of staff regarding service users decorating their personal space. The major trend among staff being that they should be able to do some decoration. Yet, French staff tended to be approving of more interventions than the UK staff, which tended to support that service users should bring personal belongings and small objects only.

Regarding socialisation, there was no evidence that service users' friendships were discouraged. Staff in both countries were satisfied with the design of social areas in terms of socio-friendliness. If service users were lonely, they had the use of a variety of options, with bedrooms being one of the main options, not necessarily linked with isolation. Both foyers and wards had sufficient day areas for service users to socialise in the opinion of most staff. Additionally, as mentally ill people find it hard to quit smoking, smoking had gradually been permitted in the wards. Staff, however, suggested that smoking should be allowed in designated lounges only. New data from the current situation would shed more light, though.

The last group of issues regarding personalisation and choice concerned the psychosocial aspects of space and the elements that could facilitate the reduction of stigma. To begin with, motivation for discharge was not spatially connected for most staff – even if service users' homes in the community were in poorer conditions for social, spatial or health-related reasons – but related to staff input and care programme, which needed more effort for the more stabilised stages, i.e., the foyers. Service users' willingness to leave was more "black and white" in acute care, according to staff responses, while in foyers staff needed to take the relevant steps and procedures to encourage service users to leave the facility.

Staff in both contexts tended to consider that the optimum foyer/ward environment should comprise more hospital than home-type traits, putting emphasis on safety and security rather than personalisation and choice related aspects. Regarding location, acute care staff prioritised a central position for the facility in relation to its catchment area. Additionally, in acute projects in health care schemes or in the vicinity of public amenities, people functioned defensively towards the unit, according to staff. Yet, inner city settings could provide anonymity and options for foyer service users' interaction with the community.

Proceeding to the interior of the foyers/wards on psychosocial perspectives of space, staff characterised a therapeutic environment mostly as calm and quiet, bright, airy and naturally lit, with a balance between private spaces and those favouring interaction. Overall, domesticity and quality related characteristics formed requirements that were so varied that there were no discernable differences between the countries. Additionally, both elements of stimulation and calmness were considered by staff as beneficial for service users, either as elements of the therapeutic regime or the environment, yet with French staff valuing stimulation more than calmness and vice versa for the UK staff.

Regarding service users' positions on privacy aspects, the majority of service users preferred single room accommodation, especially at the acute stage. However, some service users that were already sharing seemed to prefer sharing. There was no connection between the stage of a respondent's illness and single room provision and the propensity for them to stay in their room for many hours. The pattern of time spent in the room was mostly related to the ward. Acute service users tended to prefer passive or quieter activity but still, the priorities among the two groups were similar, with major preferences including listening to music and reading. Additionally, en suite accommodation was preferable according to service users, mostly among the foyer residents. Moreover, almost all service users preferred mixed gender facilities.

On service users' territoriality, areas for service users' retreat were mostly their bedrooms, especially for ward service users. Alternatively, for that purpose service users used a common room and less frequently the quiet room, a choice that could be influenced by the lack of designated areas such as quiet rooms in the case studies. Foyer service users made changes in their rooms more often than acute service users and in more private and spacious accommodation, foyer service users could be more involved in their room decoration. Regarding the territorial marking of spaces or furniture, service users in acute care and foyers tended not to have preferred places in the ward. However, occasionally in those where foyers scored high on institutional points and presented major institutional traits as seen in the previous chapters 5 and 6, service users might have had their particular chair or place on the sofa. Yet it was not clear if that was a territorial marking or an indication of personalisation of space.

Regarding socialisation and more precisely the size of the facilities, service users tended to agree with the ward numbers currently in their unit, irrespective of the stage of the illness, the country, the size of the facility and the number of service users per bedroom. There was a possibility that service users in wards where there was no choice of day-spaces and where service users had to be in the same room with no other alternative for most of the day, experienced an increased sense of crowding in the ward. But that needs more research for a definite answer.

Additionally on socialising, according to service users, service users tended to make friends in the facilities. They mostly met in lounges and then in bedrooms, which tended to be the areas service users would go to seek company if lonely. As far as the reception of visitors was concerned, the unit policies determined the framework available to service users. That varied from a dedicated visitors' room, common areas, bedrooms or no visitors allowed in the premises. For the acute service users, receiving visitors did not happen for at least some period of their stay if they were under section, which was quite frequently the case. As the number of service users having a visitors' room at their disposal did not enable statistical evaluation, one cannot know the true impact of such a room. Acute service users tended to be satisfied with the privacy they obtained regarding visits.

Next we will discuss the psychosocial aspects of the facilities and the elements related to reduction of stigma that were encountered in the service user interviews. To examine the foyers wards location to fit service users, one has to think of the elements of the urban network that service users use during their time out of the facilities. According to them, that involved mostly walking, visiting markets and leisure places for both samples, whilst cafes and restaurants as well as meeting family and friends were also high among foyer service user preferences. Regarding the desired degree of external, i.e., facade design, integration of the facility to its surroundings, the homelike appearance of the foyers/wards was more appealing to both service user groups, especially among the French service users.

Finally on the psychosocial aspects of space that related to the interior, service users in acute and post-cure facilities varied considerably regarding the morale boosters in their life in the units. Acute service users placed more weight on issues related to the environment of the facilities than the more stable ones. For the latter, going out, activities, interaction with other people and the therapeutic regime played a stronger role. Regarding environmental factors, friendliness, comfort and natural elements or views were the main morale boosters. Similarly, for foyer service users, the issues that the service users cared most about were relevant to life outside the unit. By contrast, acute service users gave more importance to the quality of their environment, and less to external factors. Service users tended to rate interpersonal relationships or their independence more than the quality of the foyer/wards environment, yet with acute service users valuing the latter more than the foyer service users. Service users appeared satisfied with the size of the ward they were in, irrespectively of its actual size and therefore the responses did not produce any indicative spectrum size of the wards/foyers as far as service users were concerned. French service users tended to be happier with the existing furniture, with some dissatisfaction appearing in the foyers where furniture was in poor condition.

Chapter 8

Conclusions

8.1. The cross cultural comparison

Facilities varied regarding policy, organization and architecture, indicating the unevenness of the mental health service provision and pointing to the lack of a clear model and path that service users could follow from the beginning of an acute episode to the return home and the follow-up there. This was partially a reflection of the complexity of the illness, as progress did not develop linearly and there were frequent recurring episodes and relapses, but it also illustrated the fact that the mental health services in both countries had not emerged from the experimentation phase, which would enable the development of a 'tried and tested' care model to have a more global implementation. From this, it is easy to understand that this variety of systems' options and approaches as well as the extent of local variations would be reflected in the architecture of the environments that housed these efforts. Architecturally, the cases were shown to differ along the dimensions of safety and security or privacy and autonomy (its opposite pole), in terms of the competence or dependency of the service users, and finally with respect to how personalisation and choice, as opposed to structure and regimentation, were incorporated into the buildings and care regimes studied. Many of these factors related to the design of and the stimulations provided by the built environment itself.

The ways in which safety was incorporated into the buildings depended on the characteristics of the service user group that they were required to house. The increasing severity of cases in most UK units brought them to the limits of their purpose and the lack of a comprehensive network of provision could result in compromises in the admission and discharge policy. In units that faced this reality, bed blockage increased the spectrum of illness stages that the wards were initially designed to cope with. Service users were more dependent in the UK, as they were closer to an acute episode, yet a lack of internal resources, inadequate staff presence and lack of a neighbouring supporting network, even in some facilities in France, led to institutional behavioural patterns and compromises with respect to service users' competence. By contrast, internal resources and locations that enabled a wide range of external activities and options to be offered to service users, combined with open ward policies, increased their integration into the community. Personalisation and choice also differed considerably in how this was interpreted by the various facilities studied, as these varied greatly from one another in terms of whether or not service users were expected to share a bedroom, the extent to which gender segregation was enforced, visitor policy, access to spaces and retreat or socialization options within their premises.

In that sense, safety and security were deemed to be more necessary and so there were more evidence in the UK, whereas competence aspects, in the re-integration sense, reflected more the purpose of the French foyers and so were manifested there to a greater extent. This could have been partially due to a fragmented approach to viewing mental illness, perhaps as a result of inadequate resources, which meant that decision-makers in both contexts had to deal with 'what was more urgent at the time'. They therefore seem to have placed a stronger focus on crisis containment at the beginning, hence the need for increased safety, and may have considered re-integration to be a secondary priority, to be dealt with later, once the physical danger was over and a return to the community was imminent, leaving psychosocial aspects as a less urgent priority to be dealt with even later, if or when resources would permit. However, this strategy would only really have worked well if the facilities had been housing an illness that evolved or responded to therapy positively and linearly, and perhaps also fast enough so that the stages in between that of the original acute stage and the eventual return home did not last so long that the service user to developed or adopted institutional behaviours or lost the skills necessary for conducting 'life as usual' in the community after the mental health episode was over. As this was clearly not the case with mental illness, which tends to have a more tortuous, unpredictable and non-linear trajectory, the prioritisation of safety and competence at the expense of the more life-affirming dimension of personalisation and choice can be regarded as having impoverished some of the environments that were studied.

Apart from this difference in the severity of the pathology of the service user population in the UK compared to France, and the fact that most UK units were closed, again due to the severity of cases, the fact that more rehabilitation tended to happen in the French units (as a rule, but not necessarily in all of the units that were studied) no major differences were detected, and especially no major differences in the psychosocial aspects, which, as we have seen, was the parameter that did not appear as straightforwardly pressing as the other two. As the least institutional unit (or the most domestic) according to the checklist was in the UK, pathology was not a sufficient reason to increase the institutional character of the buildings. Other differences concentrated on the location of the French units, which were more integrated in the community than those of the UK. However, even if the French service users were closer to rehabilitation, which was not a necessary requirement of the provision of activity functions in the premises, especially in cases where service users used external networks for that purpose.

8.1.1. Safety and security

Regarding the location of the facilities, foyers tended to be independent and adjacent or integrated to housing, whilst wards had different types of connections to the mental or general health care network, or occasionally to public network facilities that were related to security, such as police stations. By contrast, acute facilities did not have an immediate neighbouring connection to housing. This was supported by the fact that, regarding the location of the buildings, the UK cases scored higher in institutional points according to the checklist than the French ones. Staff and service users, however, did not place emphasis on safety and security issues regarding the location of the facilities. Acute care staff in the UK prioritised a central position for the facility in relation to its catchment area, and French staff rated the importance of the location as offering stimuli to the service users, such as a more central placement that was served by public transport.

According to service users, their preferences were for their time spent out of the facilities, which involved mostly walking, visiting markets and leisure places for both samples, whilst cafes and restaurants as well as meeting family and friends were also high among the preferences of foyer service users.

The safety of gardens and courtyards could be an issue for some of the foyers as well as the wards. In both contexts there were examples of gardens without fences around the perimeter or fences that were easy to trespass, a finding that broke with the institutional stereotype of a building contained by surrounding walls. Yet, the lack of security of those areas could result in locked doors to external areas or rules that prevented service users from using those areas in acute settings. There were also cases, either in urban contexts for foyers or in health care complexes for wards, where there was no garden or courtyard available or close to the ward entrance. In acute wards, the lack of secure external areas might exclude service users from having access to fresh air, and even if such areas existed, the lack of a shelter or a sitting arrangement could prevent service users from using it. However, a 'secure' external area meant different things among the wards, from 'fully enclosed' to just 'fenced'. From the staff perspective, the garden was important in places where service users tended to be ward bound, and it fell in the needs scale where they had access to open space. In more acute settings, it functioned as an opportunity for relaxation and passive activity and for more stabilised service users as an opportunity for gardening, sports or social activity such as meals. Service users, especially the ward-bound, used a garden when they had access to it according to their state of mind. More stable service users were less passive, or even did not use the garden at all if they went out during the day.

An additional restriction on access to the outside, particularly for sectioned service users, was the siting of the ward on an upper floor. Moreover, steps increased acute ward staff's difficulty in escorting people, or required them to run down the stairs behind somebody who was absconding. Foyers did not have such restrictions to service users' access to the outside and tended to develop over more floors than wards. In more detail, safety design was taken into account more in the staircases of the wards, where fire regulations were stricter as well. Stairs, and the existence of more than one storey, were raised as a problem from staff in both contexts. The number of storeys, however, did not seem to affect the staff's sense of safety.

Observability inside the foyers and the wards raised several safety and security issues. Occasionally, windows to overlook areas such as staircases, corridors or lounges were employed. There were also cases where CCTVs controlled the entrance, a practice that would have sounded institutional in the past but which would appear to have lost its custodial reference as it appears in public buildings and even housing nowadays. Alternatively, the office doors remained open, compromising staff's privacy and confidentiality. In the wards, the office or the nursing station tended to have a better control of the entrance, yet staff still had to leave the door open, unless confidential issues had to be discussed. The change in what staff considered to be best practice, -i.e., to have the door closed for confidentiality and concentration on the job that needed to be done in the office - indicated that there were compromises being made in the operation of the unit on a day to day basis, either because of the inadequate design of the facilities regarding natural and unforced observation or perhaps because there were insufficient staff to attend to the ward whilst doing administrative work at the same time.

Arrangements varied regarding the degree of privacy vs. control that the buildings afforded, ranging from a glazed nursing station close to the entrance, to a reception point with glazing to watch the entrance, to an open reception or an office close to the entrance and even an office in a separate part of the building. Staff opinions regarding the nursing station or the staff office were divided too. Monitoring equipment for the entrance was a common demand among staff in both contexts. In open units, the emphasis was placed on the control of the entrance, whilst in most wards just controlling the entrance or the entire ward from a single point did not suffice. Round mirrors were avoided.

Finally, a very important aspect of the safety of the service users was staff observation at night, especially in acute facilities. In wards, staff checked inside the rooms, and agreed with this practice, despite the presence of observation panels that were deemed necessary. Architects used a variety of means to lessen the effect of service users' loss of privacy through observation panels. However, even in most foyers staff made rounds at night. Service users tended to prefer having their door closed or locked at night; the acute mostly felt safer that way, whilst the rest reported feeling more comfortable.

A corridor layout could cause problems in most wards, either being inadequate, with doors opening against the corridors' width and natural movement flow, or because of obstacles in the form of fixtures that service users could hold on to when staff needed to escort them, or twisty parts and parts with poor visibility. In foyers, these issues were not really a concern. By contrast, staff admitted difficulties in emergency situations due to the presence of narrow and twisting corridors in almost all the UK case studies but this problem was not reported in the foyers.

Regarding architectural detailing and safety, there were fittings and fixtures related to safety that were encountered only in the wards, and those consisted of windows with restricted opening and unbreakable glass, bedroom doors that opened outwards to avoid barricading, plastic mirrors and non-weight bearing hangers - sometimes at lower than the normal height as well - and curtains. Also, alarm buttons and personal alarms were employed in most wards. According to staff, buildings for more unstable service users needed more alterations to improve safety, even though the checklist had demonstrated that they were already designed to include a greater number of secure and institutional features. Alterations that staff considered necessary involved several details of the buildings, instead of few details that could form a general rule. Foyers, on the contrary, appeared adequately safe and staff rarely had to resort to any alterations to improve safety after the opening of the foyers. Service users, and especially ward service users, tended to be satisfied with the safety levels in the premises and there was no clear, statistically important information regarding details that needed attention because they were possible hallucination triggers that needed to be avoided.

Seclusion rooms were occasionally parts of the wards, either in a direct connection with the service users' bedroom area, which caused emotional distress to service users, or far from it, in the staff office areas, which appeared less institutional but proved difficult when violent service users needed to be transported. The existence of a toilet in a seclusion room raised safety issues and had to be removed. There was no substantial data to support the necessity of a seclusion room in the wards, something that could be addressed in subsequent research.

Regarding maintenance of the wards, where the risk of harm and self-harm was higher, staff tended to respond to damage fast. In France, occasional poor conditions in facilities were mostly the result of the effects of time on some buildings that had not been not renovated in the last 30-40 years, rather than damage caused by incidents of violence. Service users in both countries were concerned about poor condition and maintenance, with hygiene being the commonest concern, and they also reported problems from odours.

8.1.2. Competence

There was a great deal of difference between the two contexts in respect of the activity available to service users, something that could be explained by the fact that foyers' service users were closer to independence. Foyers tended to present a great variety of options among themselves in dealing with activity, from extended provision inside to no internal activity whatsoever. In the latter case, when foyers tended to be located in urban areas, there was opportunity for a variety of external activities and options in the community. In rural areas, however, external options could be scarce to non-existent. In wards on the other hand, activity options tended to be limited and external options were not accessible to many service users. Foyers also varied in the spaces available for internal activity - from several equipped areas to one activity room that was not designed according to its purpose. Activity was even observed taking place in the common areas of one foyer - whereas in most wards it mostly took place in the common areas, especially if the ward was sharing grounds with a day centre, and the presence of a dedicated activity room was rare.

According to staff in both contexts, facilities needed more internal activity spaces and equipment. Staff considered that the location of foyers needed better to address service users' needs by providing more integration and activity opportunities. Focusing on the type of activity, the majority of staff deemed both internal and external occupations as necessary. There were divergences among staff in regard to the proportion of activity that should be provided within the unit as opposed to outside it, with staff working with acute service users opting for more ward-based options. This tended to shift towards more external activity options when service users approached more independent living. Here it should however be mentioned that ward staff perceived that structure, and especially activity, presented a challenge to service users at more acute stages. Acute and foyer service users' perception of needs regarding activity also differed, with foyer service users expressing their dissatisfaction more. Acute service users could attribute to activity some compensation for the fact that they could not go out and for the boredom they encountered in the wards, whereas foyer service users mostly complained about the lack of activity. Notwithstanding, service users tended to be satisfied with the type of activities on offer, especially OT, but they would like sports to be included as an option. In general though, the less exposure service users had to the community the more this increased their appreciation of the activity on offer, whereas service users that spent much time externally bothered less about internal activity.

Besides structured activities, the research also investigated two major types of activities that were not necessarily structured but were essential for everyday life: food preparation and personal space maintenance. Concentrating on the everyday activity of food preparation, the spatial configuration varied from a preparation room without a cooker to having both a professionally equipped kitchen and a homelike one. Cooking arrangements were unrelated to the stability of service users and their proximity to independence, and service users' involvement varied from nothing - even the lack of a kitchenette to prepare a beverage or have a glass of water - to cooking meals for everyone in professional kitchens. Staff objected to the practice of service users providing the ward meals in a professional kitchen, and did not regard everyday meal preparation as an indication of progress, but they also maintained that service users could individually use a domestic kitchen under supervision. However, a considerable number of staff considered that cookers were unsafe. Similarly, if food needed to be cooked in the unit or reheated there, there was no clear agreement among the service users as to how the service should be provided, with a small tendency for acute service users to want to be involved in food preparation. The microwave was proposed as an alternative by some of the staff and service users.

So far as the unstructured activity of bedroom maintenance was concerned, domestic staff were employed to clean service users' bedrooms in both acute wards and foyers. That applied even in facilities where service users worked or followed day-care programmes outside. Staff and service user opinions agreed with the current state regarding maintenance.

Foyers varied regarding the flexibility of areas used: from specialisation of areas with no multiuse to extended multiuse or even flexibility as a result of sharing premises. Neither of these options was found in the UK. By contrast, the UK could occasionally present tendencies that were reminiscent of the 'core and cluster' model, be they several wards at the periphery of a day centre or other community care facilities open to external service users as well, which was achieved by breaking larger organisations into smaller domestic units and providing external administration or support facilities for them to share. Yet, problems in the implementation of this model, such as a lack of staff to escort service users, prohibited the interaction of the wards with their adjacent day centres and tended to make the services provided inaccessible to ward service users. By contrast, the 'core and cluster' model appeared more successful in independent in-patient schemes that removed the administration and OT to the periphery spatially, while it remained centrally as provision, as it axially served clusters of in-patient accommodation, all however connected under one management. The latter could be a factor that contributed to the apparent success of this option. Staff barely mentioned issues related to the 'core and cluster' model. Only the lack of a female-only area was raised by three UK staff members and there was an isolated mention of the problems that rose from multiuse.

Regarding the sense of orientation, mental health facilities often had double loaded blind corridors in combination with deep cores, sometimes even in wards that accommodated small number of service users. Large complex layouts could however increase that phenomenon of loss of orientation. The lack of focal or reference points or local colour schemes was not used in those cases to alleviate the disorienting effect of the layout. Furthermore, the existence of turning points with no areas of focus or the twisting form of the aforementioned spinal or dark corridor recessions, accentuated the problem. It is important to note that the latter two effects were created purposely to break down the long hospital corridor references, but instead created areas of poor visibility that could increase anxiety, could function as hiding places and causing difficulties to staff escorting service users during a crisis. Similarly, fire doors could interrupt the opportunity to walk naturally in a corridor by breaking continuity.

On the contrary, open organisations that allowed external views and local sitting areas with or large windows in corridors enabled a good sense of orientation. Additionally, linearly developed single-loaded corridors with external views eased orientation and introduced daylight. This type of solution, resulting in longer corridors, could be seen by architects as bearing institutional references, as they could be related to the stereotype of the long hospital wards/corridors. One has nevertheless to recognise in that case that those long corridors provided ward-bound service users with the opportunity for walking. In a foyers, where service users had the opportunity for walks outside, smaller, compact layouts with external references resulted in a building in which it was easy to orientate. Yet despite the fact that from the architectural research on the layouts, the absence of layout simplicity, legibility and ways for daylight to enter the buildings' core was clear, orientation difficulties were seldom mentioned by staff and not at all mentioned by service users among the problems they encountered in the foyers or the wards. However, staff and service users expressed the sense of danger aroused by dark or twisty building cores.

Regarding physical accessibility, UK facilities had accessibility provisions (i.e., the buildings had been designed to some extent to cater for disabled building users), yet there was still room for improvements. On the contrary in France, accessibility issues, both those that concerned sanitary facilities and vertical communication, were frequently neglected. Staff said that service users tended to be peripatetic, yet most of them had encountered problems with service users that for mental health pathology reasons needed assistance when bathing. The majority of service users preferred ordinary bathrooms, as opposed to accessible ones, and very rarely were staff or service users concerned about stairs.

8.1.3. Personalisation and Choice

Privacy was a major psychosocial element that related to many expressions of the life in the facilities and involved many areas as well. Privacy in bedrooms differed between the two countries. In the UK there was an increased tendency for single room accommodation, both as an upcoming trend and as what the fieldwork indicated, whilst in France foyers presented greater diversity, between single or shared accommodation, and the research identified facilities that offered a choice of single rooms, double share accommodation and even triple share occasionally (though this was in older foyers that had not been renovated) as sometimes service users might choose the cheaper option of sharing. Staff in shared accommodation facilities tended to find service users' withdrawal opportunities less satisfactory than in facilities that provided accommodation in single rooms. Staff and service users also preferred single room accommodation over shared bedrooms, especially in the UK, yet service users that were already sharing tended to be satisfied with that arrangement. The propensity for UK service users to stay in their room for many hours was mostly related to the design and operation of the ward and not to the stage of their illness. However, acute service users tended to prefer passive or quieter activities more often than those who were well on the way to recovery, but the priorities among the two groups were still similar, with major preferences including listening to music and reading. Regarding sanitary facility provision in bedrooms, en suite shower accommodation throughout was limited. Some en suite showers were found but the most common observed solution was a basin in the bedroom instead. Under the same prism of reduced privacy, foyers could have bathrooms with more than two showers. Elsewhere, a lack of mirrors in service users' bedrooms encouraged service users to use common washing facilities for personal grooming. Here it should be mentioned that the provision of those facilities did not per se determine quality in private space. Unique cases related to privacy in sanitary facilities, included the freestanding toilet in triple-rooms in France, which was an extreme case, and in another there was more than one basin or toilet cubicle in the common bathrooms, which indicated the degree to which some institutional remnants could still find their way into today's world. Moreover, in another UK example, bathrooms opened directly onto the main corridor. On the other hand, for the rest of the projects the self-cleaning toilet in one foyer was considered a luxury. Also, in one case special consideration had been given to how staff might observe service users through the clever use of a mirror in combination with using the sanitary facilities to protect the privacy of the bed area, satisfying both the increased needs for observation and lessening this intrusion on privacy. The aforementioned examples indicated the major inequalities and differences, even in the same country, between institutional practices and best practice examples met in mental health facilities. Regarding privacy issues, staff, especially in France, suggested that service users' bedrooms should have en suite facilities. The tendency for French staff to recommend en suite bathrooms as compared to the UK could be accounted for by the stage of the service users' illness, as the possibility of self-harm was higher among acute service users and some staff might be more prepared to find a compromise regarding the issue of privacy. Service users, mostly in France, preferred en suite showers and this tendency would have been even higher if finances were not concerned.

In respect of storage for service users' personal belongings, the only form of locker that afforded some privacy for service users regarding their personal belongings was an isolated case and concerned individual food-lockers. On the contrary, occasionally there were lockers for staff. According to staff, storage tended to suffice in acute facilities, yet where service users stayed longer they tended to have more personal belongings and the existing storage was then deemed to be inadequate, in size or variety that could accommodate a range of possessions from small objects to large suitcases. Service users tended to be satisfied with the available storage, yet they were concerned about thefts and the fact that people could enter their rooms during their absence and steal from them, as rooms could not be locked or domestic staff would forget to lock them.

Regarding access to telephones, service users had personal land-lines only in one foyer and the rest of the facilities had public payphones with limited privacy, and only occasionally was there some seating arrangement there. Incoming calls were taken either by the staff office or the reception. Access to public computers was provided only in facilities that had IT workshops. However, staff agreed about the desirability of electronic equipment that could be brought into the facility by service users, yet there was no mention of an internet connection.

Finally on privacy issues and regarding the gender policies, in the UK at that time, the tendency was for mixed gender wards -although there were talks about changes to this policy as well as the provision of single gender areas within mixed gender wards. In France, there were either single or mixed gender foyers, as well as mixed gender comprising of single gender parts with single gender sitting arrangements, even though in these cases there was no strict policy that those common parts could not be used by both genders. In most mixed gender facilities, in both contexts, at the time when the fieldwork took place there was no provision for single gender sanitary facilities. This is lately undergoing change in the UK, as latest policies favour single gender wards or shared ones that provide for single gender sanitary facilities or a female only lounge at least. Staff and service users in both contexts supported the idea of mixed gender facilities over single gender ones, yet a few staff stressed the need to prevent relationships among service users as this could interfere with individual care programmes.

Regarding the psychosocial aspect of service user territoriality and more precisely the areas available for service users to withdraw to, staff in single room accommodation found quiet spaces more adequate, whilst staff of shared accommodation was more concerned with adequacy of quiet spaces. According to staff and service users, service users (especially those of wards) tended to retreat mostly to their bedrooms, followed by the use of common rooms, as quiet rooms were not always available, and in that sense their actual use could not be checked. Staff tended to suggest that service users should be able to do some decoration, with French staff being approving of more interventions than the UK staff, who limited interventions to personal belongings and small objects only. That was in accordance with service users' practice, as foyer service users made changes to their rooms more often than acute service users, especially if they had more private and spacious accommodation. Regarding territorial marking of areas by service users, there was no indication of such practices in the wards, yet such indications regarding specific chairs or sofas could occur in those foyers that scored high on the checklist's institutional scale.

Regarding areas available for service users to socialise, there was a great variety in provision that was unrelated to the type of the facility being studied. Facilities differed regarding the square metres of common areas per service user but these did not determine issues such as the variety of those areas, the quality of space, including comfort, and the actual room arrangements, i.e., if they were socio-petal or socio-fugal, which were very important to service users' decisions not only to use the space but to participate in social life and engage in interpersonal relationships with other service users. For example, the actual - relatively large - amount of common areas per service user did not prevent service users from forming queues outside offices in the corridors, claiming staff attention, but this activity mainly occurred in facilities that scored low on the checklist. Alternatively, in areas that had amongst the highest amounts of common area per service user, the furniture allocation could be such that service users could not be guaranteed a seat there or could not even relax there, if structured activity could exert a prior claim upon the area.

Overall, there was a great variety regarding common areas among the case studies: sometimes the common areas were compact, gathering all day activities, or they could be divided into more specialised areas such as dining rooms, main lounges, smoking lounges or quiet rooms or even games rooms or studies, offering more choice but then again being different from the homelike model of a dining room and a lounge. There was variety in the importance they received in the layout, from being centrally placed in the life of the facility to areas developing in the core of the building or in the basement lacking direct sunlight and views. There were cases where attention was paid to comfortable seating area furnishings: sofas, coffee-tables and soft lighting, and cases where service users had to open folding chairs to sit on for the sake of multi- use, or standard NHS waiting room chairs placed around the walls. These antitheses were not country - or facility - related as they could be met in both contexts. In short, common areas did not always function as socialisation opportunities as they could have done, an outcome that could be related to the therapeutic regime and structure, or the decoration of those areas could ignore homelike factors that could otherwise have encouraged service users to consider them as places to relax in or socialise rather than as 'waiting rooms'.

Service users' friendships tended to be encouraged by staff, and most service users admitted having friends in the foyers/wards -yet the social factor of service users conducting friendships could decrease in wards/foyers that scored low on the checklist in terms of "Room and Space" features, where acquaintances were made mostly in lounges, but also in bedrooms. Service users tended to be satisfied with the service user numbers currently in their unit, irrespective of the actual size of the facilities. Yet, in wards that had no choice of day-spaces, an increased sense of crowding could be experienced. Overall, staff in both countries tended to be satisfied with the sufficiency in terms of size and the design of social areas with regard to socio-friendliness. The smoking lounges though, tended occasionally to be small for the number of service users that used them. Staff suggested service users should be able to smoke in dedicated lounges but the rest of the premises should remain smoke free.

Additionally on the subject of service user socialisation and in particular their connections with the community, the visitors' policy should be mentioned. This was not related to the facility type, but was mostly dictated by the management's position and the structure the facility desired to obtain. Policies varied from no access to visitors inside the foyer/ward, especially where service users spent a substantial proportion of their day outside, to visitors' access in dedicated visitors' rooms, in the core or attached to the in-patient area. These were sometimes equipped with coffee making facilities, and placed at the entrance so that children could visit and have access to the common areas or even occasionally to the bedrooms. Sometimes staff attributed the origin of their problems to a service user's family, and for that reason staff had to be more cautious regarding visits at early acute stages, and other staff said that service users would like to be able to bring people into their bedrooms, which as a rule was not encouraged in most cases, but more data would be necessary to define staff position on visiting policies.

At the same time, the rest of the service users, according to staff opinions, needed to retain their privacy - as opposed to other people's visitors intruding in the life of the ward - especially since most of the facilities lacked a dedicated visitors' area. Acute service users, which were the ones that most of the time could not leave the premises, tended to be satisfied with the privacy they obtained regarding visits, even if for some of them restrictions applied to their privacy because of their pathology or if there was a lack of a dedicated area to meet visitors as much as possible in private. On the contrary, some service users much closer to the return to the community, especially in foyers with younger people, might prefer bringing visitors to their bedrooms.

The remaining psychosocial elements that this research dealt with concerned the appearance of the exterior, as regards the interface of the wards/foyers with the community, and the messages - much related to stigma - conveyed by the exteriors as well as the atmosphere of the interiors. The facades of the wards and the foyers were very much determined by their location in relation to the health care service or the community. As foyers were embedded in the community, and even in residential complexes, they tended to merge better with their surroundings than the wards, which tended to be integrated in extensive health/mental health care schemes, as clusters to variations on a 'core and cluster' type of health care model. This appeared clearly in the architectural checklist, where only wards that developed independently -spatially-speaking - from health care schemes achieved a more homelike appearance. The independent location in the community for the foyers, however, was of its own right sufficient for the building to achieve an integrated facade, as here the architects' intentions towards greater or lesser integration in the neighbourhood played their part, from the placement of the building in the plot, to the breaking of its volumes and details such as facade materials or openings.

For staff, mostly in the UK, issues concerning safety and anti-ligature elements and the control of were more essential than homelikeness. For foyer staff mostly, one-way integration was important - to cultivate service users' bonds outside rather than bringing the community in - and at the same time this strategy was seen to protect the territoriality zone of the facility from vandalism, NIMBYism and intrusions as well as helping to manage service users' decent behaviour externally. In short, staff in open facilities were mostly concerned with the social interface of the foyer and the neighbourhood. Staff did not make any connections with the actual appearance of the building, whether that was achieved through more homelike detailing or through the reduction of stigma through 'blending in' with the surrounding buildings. Both service user groups, especially the French, favoured the integration of the facility to its surroundings, as for them the homelike appearance of the foyers/wards was more appealing.

8.2. Further research

The fieldwork has concentrated on two specific countries, France and the UK and despite the fact that few culturally-related differences were identified, the context has proved important for the perception of what 'domestic' means. In that sense, direct analogies to other geographical contexts might need a more thorough examination in order to be translated to another geographical context, especially if variation in the mental health service provision differentiates the needs of the particular service user group.

This was a people-centred study that investigated what people, service users or staff perceived as most beneficial for the service users. In that sense, the findings might have been limited due to hidden motives or other personal fears or restraints the respondents experienced in expressing their inner thoughts. In any case, it was not a controlled epidemiological study based on service users' behaviour before or after spatial interventions. The latter would be feasible only if the study investigated specific spatial parameters, instead of the whole spectrum of the domesticity concept.

Having decided to address the major and overarching topic of how the analogy of domesticity was interpreted for the building type, and the extent to which it was either relevant or useful as a design intention, the study had to cover a plethora of topics. It therefore could not go into great depth in researching each and every one. In that sense, research in depth on specific subjects such as a more precise investigation of the facility's size, or more detailed research on the types and the spaces required for internal activity could be the next step.

Neither did it deal in detail with issues such as colours or lighting that might need epidemiological research tools as well as qualitative environmental evaluation techniques in order to measure the specific impact of those parameters on the pathology or the well-being of service users. Under the same prism, it did not cover art, which is strongly promoted in the design of health care facilities, and has an allocated percentage of the building's budget in several western countries such as the UK or Sweden. However, as previous research on the architecture of community mental health facilities was very limited, the study did cover a broad spectrum of questions, including general planning aspects such as the location and the general organization of the services provided, as well as the overall concept on the definition and measurement of the concept of domesticity and many detailed aspects of the design and equipping of the building. As such, it has provided answers to many of the assumptions and also the more contentious issues regarding architecture for people with mental health problems, and has established a robust foundation on which to base future architectural research.

8.3. The significance of architecture and design

The findings support the view that architecture and design are important and vital parts of the recovery process, and not just an inert physical setting in which this recovery can take place. Current architectural thinking and research in health care environments in general supports the view that the recipients of care as well as employees are aware of and influenced by the architecture and design of the buildings they inhabit. This project has shown that architectural decisions regarding the design of mental health units have direct implications for the policy and the organization of the ward, as spatial issues might influence the function of the facility. It therefore confirms the view that architectural design has a significant role to play in aiding patients' recovery, boosting staff morale and enhancing the quality of life of both user groups.

Normalisation theory has hitherto been considered by many experts to be a useful tool in the design of mental health facilities, as it could provide an alternative framework of assumptions that would allow questions to be raised about the previous medical model. Normalisation was thought to minimize stigma and institutional references and therefore facilitate the re- integration of the mentally ill in the community. Normalization theory focused very much on the need to reduce stigma and the psychosocial aspects of care. However, one should bear in mind that this return to the community and in particular the return home, came with arguments about its reduced costs compared to specialized care and provided attractive arguments for cutting down on the expenses that were normally associated with mental health care provision, especially when more life threatening or chronic diseases, such as cancer, coronary illness or diabetes claimed funding from health care systems. In that sense, low cost as opposed to specialized care solutions gave normalization theory a very attractive profile.

With the benefit of hindsight, it is possible to see that normalisation theory may have been overly-prejudiced against clinical intervention and underestimated the complexities of therapeutic needs and rehabilitation interventions, which could not always be addressed in environments organized as homes. Consequently, it could not necessarily provide the necessary flexibility in the application of its principles, so that it could include service users' specific needs and their environmental implications. Oversimplifications of the theory, i.e., a direct application of residential architecture principles in acute contexts, or the exclusion of therapeutic activity interventions from accommodation facilities, could considerably compromise the therapeutic role of those environments.

There is a fine line between a therapeutic space and a homelike space. While a hospital might carry the stigmatizing semiology of the past, it still involves the idea of therapy and the possibility of cure. In mental health facilities, service users have to know that they are there for a reason and that this is the place that they came to in order to be able to move on in due course, to less protected accommodation. Home is the final step of the procedure, so it may raise confusion in the minds of some service users about the work done in the units, if the unit itself looks too homelike. Yet, evidence suggested that a poor quality environment did not increase the effectiveness of the place; on the contrary, a high quality environment was related to increased service user and staff satisfaction.

Service users' realization that they were not in a permanent condition but in a transition to the next level of care, was more related to the therapeutic regime and policy than to the design of the building. The buildings therefore should rather facilitate the therapeutic interventions of both medical, nursing/nurturing and psychosocial nature, enabling best practice, rather than aim to replace those by acting as the conveyors of ideological messages and staff then having to adjust what they aim at as best practice because the space hinders it: if staff locks access to courtyard because of absconding or drug-trafficking incidents there is perhaps something wrong with the design of the courtyards, or if staff reclaim a service users' bedroom to create a staff area it could mean that staff areas were inadequately planned from the start, and if staff cannot prepare a dish with service users in the kitchen it is perhaps because the kitchen design did not meet the specifications for that purpose. The excuse often used by architects that 'staff do not bother to perform their job' is by no means an excuse for failing design practices, neither is staff shortages an excuse for architectural solutions that did not take them into consideration from the outset. In short, if staff has to change what they consider as best practice because of the building, it might also mean that the building hinders its purpose and that compromises have to be made out of necessity, and where there is lack of resources more investment in thinking at the design stage might be the indicated course.

Since from its historic onset community mental health care was seen as the replacement of the hospital and the return of service users to home, it was to some degree expected that this debate between the hospital ward and home should form the axis of the mental health care accommodation buildings debate, with hospital and home occupying the two ends of this axis. Yet, home, was inadequate as a structure to address the parameters of an integrated form of mental health care, and this was clearly experienced by staff and service users. At the other end, an environment that was too clinical, such as the hospital ward, did not accord with the nature of mental health illness, which is not related to physical dependency. In the latter, normalization theory could be of assistance as it contains the idea of domestic elements for the reduction of stigma and the psychosocial support of the service users. In that sense, the idea of bringing in the nurturing design elements of domesticity where appropriate could be envisaged, where they do not contradict other important elements that are parts of the complexity of mental health care. This is especially important as the trajectory of mental health is rarely experienced as a linear one from ill health to wellness, but is rather characterised by unpredictable and episodic phases of progression and regression. This places additional demands on buildings, which need to be particularly responsive and adaptable to a wide range of service users' needs.

Therefore, the architecture of mental health facilities should be a hybrid of a domestic and a health care environment, which also takes into account the rehabilitation procedures at the earliest possible stages of their involvement in the mental health system and where a domestic atmosphere and organisation plays a key role, but where also the three parameters model of safety, competence and personalization and choice is taken into account as a basic therapeutic element, which according to service users' pathology and care regime implies the relevant architectural and design adaptations.

Going into more detail into the three parameters, their role is essential for viewing mental health buildings in an integrated fashion, as they bring together the major aspects existing in today's pre-paradigmatic design framework, where there is no stable and agreed architectural stereotype or design prototype to guide the process from strategic briefing towards a design solution. Safety and security, which is the parameter that corresponds most closely to a model of the medical aspects of care, and therefore relates to the specialists' interventions that underpin the treatment of medical symptomatology and address the issue of dangerousness, can be seriously compromised by normalization theory as currently applied in acute care environments and to some extent in foyers as well. Staff and service users stressed their concern about the compromises that appear to have been made about the safety of their environment and the related issues such as that of observability, upon which considerable emphasis was placed. It was clear that inadequacies in addressing safety through design resulted in changes to the regime towards more institutional directions, such as limiting the service users' access to activity or to the open air, and therefore compromising service users' competence and psychosocial needs.

Competence on the other hand refers to the rehabilitation aspects of mental health care necessary to counter the disabling effects of the illness and the results of institutionalization. Under normalization theory, the place of those efforts is mainly at the periphery of accommodation, at least so far as structured activity is concerned. Under this prism, rehabilitative activities do not belong in the narrow concept of home, as organized activity and education in a normal context take place outside the domestic premises. However, as the mentally ill spent considerable amount of their time in acute care environments under section, in accommodation that was intended to be 'normal' and that therefore did not provide any additional facilities, they were denied access to structured rehabilitation services that required organized space for them, unless there were the human resources to transfer them safely to those areas, and the research indicated that for the time being at least, this was not the case. These conditions result in boredom, which was one of the major problems encountered by service users in the service, as well as further skill loss and increased passivity, all of which are strong elements of institutionalization.

The same could happen to open facilities, which, because of their location in the periphery of the service as can happen in rural areas, cannot practically have access to the necessary spectrum of services in their immediate locality. So, instead of a normal environment reducing the institutional factors, it may further promote the incapacitating effects of inactivity and inadequate stimulation, through the lack of opportunity that a more specialized environment designed to support and reinforce service users' competence would provide. The excuse for that particular lack of provision, that rehabilitation starts after stabilization, has by now long been considered as obsolete, as current thinking aims at the re-integration of the service users from the beginning of the crisis, shifting the nature and the intensity of the interventions according to service users' progress.

Finally, the parameters of personalization and choice, which refer to the psychosocial aspects of care and the reduction of stigma, could benefit from normalization principles, as they incorporate domestic aesthetics or qualities, such as not sharing bedrooms or sanitary facilities with strangers, or being able to relax in the lounge without the intrusion of other people's visitors. However, personalisation and choice still need comply with the previous two parameters, in order to enhance service users' quality of life. Where this delicate balance is achieved, and as this research has indicated a reconciliation of all the parameters is feasible, this can promote therapy. Yet, even in this final parameter a totally 'domestic' solution is not what is required -as in this way visitors would indeed remain in the main lounge-but 'domestic looking in appearance' is perhaps the more appropriate term.

In this sense, bedrooms should have curtains, although admittedly these cannot bear weight in acute environments to comply with safety, because as well as protecting service users' privacy from the exterior they also enable service users to control their exposure to natural daylight as well as giving the room a domestic touch. When specifying elements of interior decor such as curtains, however, it is important to pay attention to matching them with the bedspreads if that is what domesticity would mean in that geographical context, and have them in different colours or patterns among service user bedrooms instead of going to an institutional, uniform or even 'buy in bulk' approach. Counteracting homogeneity is one way in which domesticity could make a useful contribution. Providing mirrors in the bedrooms is another example, even if they need to be unbreakable in acute environments, because this ensures that service users do not need to leave their bedroom without being well-groomed, if they do not wish to do so or because they feel uncomfortable in performing intimate acts of personal grooming in a shared, and therefore more public, bathroom.

In similar vein but at the opposite end of the architectural spectrum in terms of building scale and appearance, personalisation could equally-well mean taking care that the new facility merges with the surroundings in a way that does not compromise the rest of the parameters, such as safety for instance, by incorporating dangerous balconies within the facades, or by such a simple gesture as that of removing the sign at the entrance to indicate the purpose of the facility, as this truly does not serve any practical purpose but costs service users' their anonymity.

Providing a comprehensive list of all the possible ways in which the three parameters could be translated into design choices and best practice examples is well beyond the scope of this research, as there are literally hundreds of design choices to be made in order to specify even the simplest building. With this in mind, the main message to result from this research is that the design of residential architecture for the mentally-ill is not just about critically looking generically at the broader framework nor even about providing individual tailored solutions to case-specific problems. The designer should have the model in mind, and use the checklist, that is in fact a list of design questions that need design decisions, as a possible useful reference tool. The message is about the need to change attitudes and challenge existing assumptions in order to develop more reflective and responsive architectural practices.

Moreover, the buildings that responded better to the therapeutic regime were the ones that involved a planning team that included users, from the beginning. The team could go through the design decisions having the three parameters in mind -as they can be both complementary and contradictory-and it is the team that can place the necessary gravity on each of these three, in order to guide the actual design decision-making process in each case, by shifting the importance of each one on a multi-dimensional grid, according to the care regime from the medical perspecive, the re-integration or psychosocial targets and principles associated with a service delivery perspective, and the personal goals and projects of the building's end users.

The end product will then not be domestic versus institutional -or 'normal' versus 'specialized' to lessen the loaded semiology of those words-but a building that is fit for purpose, a well-designed environment that affords dignity to the service users, transferring the message that this is an environment that was built with care and is well maintained and taken care of. This approach would finally acknowledge that the purpose of the units is to provide a therapeutic regime that will enable service users to recover from the crisis situation in an environment that is and feels safe, that prepares them for the next, more independent stage of living and at the same time respects their psychosocial needs.

References

[1] Abrahamson, D (1993) "Housing and Deinstitutionalisation: theory and practice in the development of a resettlement service" in MPI. Weller and

[2] M. Muijen (eds) Dimensions of community mental health care. London: Saunders

[3] Ackroyd, E (1993) "An experiment in human relationships", Medical World, (Nov/Dec): pp76-77

[4] Aggelidis, G, Azoridou, D, Brisimi, G, Gaitagi, C, Zela, P, Tatsi, S, Tzouma, C and Kapanidis K (1993) "Psychiatric care in protected residential space in the community", Tetradia Psychiatrikis (psychiatric notebooks), 44, Oct-Dec: pp. 34-45

[5] Agorastidis, C (1986) "the new system of psychiatric services and the Psychiatric Departments of the General Hospital", Galen, 28, (5): pp. 797-801

[6] Agorastidis, C (1989) "The de-institutionalisation of the chronic psychotic in practice", Galen, 31, (3): pp. 286-292

[7] Agorastidis, C, Agelidis, G, Georgakas C, Liallina, M, Doga, E, Karakoli, A, Mougias, T, Tzanakaki and Chalari, K (1986) "the admission and discharge rates in the psychiatric hospitals of Greece in the five years period 1980-1984", Galen, 28, (4): pp. 634-638

[8] Alexandris, B (1993) "The relationship of chronic psychotic patients with everyday-life objects: coffee, money, clothes", Tetradia Psychiatrikis, 41: pp.38-40

[9] Alexandris, B, (1990) "Boarding house - Hostel: theoretical background and former experiences" in P. Sakelaropoulos (ed) Risk and Psychiatry. Athens: Papazisi

[10] Amiel, R (1976) "Psychiatric Architecture and Sociotherapy" World Hospitals, 12: pp.69-74

[11] Abatzoglou, G (1995) "Boarding houses, de-institutionalisation, critical presentation and proposals", Tetradia Psychiatrikis (psychiatric notebooks), 51, Jul-Sept: pp. 51-53

[12] Andersen Consulting and Burtson-Martsteller (1993), The future of the European Health Care

[13] Anderson, S, Good, L, and Hurtig, W, (1976) "Designing a Mental Health Centre to Replace a County Hospital" Hospital and Community Psychiatry, 27(11), November: pp. 807-813

[14] Anderson, T, (1990) "Provision for the elderly mentally ill", Landscape Design, 189, April: pp 22-25.

[15] Anme, T (2000), "Positive ageing: cross cultural perspectives, social affiliation and healthy longevity" in A. Dickinson, H. Bartlett and Wade S (eds) Old age in new age, Proceedings of the British Society of Gerontology 29th Annual Conference in Oxford, 8-12 Sept 2000. Oxford: Oxford Brooks University.

[16] Appleby, L, (2002) "changing inpatient mental health care" presentation in "With Design in Mind" in RIBA in 19/06/02. London: Isle of Wight Healthcare NHS Trust

[17] Architects' Journal (1993) "Residential and communal uses", 198, (10), Sept 15: p.10

[18] Architectural Record (1981) "A mental health centre infills a tight urban site", 169, (101), August: pp 92-93

[19] Architectural Record (1983) "Bricks in the service of brains", 171, (7), June: pp 86-93

[20] Architectural Record (1983) "Designed to "fit in" ", 171, (71), June: pp 94-97

[21] Architectural Record (1981) "A hybrid hospital and home", 171, (71), June: pp 98-101

[22] Architectural Record (1992) " New Lower East Side buildings for the disadvantaged", 180, (3), March: p.30

[23] Architectural Review 1 (1988), "Boekel blocks", 138, (1096), June: pp.76-77

[24] Architectural Review 2 (1988), "MK creativity", 138, (1096), June: pp.66-69

[25] Architectural Review 3 (1988), "Webb-like in Wembley", 138, (1096), June: pp.71-72

[26] Ashton, J, (1976) "Community mental health in Britain and the USA" Update, November: pp1083-1087

[27] Aurouseau, P and Cheverry, R (1969) L' hopital des adultes. Paris: Masson

[28] Anderson, S, Good, R and Hurtig, W (1976), "Designing a mental health centre to replace a country hospital", Hosp Community Psychiatry, 27, (11): pp.807-813

[29] De Syllas J. and Duggan F.(1994). Living in the Community. Avanti Architects Limited London, unpublished., Avanti Architects Limited, London, United Kingdom

[30] Åagley, C, (1974) "The built environment as an influence on personality and social behaviour: a spatial study" in D. Canter and T. Lee (eds.) Psychology and the built environment. England: the architectural press

[31] Baker, A, Davies, R, and Sivadon, P (1960) Services Psychiatriques at Architecture Geneve: Organisation Mondial de Sante Publique

[32] Baldwin, S (1993) The myth of community care. Chapman and Hall

[33] Barradell, E, (2000) "Chair wars: an ethnographic analysis of the symbolism of chairs as a form of defence in a residential home" at Dickinson, Bartlett and Wade (eds) Old age in a new age, Proceedings of the British Society of Gerontology 29th Annual Conference, 8-10 Sept, Oxford: Oxford Brooks University

[34] Beard, H, Rudyard, P, Malamud, TJ (1982) "The Fountain House Model" Psychosocial Rehabilitation Journal, V, (1): January

[35] Bechtel, B, (1997), Environmental Psychology: an introduction, Thousand Oaks, California: Sage

[36] Bell, N, (1992) Pink doors and doorknockers, Shiring: Dementia Service Development Centre

[37] Bell, P, Fisher, Baum A, and Green, T, (1996) Environmental Psychology, (4th ed) Fort Worth: Harcourt Brace

[38] Benians, P, (1982) "Back home" Health and social services journal, Oct 21: pp1257-1258

[39] Bergsland, K, (2002) "A European comparison-Haugesund Hospital, Norway" presentation in "With Design in Mind" in RIBA in 19/06/02. London: Isle of Wight Healthcare NHS Trust

[40] Bevan, R, (1998), "Making over the asylum" Building design, October 23: pp12-14

[41] Bhurga, D, (1993), "Setting up services for ethnic minorities" in Weller and Muijen (eds) Dimensions of Community Mental Health Care, London: Saunders

[42] Blask DE, Brainard GC, Dauchy RT, Hanifin JP, Davidson LK, Krause JA, et al. 2005. Cancer Res 65(23):11174-11184.

[43] Bobrow, M, and Thomas, J, (1983) "For health care providers too: an outlook of stressful -but hopeful-change" Architectural Record, 171 (7), June: pp 102-103

[44] Bonnet, C, Dunard, M, Ettienne, B, Herblot, S, and Mathieu, S, (1993) "Contrainte et espace therapeutique" Soins Psychiatrie, 150, Avril: pp 28-32

[45] Bouras, N, (1980) "The interaction of the social environment within the psychiatric hospital", Iatriki, 37, pp 192-199

[46] Bourdieu, P, (1997) Outline of a theory of practice, Cambridge: Cambridge University Press

[47] Bradley, S, Pajakowska, R, Bellew, P, Shaw, M, Eger, S, and Thompson, I, (1994) Care in the community, the architect's journal, 8 December p25-34

[48] Brand, S., 1994, How Buildings Learn: What Happens After They're Built, New York: Viking Press.

[49] Brook, R, (2002) "The impact of a caring environment" presentation in "With Design in Mind" in RIBA in 19/06/02. London: Isle of Wight Healthcare NHS Trust

[50] Brookes, M, (1990) "Pressures on the hospital landscape", Landscape Design, 189, April: pp 36-37.

[51] Building (1986) "Health and Housing in new London Square" 251 (7460/35) August 29: p 9

[52] Burnidge, C, and Aitken, I, (1994), "Counsel Collective" HD, February: pp20-23

[53] Butcher, A, (1981) "Upgrading rehabilitation" Health and social service Journal, August 28: p 1052

[54] Calderhead, J, Hospitals for people, London: King Edward's Hospital Fund for London

[55] Castle, G, (1991) Housing and Community Care: a guide to the National Health Service and Community Care Act 1990, London: National Federation of Housing Associations

[56] Cayla, J, (1992) "La loi du 30 Juin 1838 et l' organisation des soins aux malades mentaux", Soins Psychiatrie 142/143, Aout-Septembre: pp63-66

[57] Campbell, W, (1979), "The therapeutic community: a history", Nursing Times, November 15: pp 1985-1987

[58] Carson, J, Glynn, T, Gopaulen, J, (1993) "The influence of normalisation on psychiatric service" in Weller and Muijen (eds) Dimensions of Community Mental Health Care, London: Saunders

[59] Carter, P, (1999) "The need for strategic planning" in RfBA Client forum: Therapeutic environments for mental health, on the 26/01/1999. London: pp 16-19.

[60] Cavadino, M, (1989) Mental Health Law in context, Hants (England): Dartmouth

[61] Chu, D, Trotter, S, (1974) The Madness establissement, ed the Centre for study of responsive Law, NY: Grossman bubl

[62] Cole, A, (1980) "Alternatives to mental hospitals", Nursing Times, April 17: pp 673-4

[63] Constandopoulos, A, (1994) "Conference on new psychiatric care facilities of the Greek

[64] "NHS" Health Review (Epitheorisi Ygeias), January-February: pp 28-32

[65] Chartocolis, P, (1989) "Introduction to psychiatry". Athens: Themelio.

[66] Chrysikou, E, (2012). From Normalisation theory to a "Fit for Purpose" architecture for the mentally ill. World Health Design, 5(3), pp.68-77.

[67] Chrysikou, E., Kandylis, D., Aspradakis, K., Fokas, K., Kaprinis, G., (1998). Architecture of organisation of protected living and psychosocial re-establishment units. Greek Psychiatric Association, 15th Conference of Psychiatry. Lemnos, 29 April – 3 May 1998.

[68] Cox, A, and Groves, P, (1990) Hospital and Health Care Facilities, London: Butterworth

[69] Crawford, R, (. . .) History of the Clubhouse Movement, Mosaic Clubhouse fact sheet, London

[70] Crisp, N, (2002) "the end of the beginning" presentation in "With Design in Mind" in RIBA in 19/06/02. London: Isle of Wight Healthcare NHS Trust

[71] Davies, C, (1988), "Architecture of caring" Architectural Review, 138 (1096), June: pp15

[72] Davies, M, (1990) "When in Rome. . ." The Health Service Journal, 21 June p915

[73] Davis, C, Glick, I, and Rosow, I, (1979) "The architectural design of a Psychotherapeutic

[74] "Milieu" Hospital and Community Psychiatry, 30 (7) July: pp:453-460.

[75] Dawson, S, (1993) "Ironmongery and security" AJ focus, 7 (1) June pp11-31

[76] Deahl, M, Douglas, B, and Turner, T, (2000) "Full metal jacket or the emperor's new clothes?" Psychiatric Bulletin, 24, pp207-210

[77] Dibuis, J (1995) «La rehabilitation dans le monde», in Vidon (ed) La rehabilitation psychosociale en psychiatrie Paris: Frison-Roche

[78] Dickerman K, Barach P, and Pentcost R. (2008), We shape our buildings, then they kill us: why health care buildings contribute to the error pandemic, World Health Design, April pp: 49-55

[79] Diebolt, E, (1997) De la quarantaine au quarantaine: histoire dy foyer de postcure psychiatrique de l' Elan. Paris: L' lan Retrouve

[80] Dilani A (2008), "Psychosocially supportive design: a salutogenic approach to the design of the physical environment", in World Health Design, July, pp 47-55

[81] Doerner, K, (1981) "Madmen and the Bourgeoisie, a social history of insanity and psychiatry". Oxford: Basil Blackwell.

[82] ECITE (1995) "Parts from the Report conducted on behalf of EC, on the visit in psychiatric hospitals, Autumn 1995", Tetradia Psychiatrikis (psychiatric notebooks), 54, April-Jube: pp. 23-33

[83] Edelstein E, Doctors S, Brandt R, Denton B, Granz G, Mangel R, Martin M and Chong G (2008) "The effects of colour and light on health: transdisciplinary research results", World Health Design, April pp: 57-61

[84] Edwards, A, (1975) Mental health services, 4th ed, London: Show and Sons

[85] Ekdawi, M, and Conning, A, (1994) Psychiatric rehabilitation, London: Chapman and Hall

[86] Elderfield, G, (2002) "the Sevenacres story -with patients in mind" presentation in "With Design in Mind" in RIBA in 19/06/02. London: Isle of Wight Healthcare NHS Trust

[87] Ellis, J, (1988) "West Coast care" Architectural Review, 138 (1096), June: pp58-65

[88] El-Kabir, D, and Ramsden, S, (1993) "A pragmatic approach to the health care of the single homeless: its implications in terms of human resources" Weller and Muijen (eds) Dimensions of community mental healthcare, London: Saunders

[89] European Commission, (1996), The state of health in the European Community, Brussels: Routledge

[90] Enser, J, (1999) "Summary" in RIBA Client forum: Therapeutic environments for mental health, on the 26/01/1999. London: p 44.

[91] European Observatory on health care systems (2001), "Health Care systems in transition", WHO regional office for Europe, Copenhagen: WHO

[92] Eutichiades, A, Marketos, Sp. (1981) "Treatment of psychiatric patients and legislation at the 10th century in Byzantium", Materia Medica Grecá, 9 (2), April 1981.

[93] Fisher, J (2007) Medical design, Daab

[94] Fisk, J, (1999) "Buildings for mental health -users' and managers' needs" in RIBA Client forum: Therapeutic environments for mental health, on the 26/01/1999. London: pp 20-25.

[95] Ford, N, (1990) "A healthy outlook for Wales", Landscape Design, 189, April: pp 25-29.

[96]   Ford, R, (2002) "How I woke up" presentation in "With Design in Mind" in RIBA in 19/06/02. London: Isle of Wight Healthcare NHS Trust

[97]   Foque, R, and Arretz, L, (1998) «Architecture for mental health care and Psychiatry in Belgium» publication based on presentation in XII Congresso argentino y VII congressointernational de psichiatria de enlace, psichologia medica y psichotherapia, Ieras Jordanas Universitarias de residentes se salud mental, 17-20 June, Antwerp: FDA

[98]   Freeman, H, (1997), "Standard of living: and environmental factors as a component of Quality of Life in mental disorders" Katschnig H, Freeman H, Sartorius N. Chichester,, London: John Wiley & Sons

[99]   Freeman, H, Fryers, T, Henderson, J, (1985) Mental health services in Europe: 10 years on, Copenhagen: WHO

[100] Frisk, J, (1999) "Buildings for mental health -users' and managers' needs" in RIBA Client forum: Therapeutic environments for mental health, on the 26/01/1999. London: pp 20-25.

[101] Fouqault, M, (1964) Histoire de la Folie, a l' age classique, Paris: Plon

[102] Gajos, M, (1980) "A programme for long-stay patients" in Nursing Times, January 31: pp 204-207

[103] Garety, P (1988) "Housing", in A. Lavender and F. Holloway (eds) Community care in practice John Wiley and Sons

[104] Giddens, A, (1984) The constitution of society Caimbridge: Polity

[105] Gainsborough, H, and Gainsborough, J, (1964) Principles of Hospital Design, London: Architectural Press

[106] Georgiou, G, Vargopoulos, D, and Hatziioannou, A, (1993) "The psychiatric PROVLIMATIKI from prehistoric era until early Renaissance", Galen, 35 (6): pp 631-39

[107] Goldie, N, Pilgrim, D and Rogers, A, (1989) Community Mental Health Centres: policy and practice, London: Good Practices in Mental Health

[108] Good, L, Siegel, S, and Bay, AP, (1965) Therapy by design, Springfield-Illinois: Charles C Thomas

[109] Goodman, H, (1976) "Architecture and Psychiatry: What has been achieved" World Hospitals, 12: pp 75-79

[110] Golembiewski, J, (2010) "Start making sense; Applying a salutogenic model to architectural design for psychiatric care". Facilities, 28(3), pp 100-117.

[111] Gournay, K, (2000) "The National Service Framework: overview and specific implications for residential services", The mental health review, 5(1), March: pp 6-11

[112] Great Britain Department of Environment and Department of Health, (1992) Housing and Community Care, joint circular, London: HMSO

[113] Great Britain DHSS, (1981) Reform of mental health legislation, London: HMSO

[114] Griffin, W, Mauritzen, J, and Kashmar, J, (1969) "the psychological aspects of the architectural environment" in American Journal of Psychiatry, 125 (8), February: pp 93-98

[115] Groat, L, (1995) "Introduction: places aesthetic evaluation and home" Groat (Ed) Givingplaces meaning, London: Academic Press

[116] Gueguen, JP, (1993) "L'hospitalisation de nuit en psychiatrie" Soins Psychiatrie, 150, April: pp 9-11

[117] Guigon, C and Bardiot, G (1993) "Pratique infirmiere en accueil familial therapeutique" Soins Psychiatrique, 150, April: pp 25-27

[118] Gutkowski, S, Ginath, Y, and Guttmann, F, (1992) "Improving Psychiatric Environments through minimal architectural change" in Hospital and Community Psychiatry, 43 (9), September: pp 920-923

[119] Hafner, H, and An der Heiden, W, (1996) "Background goals of evaluative research in community psychiatry" in Knudsen and Thornicroft (eds) Mental Health Service Evaluation, Cambridge: Cambridge University Press

[120] Hafner, H, and An der Heiden, W, (1996) "The Manheim project" in Kundsen and Thornicroft (eds) Mental Health Service Evaluation, Cambridge: Cambridge University Press

[121] Hagedorn, R, (1990) "Environment and occupational therapy", Landscape Design, 189, April: pp 21-22

[122] Halpern, D, (1995), Mental health and built environment: more than bricks and mortar?, London: Taylor and Francis

[123] HD (2000), "Close to home", April: pp15-20

[124] HD (1997), "A bright outlook", February: pp13-15.

[125] Harriman, M, (1992) "Designing for daylight" AIA 81 (10), October: pp 89-93

[126] Harrison, L, (1991) Implementing the white paper: working for patients, Bristol: SAUS

[127] Helman, C, (1994) Culture, health and illness, Oxford: Butterworth

[128] Heineman Higham, P and Towers, C, (2000) "Achieving homeostasis of internal and external environments: researching relationships and transitions into residential care" in A.

[129] Dickinson, H. Bartlett and Wade S (eds) Old age in new age, Proceedings of the British Society of Gerontology 29th Annual Conference in Oxford, 8-12 Sept 2000. Oxford: Oxford Brooks University., pp 315-318

[130] Hogget, B, 1996, Mental Health Law, (4th ed), London: Sweet and Maxwell

[131] Hollingsworth R, Hage, J, and Hanneman, R, (1990) State intervention in medical care: consequences in Britain, France, Sweden and the US 1890-1970, Ithaca: Cornell University Press

[132] Howel, S, (1991) "Deinstitutionalisation of the mentally ill; implications for the social housing policy in the US" Journal of architectural and planning research, 8 (4), winter: pp331-342

[133] Hoyes, L and Means, R, (1991) "Implementation of the white paper on community care, Bristol: SAUS

[134] Hudson, J, Watson, L, and Allan, G, (1996) Moving obstacles: housing choices and community care, Bristol: The Policy Press

[135] Ittelson, W, Proshansky, H, Rivlin L, (1970) "The environmental psychology of the Psychiatric Ward", in Environmental psychology: man and his physical setting, New York: Holt, Rinehart and Winston, pp 419-439

[136] Judd, S, (1998) "Building for dementia: a matter of design" in Judd et al Design for dementia, Stirling: Dementia Services Development Centre

[137] Kandylis, D, "The return from the Asylum of Leros in the society of Larissa". Volos: Wres.

[138] Kane, E, (1999) "New directions for psychiatric care" in RIBA Client forum: Therapeutic environments for mental health, on the 26/01/1999. London: pp 12-15.

[139] Kasmar, J, Griffin, W, and Mauritzen, J, (1968), "The effects of environmental surroundings on outpatients' mood and perception of psychiatrists" Journal of Consult. Clin. Psycholog. 32: pp 223-226

[140] Kelly, M, (1993), Designing for people with dementia in the context of the building standards, Stirling: Dementia services development centre

[141] Kennard, D, (1983), An introduction to therapeutic communities, London: Routledge and Kenan Paul

[142] Kirc, C, (1993) "A manager's view: the new tasks" in MPI. Weller and M. Muijen (eds) Dimensions of community mental health care, London: Saunders

[143] Kostantopoulos, A, (1994). Conference for the new psyciatic facilities of ESY (National Health System) Health Review (Epitheorisi Ygeias), January-February 1994 pp28-32.

[144] Korman, N, (1984), "The progressive upheaval", Health and Social Service Journal, August 9: pp 950-952

[145] Lavaud, A, (1993) "Les appartements therapeutiques", Soins Psychiatrie, 150, April: pp12- 14

[146] Leff, J, (1995), "Beyond the asylum" in Health Service Journal, June 22: pp 28-30

[147] Leff, J, (1999) "The evolution of modern psychiatric care" in RIBA Client forum: Therapeutic environments for mental health, on the 26/01/1999. London: pp 8-10.

[148] Lelliott, P, (1996), "The cost of living" Health Service Journal, February 1: pp26-27

[149] Leniaud, JM (1992) "Architecture psychiatrique et patrimoin monumental" Soins Psychiatrie, 142/143, Aout-Septembre: pp59-64

[150] Leopold, H, and McStay, P, (1980), "The psychiatric group home-1", Nursing Times, May 8: pp 829-832

[151] Leopold, H, and McStay, P, (1980), "The psychiatric group home-2", Nursing Times, May 15: pp 866-868

[152] Lombard, M, (1993) "Apprendre a se reprendre en charge" Soins Psychiatrie, 150, Avril: pp 4-7

[153] Lygetsos, G, (1986) "The psychiatric hospital; the present and the future" Encephalos 23: pp286-289

[154] Madianons, M, (1980) "Social Psychiatry: historical review, definition and ideology", Encephalos 17: pp159-165

[155] Madianons, M, (1994) Psychiatric Revolution and its development, from theory to practice, Athens: Ellinika Grammata

[156] Madianos, M, (1995) "Psychiatric Revolution in Greece: DIAXRONIKA comparative data", Tetradia Psychiatrikis (psychiatric notebooks), 51, Jul-Sept: pp. 9-19

[157] Madonakis, I, (1983) "Part-time hospitalisation in psychiatry" Encephalos, 20: pp 206-208

[158] Malkin, J, (1992) Hospital Interior architecture, NY: Van Nostrand and Reinhold

[159] Manoleas, P, (1991) "Designing mental health facilities: an interactive process", Hospital and Community Psychiatry, 42 (3), March pp: 305-308

[160] Marie-Cardine, M, and Terra, J, (1992) "Le secteur psychiatrique en France: un bilan dificile" Soins Psychiatrie, 142-142, Aout-Septembre: pp14-18

[161] Markus, T, (1993) Buildings and power: freedom and control in the origin of modern building types, London: Routledge

[162]   Marshal, M, (1998) "Therapeutic buildings for people with dementia" Judd et al Design for dementia, Stirling: Dementia Services Development Centre
[163]   MARV (1991) Building for mental health: stick to your principles, London: PNL Press
[164]   Matsa, K, and Michalakeas, A, (1998) "Dafni in the OVT-CRY of the psychiatric reform"
[165]   Tetradia Psychiatrikis (psychiatric notebooks), 61, January-March: pp. 10-15
[166]   McCurry, P, (1999) "Hope for London's mental health", Community Care, June pp: 17-23
[167]   Megalooikonomou, T, (2007). In: Psychiatry department of AUTH (Aristotle University of Thessaloniki) , Society and medical health conference. Thessaloniki, Greece, 20-21 October 2007.
[168]   Megaloikonomou, T, and Baldi, C, (1995) "Residential re-establishment and social reintegration" Tetradia Psychiatrikis (psychiatric notebooks), 49, January-March: pp. 83-89
[169]   The Mental Health Act Commission (1997) The national visit, London: The Mental Health
[170]   Act Commission and Sainsbury Centre for Mental Health
[171]   Middleton, R, (1993), "Sickness, madness and crime at the grounds of form", AA files, 25, Summer: pp14-29
[172]   Miles, M, (1990) "A ward with a view", Landscape Design, 189, April: pp 40-42. Miles M 2, (1990), Art and Mental Health Hospitals Dundee: British Health Care Arts Centre
[173]   Miles, M, (1994) "Art in hospitals; does it work? A survey of evaluation of art projects in the NHS", Journal of the Royal Society of Medicine, 87, March: pp 161-163
[174]   Milioni, C, and Condopoulou, E, (1998) "Evaluation of the therapeutic environment of the traditional psychiatric hospital and the hostels for the schizophrenic" Tetradia Psychiatrikis (Notebooks of psychiatry), 61, January-March: pp 30-42
[175]   Monetti, V, (1992) "L' asile psychiatrique et la traitement moral au 19 siecle", Soins Psychiatrique, 142/143, Aout-Septembre: pp 55-58
[176]   Morris, I, (1991) "Residential Care" Bennet and Freeman (eds) Community Psychiatry, Longman: UK
[177]   Morris, I, (1993) "Working with people with long term mental health problems: the process of psychiatric rehabilitation" in Weller and Muijen (eds) Dimensions of community mental health care. London: Saunders
[178]   Muijen, M, (1993) "Mental health services: what works?" in Weller and Muijen (eds) Dimensions of community mental health care. London: Saunders
[179]   Myerson, J, (1993), "Sensual Healing" in Design (CHECK ON INTERNET), April.
[180]   NAHA, (1984) Community Care: NAHA's position on Community Care (mentalluy handicapped and mentally ill people), July: NAHA
[181]   NHS Excecutive, (1996) Health service Guidelines: LASSL(96)16 and HSG(96)6, 19February, Department of Health
[182]   NHS Excecutive, (1995) Patient Empowerment: Privacy, dignity and the mixed sex ward guidance for best practice, NW Regional Health Authority
[183]   Nightingale, M, (2002) "Sevenacres -the design solution" presentation in With Design in Mind in RIBA on 19/06/02. London: Isle of Wight Healthcare NHS Trust
[184]   Norman DA (2002), the design of everyday thinks, NY: Basic Books
[185]   Oliver, J, Hurvey, P, Bridges, K, Mohamad, H (1996), Quality of life and mental health services, London: Routledge.
[186]   Osmond, H, (1970) "Function as the basis of Psychiatric Ward", (slightly condensed version from Mental Hospitals, 8, April 1957:pp 23-30) in the Proshansky et al (eds) The environmental psychology: man and his physical setting, NY: Holt, Rinehart and Winston
[187]   Owen, C, Rutherford, V, Jones, M, Wright, C, Tennant, C, and Smallman, A (1996) "Housing accommodation preferences of people with psychiatric disabilities" Psychiatric Services, 47 (6), June: pp 628-632.
[188]   Papamichael, E, (1997). "National psychiatric services-The Irish model". Tetradia Psychiatrikis (psychiatric notebooks) 56 pp 93-99, Jan-March 1997.
[189]   Patsi, V, (1999), Analysis of the legislative framework of reforms of mental health in Greece, supervisor Giannoulatos, P, unpublished dissertation in National College of of Public Management of Greece
[190]   Payer, L, (1988) Medicine and culture, Gollancz: London
[191]   Payne, F and O'Gorman, C (2002) "Managing mental health", Health Management 2001; 5 (10), December-January: pp14-15
[192]   Peace, S, (1998) K100 Understanding Health and Social Care, Block 2, People and Places, London: Open University Press

[193] Peck, E, (1985), "Planning not platitudes", Health and Social Services Journal, January 17: pp 78-79

[194] Penton, J, (1983) "Experimentation urged for housing the handicapped" AJ, 178 (36) September 7: p 45

[195] Nathan H. Perkins, (2013) "Including patients, staff and visitors in the design of the psychiatric milieu: Notes from the field", Facilities, Vol. 31 Iss: 9/10, pp.379 - 390

[196] Perrera, D, (1993) "Les vacances" Soins Psychiatrie, 150, Avril: pp 20-21

[197] Pevsner, N, (1976) A history of building types, Washington DC: Trustees of the National Gallery of Art

[198] Peyron-Foucard, I, (1993) "Le CAT dix ans plus tard", Soins Psychiatrie, 150, Avril: p 2

[199] Phippen, P, (1998) "Interpreting "home": the architects dilemma" " in Judd et al Design for dementia, Stirling: Dementia Services Development Centre

[200] Pilling, S, (1991) Rehabilitation and community care, London: Routledge

[201] Pinto, M, (2002) Mental Health Care: four countries four different ways-one common trend, EUROPHAMILY-Medipsy

[202] Poggi D, and Carlier, I, (1995) "Voyage au Pays de CMP" Soins Psychiatrie, 172, Fevrier, pp: 12-18

[203] Plantamura, F, Albini, P, and Lembi P, (2014) "Architecture and Psychiatric Disease - Rethinking places of care". In: A. Yoxall and K. Christer, eds. 2014. Proceedings of the 2nd European Conference on Design 4 Health 2013, Sheffield 3rd-5th July 2013. Sheffield: Sheffield Hallam University. ISBN: 978-1-84387-373-0

[204] Pollack, A, (1997) "Landscaping for Dementia" " in Judd et al (eds) Design for dementia, Stirling: Dementia Services Development Centre

[205] Pollack, R, (1997) "Technology and design for dementia" in Judd et al (eds) Design for dementia, Stirling: Dementia Services Development Centre

[206] Ramon, S, (1996) Mental Health in Europe, ed Campling, J, London: MIND Ramon, S, (1996) Mental health in Europe, London: MIND

[207] Relph-Knight, L, (1980) "Hobart home base", Building design, June13: pp 19-21

[208] Royal College of Psychiatrists (1998) Not just bricks and mortar, Council Report CR62, London

[209] Remen, S, (1991) "Signs, Symbols and the psychiatric environment" The psychiatric hospital, 22 (3): pp113-118

[210] Robinson JW, Emmons P and Graff M (1984) A role for the architect in the environment-behavior research, In D Duerk and D Campbell (eds) EDRA 15, 1984: the challenge of diversity, Washington DC: EDRA

[211] Rogers, A, Pilgrine, D, and Lacey, R, (1993) Experiencing psychiatry, London: MIND

[212] Rush, R, (1982) "A building adrift" Progressive architecture, 582, pp 152-5

[213] Ryan, P, (1993) "Social services care management" in Weller and Muijen (eds) Dimensions of community mental health care. London: Saunders

[214] Sainsbury Centre for Mental Health (1998) Acute problems: a survey of the quality of care in acute psychiatric wards, London: Sainsbury Centre for Mental Health

[215] Saradides, D, (1995) «Brief history of reylation 815/84», Tetradia Psychiatrikis (psychiatric notebooks), 46, April-June: pp. 28-31

[216] Scher, P, (1996) "Patient focused architecture for health care" in Arts for Health, Manchester: Manchester Metropolitan University, Faculty of Art and Design

[217] Seelye, A, (1978) "The use of ordinary housing for hostels for the mentally ill" Social Work Service, 15, May: pp 45-48

[218] Shephed, G, (1991) "Psychiatric rehabilitation for the 1990's" in Watts and Bennet (eds) Theory and Practice of Psychiatric Rehabilitation, West Sussex: John Wiley and Sons

[219] Sivadon, P, (1965), "Therapeutic implications" L'evolution Psychiatrique No.3, pp 477-498.

[220] Sloan Devlin, A, (1992) "Psychiatric ward renovation: staff perception and patient behavior" Environment and Behavior, 24(1), January: pp: 66-84

[221] Smith, M, (2002) "Building for mental health-stick to your principles" presentation in "With Design in Mind" in RIBA in 19/06/02. London: Isle of Wight Healthcare NHS Trust

[222] Spring, M, (1986) "They do take sugar" Building, 251 (7460(35)), August 19: pp 20-21

[223] Spring, M, (1990) "Pillars of society" Building, 255 (7652(24)), June 15: pp 47-49

[224] Stratdhee, G, (1993) "Primary care and community psychiatric services: Changing patterns and possibilities" in Weller and Muijen (eds) Dimensions of community mental health care. London: Saunders

[225] Stefanis, K, and Madianos, M, (1980), "Remarks and perspectives for the PERIFERIAKI development of health care facilities" Iatriki, 38: pp:241-249

[226]   Stoneham, J, (1990) "Sheltered landscapes" Landscape design, 189, April: 40-42

[227]   Symons, J, (1985) "Update: Community care. 4 The mental health revolution", in AJ, May 22: pp73-86

[228]   Tan, H, (1990) "The art of healing", Landscape Design, 189, April: pp 10-11

[229]   Taylor, J, (1991) Hospital and asylum architecture in England 1840-1914, London/NY: Mansel

[230]   Thornocroft, G, (1976), "Group homes- a success?" in Nursing times, January 11: pp84-85

[231]   Tomlinson, D, (1991) Utopia, community care and the retreat from the asylums, Milton Keynes, Philadelphia: Open University Press

[232]   Torrey, E, (1993), "An American perspective: crises in service for people with serious mental illnesses" in Weller and Muijen (eds) Dimensions of community mental health care. London: Saunders

[233]   Turner-Crowson, J, (1993) Reshaping mental health services London: King's Fund

[234]   Tzouma, C, Zela, P, Gaitatzi, C, Brisimi, G, Kapanidi, K, and Aggelidi, G, (1995) «Living in protacted space in the community for mentally ill people: assessment of Quality of Life», Tetradia Psychiatrikis (psychiatric notebooks), 49, January-March: pp. 90-95

[235]   Uzzel, D, and Lewand, K, (1990) "The psychology of landscape", Landscape Design, 189, April: pp 34-35.

[236]   Vavyli, F (1992) G4.15 Planning and design issues for healthcare spaces: teaching notes. Thessalonika: Department of Architecture, AUTH

[237]   Verderber, S, and Fine, D, (2000) Health care architecture in the era of radical transformation, New Haven and London: Yale University Press

[238]   Verdoux, H (2007), "The current state of adult mental health care in France", Eur Arch Clin Neurosci, 257, pp: 64-70

[239]   Victor, C, and Scambler, S, (2000) «Loneliness, isolation and living alone in later life: a tale of two surveys» in A. Dickinson, H. Bartlett and Wade S (eds) Old age in new age, Proceedings of the British Society of Gerontology 29th Annual Conference in Oxford, 8-12 Sept 2000. Oxford: Oxford Brooks University pp203-206

[240]   Vidon, G (1995) «La rchabilitation dans tous les etats», in Vidon (ed) La rehabilitation psychosociale en psychiatrie Paris: Frison-Roche

[241]   Vidon, G (1995) «La deinstitutionalisation: ses origines,ses retombees, son bilan», in Vidon (ed) La rehabilitation psychosociale en psychiatrie Paris: Frison-Roche

[242]   Vignet, JP, (1999) «La sante mentale en France: etat des lieux» in Sante Publique, 11e anne, 2: pp127-135

[243]   Vostanis, P, (1989) "Re-establishment of the mentally ill", Encephalos, 26: pp 97-1984

[244]   Weller, M, (1993), "Where we came from", in Weller and Muijen (eds) Dimensions of community mental health care. London: Saunders

[245]   Weller, M, (1993), "Where we are going", in Weller and Muijen (eds) Dimensions of community mental health care. London: Saunders

[246]   Whittle, M, Hunt, L, Allen, N, Boyd, D and Nightingale, M, (1999) "West London Health

[247]   NHS Trust" in RfBA Client forum: Therapeutic environments for mental health, on the 26/01/1999. London: p 44-55.

[248]   WHO, (1953) Community Mental Hospital technical report, No 73 Geneva

[249]   WLHE (1997) Community based mental health facilities: safety and security by design, London: West London Health Estates (WLHE)

[250]   Williams, A, (1989) "Community home south-west London: Commentary», Building, August 25; pp 38

[251]   Williams Robinson, J, (2006), «Institution and Home: Architecture as a Cultural Medium», Amsterdam: Techne Press

[252]   Zissi, A (1995) «Descriptive date for 12 hostels,which mostly accommodate former inmates from Leros asylum», Tetradia Psychiatrikis (psychiatric notebooks), 51, Jul-Sept: pp. 54-58

[253]   Zissi, A, Barry, M, and Cochrane, R, (1998), "A mediational mode; of quality of life for individuals with severe mental health problems" Psychological medicine, 28: pp 1221-1230

[254]   Zwach, F, (1988) "Fest House Berlin" Arch